D1564309

Documents of Destruction

Documents of Destruction

Germany
and
Jewry
1933–1945

Edited with
Commentary
by
RAUL HILBERG

CHICAGO: QUADRANGLE BOOKS, 1971

Library of Congress Catalog Card Number: 77–152092

SBN Cloth 8129–0192–4
SBN Paper 8129–6165–X

*To my son David
and
my daughter Deborah*

Most of you know what it means when 100 corpses
lie there, or 500 lie there, or 1000 lie there.
To have gone through this and—apart from
exceptions caused by human weakness—to have
remained decent, that has hardened us.
That is a page of glory in our history
never written and never to be written.

Heinrich Himmler to his SS and police generals
October 1943

Today I am one of the survivors. For twenty years
I have constantly heard within my mind the
very cry of the murdered: Tell it to the world!

Jacob Celemenski
Jewish survivor

Preface

Most of the materials assembled in this reader consist of papers written by German perpetrators or Jewish victims during the destruction of European Jewry. The selections deal with small pieces of a large scene: a single occurrence, a corner of a place, a portion of a problem. In narrative historiography such particulars are often submerged in a panorama; here the detail is an end in itself. Each event is intended to stand out in relief, not merely as an illustration of history drawn from minor acts, remote locations, or unknown persons, but as a happening which, with thousands like it, *is* history.

The compendium is brief, but I have put it together with two specifications in mind. One consideration was balance, so that the destruction of the Jews might be seen from beginning to finish, in various parts of Europe, and as both German and Jewish experiences. A second aim was newness, to the extent that most of the pages were allotted to items which have never before been mentioned in print.

Although I could choose from a sizable accumulation of German and Jewish accounts, I had to face a disparity from the very start: the German material at my disposal was composed primarily of official documents; the Jewish sources were mainly autobiographical.

German documents were found by the Allies in public buildings and storage places after Germany's collapse. German officialdom had left behind reports, orders, correspondence, and conference minutes by the thousands and tens of thousands. These folders are interconnected, one explaining the contents of the other. The German Reich emerges from them as structure and *Gestalt*. But one is stymied looking beneath this pile for private expressions of thought. The personal letters and diaries of the German bureaucrats are virtually unavailable. They have been locked in drawers and cellars, if not incinerated. Similarly, the German memoir literature contains few references to anti-Jewish activities. In Germany the Jews have remained a difficult subject; it is easy to forget them in recollections of a wartime life filled with stress and duties.

A very different picture emerges from the Jewish side. The documentation of the Jewish community machinery is incomplete and localized, written in more than a dozen languages, scattered in more than a dozen countries. In Eastern Europe, ghetto offices were sometimes destroyed with the ghetto inhabitants, files and people engulfed. Much of what is known about the Jewish fate under the Nazis is consequently derived from a large number of individual statements. Unlike the German observers, the Jewish witnesses of destruction have not been reluctant to record all they have seen and felt, for if the Germans were frequently part-time perpetrators, the Jews were always full-time victims. The survivors have poured out their reflections in countless books and depositions in a major spontaneous effort at remembrance. After more than twenty-five years this production is still going on.

In the aggregate then, the German and Jewish sources differ in style and perspective. The German records, though terse, convey a sense of sweep; the Jewish narrations, while long, impart immediacy. The collection in this volume reflects the contrast between these two kinds of description.

Before making decisions about inclusions, I had the opportunity of visiting a number of archives. My search was aided in the first instance by the University of Vermont, which granted me sabbatical leave for travel abroad and a small sum for microfilm. The archivists of the YIVO Institute in New York, the Institut für Zeitgeschichte in Munich, the German Federal Archives in Koblenz, and the Yad Vashem Oral History Depot in Tel Aviv have all helped me with their knowledge and time. My special gratitude goes to Mrs. Bronia Klibanski of Yad Vashem in Jerusalem for providing access to the archives there and for sharing with me many of her insights into the catastrophe.

Each selection to follow is identified by its archival or published source. Nuremberg documents are deposited in mimeographed copies in major libraries. Documents marked "Israel Police" are certified photocopies which were sent to the Israeli government from various archives and which were used during the Eichmann trial. "Alexandria" documents are original German folders which were once kept at the Federal Records Center in Alexandria, Virginia. They are now listed in the *Catalog of the German Records Microfilmed at Alexandria, Va.*, from which rolls of film may be ordered. Except where indicated otherwise, the translations are mine.

Contents

xi

Documents of Destruction

Introduction

Two developments were intertwined in the Nazi assault on the Jews. One was a German administrative process evolving from ponderously slow beginnings to a massive climax, the other a progressive enfeeblement of the Jewish population in the German vise. The German buildup ensnared the Jews in laws, decrees, and regulations. The Germans issued instructions; the Jews reorganized their lives. The Germans became harsh, the Jews more vulnerable in their quandary. As German moves became ominous, the Jews clung to hope. The Germans pressed on relentlessly and the Jews despaired. The outer limits were reached: never before had an act been so extreme, a loss so total.

When Adolf Hitler came to power in 1933, a modern bureaucracy set out for the first time to destroy an entire people. That machinery of destruction was not a single organization but a network of offices in the party, the ministries, the army, and industry. Its onslaught on the Jews was not planned in advance but developed blow by blow. In spite of such decentralization, few operations could have been more efficient than this singular deed in the midst of a general war.

The anchorage of the entire undertaking was a definition of the term "Jew." With that definition in hand, the German administrators were able to sort out automatically the targets of destruction. Under the classification decree, a person was considered a Jew if at least three of his grandparents had belonged to the Jewish religion, or if two of his grandparents were Jews at one time and he himself adhered to the Jewish faith or was married to a Jewish partner on the day preceding the issuance of the ordinance. In drawing up this regulation, the ministerial experts sought to prevent the victim from changing his status, and thus also his fate.

Toward the later 1930's, Jews became increasingly the object of an industrial-bureaucratic attack. A multi-pronged expropriation process was aimed at them. It began with job dismissals and pressures on Jewish business enterprises. Later it encompassed forced sales of companies, discriminatory property taxes, blocking of bank deposits, compulsory labor, reduced wages, special income taxes, lowered rations, and confiscation of personal property, pensions, and claims.

In the meantime, the Jewish community was subjected to a physical concentration which involved, at first, the prohibition of intermarriages, and, later, a series of housing restrictions, movement limitations, and identification measures. The Jews of Germany now were forced to undergo document stamping, name changes, and the marking of their clothes with a star. They were placed under the orders of a Jewish council which took its instructions from the state police.

In 1939 the destruction process spilled into Poland. There the Germans herded the Jews into ghettos, packing the victims behind fences and walls. All personal traffic with the outside world was eliminated. Finished goods had to be exported from ghetto factories, and for a while foodstuffs were shipped in. Gradually the food supply diminished. The ghetto inmates were exposed to starvation, and the sick died by the hundreds of thousands.

When Nazi Germany attacked Soviet Russia, the machine of destruction was freed from all restraints. On June 22, 1941, four battalions of the Security Police crossed the eastern border into the U.S.S.R. with orders to kill all Jews on the spot. In the newly taken cities and towns, Jews were caught en masse. They were placed before anti-tank ditches and prepared graves and mowed down with rifle salvos and machine-gun fire. As the trails of blood ran deeper into Soviet territory, SS and Police reinforcements poured into the area, the army was pressed into service, and native helpers pitched in. The killings increased and efficiency became more pronounced. The victims were forced to lie in the ditches, the head of the man awaiting the bullet on the feet of the corpse below. Soon, gas-vans appeared on the scene to suffocate women and children. After two years of this carnage, the mass graves of the east contained the bodies of about 1,400,000 Jews.

Little more than a month after the launching of operations in Russia, Hermann Göring signed the order for a "final solution" of the "Jewish problem" on a European-wide scale. Civil servants and party men now began to confer about their task. The uprooting process was to be pushed in all areas under German control. Everywhere the Jews were to be defined, expropriated, and concentrated. When all preliminary steps had been taken, the Jews were to be transported to the east to be killed. The deportation machinery was laboriously set in motion, with the Reich itself first on the list so as to relieve the shortage of housing. Almost simultaneously, short-haul trains began to empty the ghettos of Poland. From the civilian-controlled territories of Norway, the Netherlands, and Luxembourg, from the military areas of Belgium, France, and Greece, from the Axis satellites of Vichy France, the Italian Republic, Slovakia, Croatia, Greater Bulgaria, and Greater Hungary, hundreds of sealed transports carried their human cargo to a rapid death.

The arrival points of the deportation trains were six killing centers in Poland: Lublin, Kulmhof, Treblinka, Sobibor, Belzec, and Auschwitz. The Lublin camp was used for shootings; Kulmhof was equipped with gas-vans; Treblinka, Sobibor, and Belzec contained gas chambers into which carbon monoxide was piped; Auschwitz had facilities for killing entire masses with quick-working hydrogen cyanide gas. For the great bulk of the deportees there was no reprieve. Men, women, and children were undressed upon arrival and killed on an assembly line. Almost three million people succumbed to the gassings before the camps were dismantled under the impact of the receding front lines.

While German society was thus pitted in a series of interlocking decisions against European Jewry, the Jewish communities became more and more isolated from the surrounding population and from one another. Between increasingly lethal German blows, a swelling Jewish bureaucracy reorganized and consolidated its resources, desperately trying to hold its course and striving above all for continuity. By 1941–1942, hundreds of such Jewish governments were operating in German-dominated Europe. In the west and south they were centralized on a country-wide basis like the *Union Générale des Israélites de France*, the *Reichsvereinigung* in Germany, or the *Ústredna Zidov* in Slovakia; but in most of Poland, the Baltic areas, and farther east in the occupied U.S.S.R., they were local Jewish councils, functioning as municipalities in closed-off ghettos.

A number of characteristics apply generally to these Jewish organizations. They were first of all continuations of the pre-war Jewish community machinery, retaining many of its leaders and much of its personnel. When, for example, the Germans decreed in Poland that each of the large communities was to have a *Judenrat* with twenty-four members, the twenty-three-man Jewish Council in Lublin simply added one man and went on with its business. As hardships intensified, various communities widened their functions in such domains as sanitation, health, food distribution, employment, apartment allocation, training and education, as well as public order. Finally, the Jewish organizations were employed by the Germans for the implementation of destructive measures: registrations, confiscations, and roundups for deportation. The Jewish councils, their police and divisions for special tasks, had now become agents of the Germans. They continued to obey orders and efficiently produced results. Several million Jews were consequently trapped, not only in the Nazi Reich but in their own communities as well.

While the Jewish apparatus was undergoing these transformations, many individuals and families sought their own ways to save themselves. At times these attempts were difficult or ingenious, as in the case of armed resistance, illicit trade, or the forgery of personal documents. Most often, however, less celebrated means were used—the principal tools of survival were mundane.

The most reliable guarantee of safety was special status: mixed marriage, foreign nationality, and, in some of the Balkan areas, conversion to Christianity. Such affiliations could mean exemption from annihilation.

A second, though less promising, haven was a position in the Jewish community. The *Prominente* lived a little better, ate a little more, and obtained privileges and deferments for themselves and their families. With the onset of deportations, the Jewish councils and their administrative personnel did not shrink as fast as the ghetto population at large.

Private resources constituted a third survival mechanism, if only because they had value in a variety of markets. Cash could buy food, space, or medicines. It could ameliorate suffering or prolong life. In such eastern ghettos as Czestochowa, Poland, or Bershad in the Roumanian-occupied U.S.S.R., money could be used to avoid forced labor. Under certain conditions, as in the Netherlands, it could pay for shelter in hiding.

Skill was yet another important asset. Because the Germans needed diamond cutters, leather workers, carpenters, and other artisans, members of these occupational groups were kept alive longer. Often, however, their families were not protected, and the workers themselves were "combed out" of the factories in repeated "actions."

The last but not always least important factor was the individual's physical condition and psychological makeup. There were situations in which time was bought by endurance, tenacity, or presence of mind. On the other hand, epidemics and roundups often did not discriminate—they caught the weak and the strong.

The Jewish communities under the Nazis were seething with terminal life. They lived from moment to moment, increasingly helpless, and with forebodings of the end. Looking back, one can still feel the ghetto, its clamor and jostling, its captives stepping over bodies and grasping after straws. One can still see the victims in the chaos, discarding all their ballast, losing every foothold, and drawn into a vortex, disappearing in the crush. World Jewry lost one-third of its people in this destruction process. In the macrocosm, that is one history, one fate, and one statistic; but each of these individuals also had a name and each suffered his own death.

1.   A Jewish Argument

When the Jews in Germany were confronted by an anti-Semitic movement in the 1890's, they responded with many assertions of their innocence and worthiness. German Jewry's principal representative in this rebuttal effort was the *Central-Verein deutscher Staatsbürger jüdischen Glaubens* (Central Association of German Citizens of the Jewish Religion), established in 1893. A smaller organization, founded by non-Jews but later predominantly Jewish in membership, was the *Verein zur Abwehr des Anti-Semitismus* (Association to Counter Anti-Semitism). The periodical of this association, the *Abwehr-Blätter*, was published for forty-two years. The following excerpts are taken from an article entitled "The Most Current Anti-Semitic Lies—Something to Counter Them" in the issue of October 1932. The number of Jews in Germany at that time was about 515,000, fewer than 1 per cent of the population.

[Verein zur Abwehr des Anti-Semitismus, *Abwehr-Blätter*, XLII (October 1932), insert.]

"DIE GANGBARSTEN ANTISEMITISCHEN LÜGEN—
EINIGES ZUR WIDERLEGUNG" [EXCERPTS]

"*Jewish World Finance*"

Today, capital formation takes place in large industry. Its largest enterprises are almost entirely dominated by non-Jewish interests: Krupp, Vereinigte Stahlwerke, Klöckner, Stinnes, Siemens, Stumm, I. G. Farben, Hugenberg, Hapag, Nordlloyd.

International connections are concentrated most heavily in those industries in which Jews are without influence or altogether unrepresented: the German-French iron cartel, wooden matches trust, oil trust, potash industry, and shipping conventions are all "clean of Jews," and so are the international chemical cartel, nylon production and all the other raw material and key industries in which Jews have no influence either as owners or directors. . . .

"Wealth of the Jews"

. . . The ten largest conglomerations of wealth are in the following hands: Ex-Emperor Wilhelm II, Count Albert von Thurn und Taxis, Mrs. Bertha Krupp von Bohlen und Halbach, Fritz Thyssen, Otto Wolff, Johann Count zu Hohenlohe-Oehringen, Count Maximilian Egon zu Fürstenberg, Count Guidetto Henckel von Donnersmarck, Count Heinrich XV von Pless, Prince Friedrich of Prussia. . . .

"Jewish Bolshevism"

Bolshevism was developed from Russian nihilism, whose founders were entirely non-Jews, some of them noblemen.

In the summer of 1922, the 18 people's commissars included two Jews (Trotsky, Dorgulevski) and among the 150 members of the Supreme Soviet, seven were Jews. Trotsky has in the meantime been shut out and banned.

The greatest supporter of Bolshevism and the actual instigator of the Russian Revolution was the Imperial German Government. Upon the insistence of Ludendorff, it gave Lenin—incidentally not a Jew but a Tatar of old noble stock—fifty million Goldmark and transported him in a parlor car from Switzerland through Germany to Russia. . . .

"Jewish Government"

. . . The anti-Semites assert that the German government is full of Jews. The 19 post-war cabinets consisted of 237 minis-

ters of whom three (Preuss and twice Rathenau) were Jews
and four (Landsberg, Gradnauer, and twice Hilferding) of
Jewish descent. The last few governments have had no Jewish
ministers.

In the German provinces, the situation is not different: none
of the provincial cabinets contain a Jew. The administration
is not full of Jews, either. For example, in Prussia, among the
twelve chief presidents, thirty-five government presidents
and four hundred provincial counsellors, there is not a single
Jew. . . .

Cultural Contributions by Jews

. . . The following are only a few examples of well known
names whose accomplishments, especially within the realm of
German culture, will not be denied by any educated and objective person.

a) Philosophers: Moritz Lazarus, H. Steinthal (founder of
national character psychology and linguist), Hermann Cohen
(Kant researcher, founder of the "Marburg School"), William
Stern (child psychology), Max Wertheimer (Gestalt theory),
Fritz Mauthner (philosophy of language), Edmund Husserl,
Georg Simmel.

b) Natural Scientists: Richard Willstätter (Pour le mérite,
Nobel prize), Haber (Nobel prize), Frank, Caro (these three:
inventors of fixation of nitrogen from the air, the importance
of which for agriculture and wartime production of munitions
is obvious), Heinrich Hertz (of Jewish descent, pathbreaking
researcher in electricity), Hermann Aron (inventor of electricity meter), Albert Einstein (Nobel prize), Leo Grätz.

c) Technicians: S. Markus (inventor of first gasoline driven
automobile), Popper Lynkeus (inventor of electric transmission lines), Arnstein (builder of overseas-Zeppelin Z.R.3), R. v.
Lieben (inventor of radio amplifiers).

d) Medical Scientists: Jakob Henle, Ludwig Traube
(founder of experimental pathology), Henoch and Finkelstein
(pediatrics), Albert Fränkel (discoverer of pneumonia agent),
Benedikt Stilling (tied blood vessels during hemorrhages),
Meyerhof (Nobel prize), August von Wassermann (producer

of first typhus serum, discoverer of research methods for syphilis treatment, organizer of protective inoculation in the army), Paul Ehrlich (Nobel prize, inventor of salvarsan). How many sick anti-Semites are profiting from these Jewish accomplishments!

e) Jurists: Julius Stahl, Jellinek, Paul Laband, Hermann Staub, L. Goldschmidt, Neander, Heinrich Dernburg, Franz Oppenheimer.

f) Artists: the musicians Felix Mendelssohn-Bartholdy, Meyerbeer, Brüll; the painters Max Liebermann, Lesser Ury; the sculptor Benno Elkan; the architect Alfred Messel.

g) Poets and Writers: Heinrich Heine ("Loreley!"), Berthold Auerbach, Franz Werfel, Jakob Wassemann, Georg Hermann, Lion Feuchtwanger, Ludwig Fulda. The flag song "Proud Flies the Flag" was written by Robert Linderer, the soldiers' song "Annemarie" by Julius Freund. . . .

The Jews in War

. . . Of 538,000 Jews in Germany, more than 96,000 were under arms, including 10,000 volunteers; about 80,000 were on the front lines, 35,000 received decorations, 23,000 were promoted, including more than 2000 to officer rank (without medical corps). One hundred sixty-eight Jews who volunteered as flyers are known by name. At the top of the list is Lieutenant D. R. Frankl who received the Pour le mérite and who like 29 other Jewish flyers was killed in battle.

Twelve thousand Jewish soldiers did not see their homeland again; they died a hero's death for their German fatherland. More than 10,000 of their names have now been recorded with personal information, unit, and number. The dead of Hamburg, Alsace-Lorraine and ceded Posen (with its relatively large Jewish population) have not yet been registered.

It is heartless to demand today that the widows and orphans, parents and brothers, brides and relatives of 12,000 fallen Jews bc deprived of equality in Germany.

2.   A Confidential Nazi Analysis

In 1944 a Nazi study of Jewish penetrations in the economy of Europe appeared in Vienna with the notation "Not in the book trade." The volume, which was to have been the first of at least two, deals with England and pre-Nazi Germany (including Austria). It is replete with tables and charts which reveal a special interest in quantities and proportions. While the author assumes a great deal about Jewish economic power, he holds these assumptions constant for all countries and all periods. For this reason, his conclusions are of interest. He finds first that the economic "Judaization" of the European countries was much greater in the east than in the west, but that at the same time the absolute size of the eastern undertakings was much smaller than the western. He discovers, second, that the high point of Jewish economic influence had been reached in 1913. After 1918 the Jewish banks of Berlin and Vienna were operating with money which they had received as callable low-interest loans from western sources. The Jews were lending these funds at higher rates for long-term purposes to small and medium-sized industries. When, in 1931, the western creditors recalled their loans, the Jewish banks, which were the epitome of Jewish power, collapsed.

[Wolfgang Höfler, *Untersuchungen über die Machtstellung der Juden in der Weltwirtschaft*, vol. I *England und das Vornationalsozialistische Deutschland* (Vienna: printed by Adolph Holzhausens Nachf., 1944), 216–17, 235–37. In the library of the University of Vermont through the courtesy of Dr. S. A. Goudsmit.]

As for low-level economic enterprises, such as trade with second-hand goods, animal byproducts, furs, and so forth, the results ascertained from inquiries into various branches indicate a fairly even Judaization of the whole of Europe in 1933. Where critical economic functions are concerned, however—and they interest us most—one will find regularly that

first, the degree of Judaization rises steeply as one proceeds from west to east

second, there is often a decline in the size of the critical economic sectors from England through Germany and Austria towards Poland and Hungary.

These contradictory tendencies result in a *crestline* of Jewish economic power within Europe, which runs north to south through east-central Europe across Berlin, Prague, and Vienna to Triest. West of this line Jews in the top strata become scarce, while to the east, in Poland, Hungary and the Balkan states, almost all trade is Jewish—but in dimensions which regularly amount to less than one per cent of world volume. Looking at the material gathered so far, the crestline seems to drop off sharply on both sides and this is especially true if we place ourselves into the year 1913 when this central European belt, in comparison with neighbor states, had reached its economic zenith. . . .

The game which Jewry played for 30 years against the German people is not over by a long shot. But from the day when they gave up their position as the protected Jews of the German and Austrian emperors, to sail on their own in the stormy sea of world politics, they have no longer had any luck. . . .

. . . Germany, which in 1913 occupied a primary economic position within Europe in many respects, and which had had every prospect of taking first place in all respects, declined in 1918 to a pillaged humiliated beggar and the sick man of the world economy. The blow came down with special force on the banks. . . .

. . . The collapse which the German and Austrian armies had suffered in November 1918 engulfed the banks of Berlin and Vienna during 1931 as a matter of logical consequence. The two thrones from which the Jews had dominated the central European economy for 80 years were thus demolished. Most telling was the result for the Viennese banks which had dominated most of the banks in the successor states of the old [Austro-Hungarian] monarchy, and which ruled directly or indirectly Austrian industry and, beyond it, major iron works, coal mines, lumber yards, sugar factories, and so forth all the way to [German] Silesia, [Polish] Galicia, and [Roumanian] Transylvania. But here too that rule had rested on funds borrowed from French, English, and American sources, and when these loans were called in 1931, the banks collapsed. . . .

All of the share capital held by the major Viennese banks (with the exception of the French-Jewish Länderbank) was annihilated between 1931 and 1935. . . . In Berlin, no banks survived without open state support, except for the Deutsche Bank and the Handelsgesellschaft. To recognize the logic of these facts, it is important to realize that in both Vienna and Berlin the large banks had lost their wealth and for the most part fallen de facto into the control of the state, before National Socialism seized power.

3.   Name Changes: 1932

From their earliest days the Nazis were interested in names: company names, street names, personal names. They wanted to eliminate Jewish names from institutions or locales which were considered German, and they were anxious to identify the Jewish character of any family that was thought to be Jewish or any business that was believed to be in Jewish hands. The identifications were a natural consequence of the oft-repeated assertion that Jewry was camouflaging itself in German trappings and exerting its influence from hidden power positions, but the name decrees—particularly the compulsory adoption of the Jewish middle names Israel and Sara—also served to facilitate expulsion and destruction.

The bureaucrat in charge of personal names was Dr. Hans Globke in the Interior Ministry. The passages

below are taken from a Globke draft which is significant primarily for its date—it was written on December
23, 1932, more than five weeks *before* Hitler took office.

[Central Archives of the German Democratic Republic through the courtesy
of Ambassador Stefan Heymann, excerpt.]

[Prussian] Minister of Interior
Berlin, December 23, 1932 [Handwritten:] date remains,
to Government Presidents (Police President in Berlin), Provincial Councillors and State Police Administrators, as well as
the other local public offices in city districts.

> At once! Not suited for
> printing in Ministerial
> Gazette

Draft by
Government Councillor
Dr. Globke
I am transmitting herewith the guidelines that are to be
observed while processing requests for name changes which
are to be submitted to me for decision. I should like to remark
explicitly that these are only designed to facilitate the preparation of a decision. Even if the criteria in these guidelines are
met, there is no guarantee of approval of a requested name
change. Kindly refrain from publishing the guidelines. [Sev-
eral initials, including Gl 20–XII]

Guidelines
for Processing Requests for Change of
Family Names

– – –

VI Jewish Names
(1) The viewpoint that a person of Jewish descent is dishon-
ored by carrying a Jewish name cannot be approved of. Therefore, attempts on the part of Jewish persons to disguise their
Jewish descent by removing or changing their Jewish name
cannot be supported. Adoption of Christianity constitutes no
reason to change the name. Similarly a name change should

not be based on references to anti-Semitic currents or a striving for economic improvement.

(2) On the other hand, repulsive Jewish names which usually give rise to sneers (such as Itzig, Schmul, ~~Moses~~ [crossed out in text]) or which produce an aversion towards the carrier (Nachtschweiss [literally: Nightsweat], Totenkopf [death-head]) may be changed in the same way as repulsive German names, but as a rule only by ~~changing the sound~~ [crossed out in original] granting a similar sounding name (Issen, Schmal, ~~Moses~~ [crossed out]), the name of a close relative, or a phantasy name, not by award of a circulating ~~German~~ [crossed out] name.

4.   Action in the Universities

The first measure published by the new Nazi regime was contained in paragraph 3 of the Law for the Restoration of the Professional Civil Service of April 7, 1933. It provided for the compulsory retirement of "non-Aryans" with the exception of officials who had served since August 1, 1914, or who were front-line veterans, or whose fathers or sons had been killed in action. Paragraph 2 of the First Implementation Decree dated April 11, 1933, defined a "non-Aryan" as anyone with at least one Jewish grandparent. The law, with the definition of the implementation decree, was applied to public schools and universities inasmuch as members of the teaching staffs were officials.

On April 25, 1933, the Nazis issued also the Law Against Overcrowding of German Schools, which stipulated that the percentage of "non-Aryans" to be admitted to each school or university was to be no higher than the percentage of "non-Aryans" in the population of the entire Reich. (It was fixed at 1.5 per cent.) The calculation of the number of "non-Aryans" was *not* to include children of front-line veterans or those who had an "Aryan" parent or two "Aryan" grandparents.

The first of the two documents reprinted below is a dismissal notice sent to a Jewish professor. The second is an action involving the denial of scholarships to Jewish students. The scholarship recipients were in effect considered civil servants. They were to be ineligible for stipends if they had been ineligible for retention in the civil service; they were to be affected by the regulation even if they had not been affected by the quota calculation.

[From the personnel records of the University of Frankfurt am Main in: Kommission zur Erforschung der Geschichte der Frankfurter Juden, *Dokumente zur Geschichte der Frankfurter Juden 1933–1945* (Frankfurt am Main: Verlag Waldemar Kramer, 1963), p. 101.]

Minister for Science, Art, and Public Education (Rust) to Professor Martin Buber, with Copies to the Rector and University Senate, April 10, 1933

Based on §3 of the Law for the Restoration of the Civil Service of April 7, 1933 I hereby deprive you of your tenure at the University of Frankfurt am Main.

[From *Freiburger Studentenzeitung*, November 3, 1933, p. 6, as reprinted in Guido Schneeberger, ed., *Nachlese zu Heidegger* (Bern, Switzerland: privately printed, 1962), p. 137.]

AWARDS OF FINANCIAL SUPPORT TO STUDENTS IN
BADEN [PROVINCE] COLLEGES

Students who during the last few years have fought for the national revolution in the SA, SS or other armed formations are entitled, upon submission of a certificate signed by their superiors, to special consideration in the award of financial support (tuition remission, stipends, etc.).

On the other hand no awards may henceforth be given to Jewish or Marxist students.

Jewish students in accordance with this regulation are students of non-Aryan descent within the meaning of paragraph 3 of the Law for the Restoration of the Civil Service and of paragraph 2 of the First Ordinance for the Implementation of the Law for the Restoration of the Civil Service of April 11, 1933. The prohibition of awards applies therefore also to those students of non-Aryan descent who have one parent and two grandparents of Aryan descent and whose father fought during the World War on the front line for Germany or its allies. Excepted from this prohibition are only those students of non-Aryan descent who have been front-line soldiers themselves or whose father was killed on the German side during the World War.

The Rector
[Martin Heidegger]

5.   The Jews Defined

Not until 1935 did the German bureaucracy come up with a definition of the term "Jew." The occasion was the issuance of a Reich Citizenship Law (one of the "Nuremberg Laws") which had declared that Jews could not be citizens. The First Ordinance to the Reich Citizenship Law established a method to determine who was a Jew and also provided for the dismissal of all the remaining "non-Aryan" officials who were Jews within the scope of the new definition.

It is to be noted that while heretofore the population had been divided only into "Aryans" and "non-Aryans," there were now two kinds of non-Aryans: Jews and so-called *Mischlinge.* Half-Jews who did not belong to the Jewish religion or who were not married to a Jewish person on September 15, 1935, were to be called *Mischlinge* of the first degree. One-quarter Jews became

Mischlinge of the second degree. The fate of the *Mischlinge* was never settled to the complete satisfaction of the Nazi party, and they were the subject of considerable discussion during the "final solution" conferences of 1941 and 1942.

Throughout the twelve years of Nazi rule, records establishing descent or religious adherence were all-important in deciding who was a Jew, a *Mischling*, or a German. An illustration of a case involving records is appended to the text of the definition decree. Reference in the correspondence of this case is made to the wearing of the Jewish Star. The Yellow Star of David had to be worn by Jews after September 14, 1941. *Mischlinge* did not have to wear it.

[*Reichsgesetzblatt* (*Reich Legal Gazette*) 1935, I, 1333.]

FIRST ORDINANCE TO THE REICH CITIZENSHIP LAW
NOVEMBER 14, 1935

On the basis of article 3 of the Reich Citizenship Law of September 15, 1935 (*Reich Legal Gazette* I, 1146) the following is ordered:

Article 1

1. Until the issuance of further regulations for the award of citizenship, nationals of German or related blood who possessed the right to vote in Reichstag elections at the time when the Reich Citizenship Law entered into force or who were granted provisional citizenship by the Reich Minister of Interior acting in agreement with the Deputy of the Führer, are provisionally considered Reich citizens.

2. The Reich Minister of Interior acting in agreement with the Deputy of the Führer may revoke provisional citizenship.

Article 2

1. The regulations of Article 1 apply also to nationals who were part Jews [*jüdische Mischlinge*].

2. Partly Jewish is anyone who is descended from one or

two grandparents who are fully Jewish [*volljüdisch*] by race, in so far as he is not to be considered as Jewish under article 5, section 2. A grandparent is to be considered as fully Jewish if he belonged to the Jewish religious community.

Article 3

Only a Reich citizen as bearer of complete political rights may exercise the right to vote in political affairs or hold public office. The Reich Minister of Interior or an agency empowered by him may make exceptions with regard to an admission to public office during the transition. The affairs of religious communities will not be affected.

Article 4

1. A Jew cannot be a Reich citizen. He is not allowed the right to vote in political affairs; he cannot hold public office.

2. Jewish civil servants will retire as of December 31, 1935. If these civil servants fought for Germany or her allies in the World War, they will receive the full pension to which they are entitled by their last position in the pay scale, until they reach retirement age; they will not, however, advance in seniority. Upon reaching retirement age their pension is to be based on pay scales which will prevail at that time.

3. The affairs of religious communities will not be affected.

4. The provisions of service for teachers in Jewish public schools will remain unaltered until new regulations are issued for the Jewish school system.

Article 5

1. Jew is he who is descended from at least three grandparents who are fully Jewish by race. Article 2, paragraph 2, sentence 2 applies.

2. Also to be considered a Jew is a partly Jewish national who is descended from two fully Jewish grandparents and
   a) who belonged to the Jewish religious community, upon adoption of the [Reich Citizenship] Law, or is received into the community thereafter, or
   b) who was married to a Jewish person upon adoption of the law, or marries one thereafter, or

c) who is the offspring of a marriage concluded by a Jew (as defined in paragraph 1) after the entry into force of the Law for the Protection of German Blood and Honor of September 15, 1935 (*Reich Legal Gazette* I, 1146), or

d) who is the offspring of an extramarital relationship involving a Jew (as defined in paragraph 1) and who is born out of wedlock after July 31, 1936.

Article 6

1. Requirements for purity of blood exceeding those of article 5, which are made in Reich laws or regulations of the National Socialist German Workers' Party and its organizations, remain unaffected.

2. Any other requirements for purity of blood, exceeding those of article 4, may be made only with the consent of the Reich Minister of the Interior and the Deputy of the Führer. Insofar as requirements of this type exist already, they become void on January 1, 1936 unless they are accepted by the Reich Minister of the Interior acting with the agreement of the Deputy of the Führer. Acceptance is to be requested from the Reich Minister of the Interior.

Article 7

The Führer and Reich Chancellor may grant exemptions from the stipulations of implementory ordinances.
Berlin, November 14, 1935
The Führer and Reich Chancellor
    Adolf Hitler
The Reich Minister of the Interior
    Frick
The Deputy of the Führer
    R. Hess
(Reich Minister without Portfolio)

[Israel Police document 1107.]

Gestapo Office in Düsseldorf/Section II B 4 to Reich Security Main Office IV B 4, Berlin, October, 1942

Subject: Petition of Emilie Heimann, of German blood, born
          Adolphs, April 1, 1899, in W.-Elberfeld, married to
          the Jew Israel Heimann, born January 27, 1900, in
          W.-Elberfeld, both living in W.-Elberfeld, Sophien
          Street 12.

Previous: Decrees of May 29 and September 2, 1942 IV B 4 a
           —847/42

Enclosure: 1 stapled

The Jewish Community List (critical date October 1, 1935)
drawn up by the Jewish Community in Elberfeld and available
to my branch office in Wuppertal carries the *Mischlinge* of the
1st degree Eva and Mally Heimann as members of the Jewish
religious community. Moreover, their Jewish father, Wilhelm
Isr. Heimann designated them as "Israelite" in the yearly
registrations of 1931 and 1932. On the basis of these records,
the decision with respect to racial classification was that these
Mischlinge of the 1st degree were to be regarded as Jews within
the meaning of §5, section 2a of the First Ordinance to the
Reich Citizenship Law and that accordingly they had to wear
the Jewish star.

The Heimanns deny that they registered their children as
members of the Jewish community in Wuppertal or that they
permitted them to take part in Jewish religious instruction.
During the examination of the records of the Jewish community in Wuppertal it was established that the Jewish community list was put together on the basis of the community's
consolidated household list by the Jew Sussmann, now
deceased, then employed in the community as a teacher. Sussmann, however, added Jews and *Mischlinge* who were known
to him, but for whom there were no household lists, to the
community register. In these cases, he made a handwritten
notation and appended any evidence available to the Jewish
community. As for the Heimann family as well as seven other
persons, there is neither a household list nor any note prepared by Sussmann. It is therefore not possible to provide an

incontestable answer to the objection of the Heimanns that their children were included in the Jewish community list without their knowledge, since they did not register the children with the Jewish community and prepared no household list. However, inasmuch as today the community possesses neither the household list for the family Heimann nor any writing by Sussmann about them and yet the H. family does appear in the community register, one may suspect that Heimann, who has been employed by the community since 1940 and who had access to all its records, destroyed the papers which incriminate his family. That there are no records of the seven other Jews can only strengthen this suspicion, since H. relies on the destruction of these records to justify the absence of a listing of his own family.

In view of the above, I request that the appeal of Mrs. Heimann be rejected and that the *Mischlinge* of the 1st degree Mally and Eva Heimann be classified as Jews in accordance with §5, section 2 of the First Ordinance to the Reich Citizenship Law. I hereby return the material sent to me under the decree of May 29, 1942—IV B 4 a 847/742.

Berlin SW 11, January 1, 1943
Gestapo
RSHA IV C 2
Arrest No. H. 16981

Protective Custody Order

First and Second Name: Wilhelm Israel Heimann
Birthday and Birthplace: January 27, 1900 in Elberfeld
Occupation: writer
Marital Status: married
Nationality: German
Religion: Mosaic
Race (to be noted with Non-Aryan): Jew
Residence: Wuppertal-Elberfeld, Sophia Street 12

is taken into custody

Reasons:

He—she—through his her—conduct endangers, according to state political findings, the substance and security of people and state, in that he she—is under deep suspicion of having used his position as employee in the office of the Jewish community in Wuppertal to remove rosters which disclosed the racial classification of his children, and which were the basis for entering his children in the Jewish community list of Wuppertal, so that it is to be feared that so long as he is free his conduct will be detrimental to the state.

6.   The Disbarment of the Jewish Lawyers

The Fifth Ordinance to the Reich Citizenship Law, dated September 27, 1938, removed Jewish lawyers from the bar, thus reducing them to "consultants." The ordinance was signed by Hitler, Minister of Justice Gürtner, Minister of Interior Frick, Deputy of the Führer (and chief of the party machinery) Hess, and Undersecretary of Finance Reinhardt. The sequence of signatures indicates that the measure was drafted in the Justice Ministry with the participation of the other offices. A short story of the genesis of the decree was told by the Justice Ministry's Undersecretary Franz Schlegelberger at his trial in Nuremberg.

The trial, incidentally, was portrayed in the motion picture *Judgment at Nuremberg*, and the chief defendant was played by Burt Lancaster. The movie character is a composite of two real persons, one of whom—the scholarly one—is Schlegelberger.

[Testimony by Franz Schlegelberger in the Justice Trial, *Trials of War Criminals* (Washington: U.S. Government Printing Office, 1951), III, 718–719.]

... When the Party started a campaign against Jewish lawyers, I went to see Hitler and told him that it was untenable to remove from their profession Jewish lawyers among whom research people of repute were included, and with whom I myself had worked. I was pleased when I succeeded in persuading Hitler that that was correct and in achieving his agreement that he would reject the wishes of the Party. To inform the agencies concerned, I called a meeting of Ministers of Justice of the Laender who were still in office in those days and informed them about Hitler's decision. The result was surprising. I encountered bitter resistance, and the meeting bore no result. Hitler asked for Guertner [Gürtner] to come to see him and asked him for information as to whether I was not perhaps a Jew myself. Then the Party began to exercise pressure on Hitler. He abandoned his decision, and the Jewish lawyers were removed from office. So as to make it possible at least for the Jews to preserve their rights, I proposed to set up the institute of the so-called Jewish consultants where former lawyers worked as consultants.

7.   An "Aryanization" Contract

The process of transferring Jewish enterprises into non-Jewish hands was called "Aryanization." Until 1938 such transfers were accomplished upon the initiative of buyers and sellers and involved terms which reflected the increasingly difficult position of the Jewish businessman. Moreover, each contract had to have official approval, which was given only if the property was sold for a fraction of its value. Late in 1938, Jewish firms were made subject to liquidation or compulsory transfer.

J. & C. A. Schneider Company in Frankfurt am Main was wholly owned by Jews and manufactured slippers.

The "Aryanization" is described in a report written by a Dresdner Bank official in Frankfurt on January 7, 1946 (Alexandria document DB-324). The Dresdner Bank in this case had been an "adviser" in the transaction.

At the end of 1937 the owners were prepared to enter into negotiations with prospective purchasers, and on June 24, 1938, a contract was made with Hausschuh-Vertriebs-G.m.b.H., a subsidiary of Jürgens-van-den Berg Margarine-Verkaufs-Union. The price was 4,250,-000 Reichsmark, an amount based on a valuation of the net inventory on May 1, 1938, which was 4,426,000 Reichsmark. In short, the entire plant, the land, buildings, machines, installations, trademark, and so forth, were not considered part of the market value. Even so, approval was withheld pending an investigation into the purely "Aryan" character of Jürgens-van-den Berg.

A contract was subsequently made with another purchaser, Bruno Seletzky, a Swiss representative of the Czech Skoda-Works. The projected amount, once again 4,250,000 Reichsmark, was reduced by the Economy Ministry by 250,000 Reichsmark, which were set aside for employee fringe benefits. But not all of the permitted four million were made available to the owners. In accordance with paragraph 8 of the contract, they were to receive the equivalent of 880,000 Reichsmark in Swiss francs. This was their only real compensation. The sum of 1,350,000 Reichsmark was allowed in German currency, and most of this money had to be handed over by the owners to the German Reich in the form of personal taxes, including special taxes payable upon emigration. The remaining 1,770,000 Reichsmark were not received at all. That was the amount judged by the Economy Ministry to have been the "Aryanization profit" of the purchaser, i.e., the difference between his payment and stated value; and pursuant to the prevailing philosophy that only the Reich was to profit from the destruction of the Jews, the 1,770,000 were to be collected by the Reich, in this case in the form of foreign currencies supplied by the purchaser. The Jewish sellers, in other words, had to relinquish in favor of the Reich the 1,770,000 Reichsmark from the sum due to them in order to close the transaction.

Paragraph 4, section 2, clause 2 deals with another serious consequence of "Aryanizations"—the loss of jobs held by Jewish employees, who are mentioned by name in Appendix 3 of the contract.

[Alexandria documents from the files of the Dresdner Bank (DB-83), Microfilm T 83, Roll 97.]

Copy

For the original, 10,000 Reichsmark have been paid as deed tax.
Frankfurt a. M.   27th December 1938
Notary (signature by Wirth)
No. 1162 Year 1938 in the deed roll
Negotiated
Frankfurt am Main, December 17, 1938.
Appearing today before the undersigned, Kurt Wirth, resident notary in Frankfurt am Main in the district of the Main Provincial Court, Frankfurt am Main, were
1. The merchant Lothar Adler, Frankfurt a. M. Schwindt Street 23
2. The merchant Friedrich, known as Fritz Adler, Frankfurt a. M. Beethoven Street 43
both acting on their own behalf as well as partners personally liable for the firm J. & C. A. Schneider, Frankfurt a. M.,
3. The director Bruno Seletzky currently resident in Zurich, Tal Street 1. The party mentioned in 1. is known to the officiating notary personally, the parties in 2. and 3. are not but were introduced to him by the [party] Provincial Economic Adviser Karl Eckardt, Frankfurt a. M. whom he knows and who was present. Thereby the officiating notary obtained cer-

tainty about the identity of the parties 2. and 3. The parties allowed the following contract to be witnessed:

§1.   *Sold Enterprise. Right of Firm.*

(1) Messrs. Lothar and Fritz Adler are selling the above-mentioned firm known until now as J. & C. A. Schneider, which produces and sells shoes, especially slippers, together with all that pertains thereto, to Mr. Bruno Seletzky.

(2) The sellers expressly agree herewith that the buyer continue to use the firm name "J. & C. A. Schneider" with or without an addendum indicating the successor relationship. The buyer is not obligated to continue the use of the firm name and may change it any time for reasons of his own.

§2.   *Sold Property.*

(1) Together with the enterprise, all properties (assets and rights) which are possessed by the firm and which were in stock as of May 1, 1938, or which should have been in stock on that date in accordance with standard bookkeeping practice, are hereby sold, provided however that there is no inclusion of any changes which occurred after May 1, 1938 as a consequence of normal business activity.

(2) Amongst sold properties are included under any circumstances the following objects, materials, lots, and rights even if they have not been entered in the books of the firm:

1) The lots, together with buildings and plant installations registered in the deed book of Frankfurt am Main

District 15 Sheet 312 Kt Sheet 204, parcels 13/8, 4, 5, 6, 7, 12/8

District 15 Sheet 421 Kt Sheet 206, parcel 4

District 15 Sheet 832 Kt Sheet 206, parcel 16/12

District 15 Sheet 857 Kt Sheet 206, parcel 19/2

District 15 Sheet 1190 Kt Sheet 209, parcels 19/2, 3, 22/1

Use and liabilities are transferred as of May 1, 1938, to the acquirer who from this date assumes also insurance and rental contracts pertaining to the lots and buildings.

The transfer has already taken place.

The parties to the contract hereby define the cession:

"We are agreed that the properties under (2) 1) should be transferred to the acquirer and consent and request to have the legal changes recorded in the deed book."

For purposes of calculating taxes and costs, the value of the single units is given as follows:

Re 15 Leaf 312 noted parcels: RM 154,500
Re 15 Leaf 421 noted parcels: RM 253,200
Re 15 Leaf 832 noted parcels: RM 25,400
Re 15 Leaf 857 noted parcels: RM 17,800
Re 15 Leaf 1190 noted parcels: RM 247,400

2) All inventory pieces used in the sold enterprise, including vehicles as well as transport and store installations with the exception of the two passenger cars which carry license plates IT 106839 and IT 111652

3) all the machines, tools and plant installations used in the sold enterprise with the exception of any leased machines

4) all the available supplies in the sold enterprise

5) all existing claims against customers, claims arising from exchanges, bank deposits, credits from prepayments and other claims or credits pertaining to the sold enterprise

6) all cash

7) all patents or trademarks of any kind used by the sold enterprise or entered in the name of the firm or its partners

8) the contractual rights vis-à-vis the Württembergische Notenbank in Stuttgart and the Dresdner Bank in Frankfurt am Main for erasing the debts entered with respect to the above-mentioned properties in the deed book in part III.

(3) Except for any express provisions to the contrary the sold properties including the real properties are being sold as they stand, without liability for any defects of any sort. The sellers guarantee, however, that the sold properties are available and not encumbered by rights of third parties with the exception of the following on real properties

a) the Dresdner Bank Reichsmark 600,000
b) the Dresdner Bank Goldmark 100,000
c) the Würtemb. Notenbank Goldmark 200,000
d) the Würtemb. Notenbank Goldmark 400,000

and with the exception of any title reservations customarily exercised by suppliers. The sellers are obligated to remove at their own cost any rights of third parties which may exist in spite of this agreement, especially encumbrances entered in the deed book so far as they do not coincide with the agreement. Excepted therefrom is the entry in Part II of the deed book which provides for cession of property to the city of Frankfurt a. M. for street construction purposes.

So far as the sellers are still indebted under the loans in Part III, they agree to the immediate erasure of these loans.

§3.   *Obligations to be Taken Over.*

[Deals with normal business obligations and tax obligations. For taxes due from March 1, 1938, buyer makes himself liable to a maximum of RM 100,000.]

§4.   *Contracts to be Taken Over.*

(1) The buyer is entitled and obligated to take over the following contracts to which the sold firm was a party and which were in force on May 1, 1938:

a) all contracts for purchases and deliveries

b) all the contracts for service employment and representation with Aryan persons, which are appropriate to the normal business activity of the firm and which are not to be enforced after December 31, 1939, or which may be dissolved as of that date on the basis of rights existing on May 1, 1938

c) all rental contracts which are appropriate to the normal business of the firm and which expire not later than December 31, 1939 or which may be dissolved as of that date on the basis of rights existing on May 1, 1938

d) insurance contracts listed in appendix I

e) the following construction contracts

1. for reconstruction of the main entrance on Mainzerland Street 281

2. for mixing room and installations and

3. for reconstruction of sanitary facilities

f) other contracts not mentioned, especially forgotten contracts of lesser importance which are appropriate for normal activity of the firm and which should be taken over as matter of full faith and credit.

(2) The following contracts are taken over in deviation from section (1)

1) employment contracts with Aryan persons named in appendix II,

2) employment contracts with non-Aryan persons named in appendix III, provided that the contracts agree with the description in the appendix especially with regard to their expiration or termination. However, there will be no employment of non-Aryan persons from the day of contract termination. They must nevertheless be available to the new management for as long as they are contractually entitled to indemnification,

3) rental contracts contained in appendix IV.

(3) With respect to the non-Aryan persons, whose contracts are to be taken over under article 2, section 2, the sellers are answerable to the buyer for the following:

1. Every contract must unconditionally expire on the date listed in appendix III.

2. Upon their separation, the persons involved must not present any settlement claims against the buyer. Any settlement claims to be granted or paid to these persons for moral or legal reasons must be arranged with final and terminal effect between the sellers and the persons involved and also paid to these persons before the buyer takes over the contractual relationship, so that the buyer is liable only for current wages or other emoluments to the day of their separation, apart from claims which these persons may develop from an employment lasting beyond the time periods listed in appendix III.

(4) The sellers are answerable to the buyer for the fact that the rental contract in respect of Kleyer Street 70 mentioned in appendix IV runs to May 31, 1945.

§5.   *Takeover, Utilization, and Liabilities.*
[Provides for considering the enterprise as being run on the account of the buyer as of May 1, 1938.]

§6.   *Introduction into the Enterprise.*
(1) The sellers are handing over the management at once to the new entrepreneur and are basically no longer active in the enterprise. However, they will be available to the new management for a minimum of 2 months and a maximum of 6 months, if the latter for any reason, including orientation in business habits, introduction to suppliers and customers, or other reasons, requires their participation.

(2) So long as the buyer does not relinquish the availability of the sellers, he must recompense Mr. Lothar Adler 5000 Reichsmark monthly and Mr. Fritz Adler 4000 Reichsmark.

§7.   *Competition Clause.*

The sellers obligate themselves not to set up or operate directly or indirectly a slipper factory in Germany until December 31, 1948 nor participate in such an enterprise directly or indirectly. The sellers obligate themselves especially not to participate or act in such an enterprise within Germany as manager, employee, representative or owner. The term activity includes also general consultations as well as service in a board of directors or service in an office which is equivalent to that of member of the board. The term participation does not include capital participation which is not at the same time competitive activity.

§8.   *Sales Price.*

(1) The sales price for the enterprise to be delivered under this contract, including properties, objects, lots, rights, and the further obligations assumed by the sellers under this contract (excepting those of §6), is to be paid by the buyer, taking account of the obligations to be assumed by him, to the sellers in the amount of

4,000,000.—Reichsmark.

(2) The sales price is due upon receipt of necessary official approval with annual interest of 4% from May 1, 1938. The sales price of 4,000,000.—Reichsmark will be discharged in Reichsmark in the amount of 1,350,000 Reichsmark, and in Swiss Francs in the amount of 350,000.—(three hundred and fifty thousand Swiss Francs) payable to the sellers abroad.

§9.   *Costs.*

[Each party pays own costs of legal and financial counsel.]

§10.   *Foreign Currency Approval.*

So far as foreign currency approval is required for the fulfillment of particular stipulations in this contract, these stipulations enter into force only after receipt of foreign currency approval. For the rest, any disapproval of foreign currency does not affect the validity of the contract.

The parties obligate themselves to make joint efforts for required approval.

§11.

This contract is concluded as of November 14, 1938, but should receive renewal certification today in notary form.

The sellers are Jews; the buyer is Aryan and a foreigner for foreign currency purposes.

The protocol, together with appendices, was read in the presence of the notary, approved by the parties, and signed by them in person as follows

signed	Bruno Seletzky
signed	Lothar Adler
signed	Fritz Adler
signed	Kurt Wirth, Notary

To §4 Article Section 2

Appendix III to the notary protocol of December 17, 1938, deed roll No. 1162/1938 signed K. Wirth, Notary

Contracts with non-Aryan employees and non-Aryan representatives

1) Contract with Mr. Fritz Ballin, sub-representative for Berlin. The contractual relationship which extended to September 30, 1939, ends in accordance with settlement agreement on June 30, 1939.

2) Contract with Mr. Arthur Bramsen, officer of the firm and principal commercial traveler in Germany and abroad (Belgium and Scandinavia). The contractual relationship which extended to December 31, 1939, ends in accordance with settlement agreement on March 31, 1939.

3) Contract with Mr. Felix Freund, representative for Southern Germany, Rheinpfalz. The contractual relationship, which in accordance with legal requirements is terminable, ends in accordance with settlement agreement on December 31, 1938.

4) Contract with Mr. M. Goldschmidt, commercial traveler for Holland, England, Switzerland, and Morocco. The contractual relationship ends in accordance with agreement on December 31, 1938.

5) Contract with Mr. S. Gromowski, representative for Pom-

erania, East and West Prussia. The contractual relationship ends in accordance with agreement on September 30, 1938.

6) Contract with Main Provincial Court Judge (retired) Hess. The contractual relationship ends in accordance with agreement on March 31, 1939.

7) Contract with Miss Oppenheim, director of the samples division. The contractual relationship ends in accordance with agreement on March 31, 1939.

8) Contract with Mr. Leon Schmerbach, commercial traveler for Southern Germany. The contractual relationship ends in accordance with agreement on December 31, 1938.

9) Contract with Mr. J. Schoen, commercial traveler for North Germany. The contractual relationship ends in accordance with agreement on September 30, 1938.

10) Contract with Mr. Ludwig Strauss, commercial traveler in the Rhineland. The contractual relationship that extended to September 30, 1939, ends in accordance with settlement agreement on March 31, 1939.

11) Contract with Mrs. Weinberger, director of camel's-hair disposition, camel's-hair removal, and camel's-hair sample division. The contractual relationship ends in accordance with agreement on December 31, 1938.

12) Contract with Mr. A. Apfelbaum, Berlin representative. The contractual relationship ends in accordance with agreement on September 30, 1939.

13) Contract with Mr. Michael Cohn, Copenhagen, representative for Denmark. The contractual relationship ends in accordance with agreement on December 31, 1938.

14) Contract with Mr. Gaston Haas, Casablanca, representative for Morocco. The contractual relationship ends in accordance with agreement on December 31, 1938.

15) Contract with Mr. Achille Kahn, Brussels, representative for Belgium. The contractual relationship ends in accordance with agreement on December 31, 1938.

16) Contracts with all other non-Aryan employees not named under 1) to 15), provided that these contracts were terminated not later than June 30, 1938, or ended by that date.

8. Jews in Health Resorts

The physical separation of German and Jew was begun in the 1930's. Some of these measures were drafted by civil servants who made a multitude of distinctions and whose work was cautious, painstaking, and slow. The letter on health resorts is an example.

[Alexandria document EAP VIII–173–b–16–14/38, Microfilm T 175, Roll 409.]

Copy

The Reich and Prussian Minister of the Interior
(signed: deputizing Pfundtner)
to provincial governments in Prussia
  chief presidents and government presidents [outside Prussia]
Rapid Letter
July 24, 1937
Subject: Jewish guests in baths and health resorts

Insofar as visits by non-resident Jewish guests to baths and health resorts are made subject to regulation, the following guidelines are to be observed by state and local authorities in charge of health installations.

1. Jewish guests are to be admitted to health baths in which there is a possibility for their separate accommodation in Jewish resort buildings, hotels, pensions, guest houses, and the like, provided that no German female personnel under the age of 45 is being employed in these enterprises.

Community facilities which serve health purposes such as mineral drinking halls, or bath houses, are to be made available to Jews; having regard, however, for the non-Jewish guests, it is admissible to prescribe restrictions as to place and time for

Jewish occupancy, for example, restrictions to specific cabins or specific times for bathing. Those of the community facilities which do not serve health purposes directly, such as gardens, sport arenas, or guest houses, may be barred to Jews.

In all other baths or health resorts, Jews may be excluded generally or partially, or restricted to existing Jewish enterprises (article 1 §1).

Health baths within the meaning of this regulation are those baths in which natural, localized, curative agents are made available in appropriate manner to the general public for health recovery.

2. The term "Jew" is defined in §5 of the First Ordinance to the Reich Citizenship Law of November 14, 1935 (*Reich Legal Gazette* I, 1333). No distinction is to be made between Jews of German and foreign nationalities.

3. Before issuance of any [specific] regulation, an opportunity should be given to the Reich Committee for Tourism to express its views.

I request that all implementory steps be taken and that an attempt be made with the cooperation of the Reich Committee for Tourism to assure observance of these guidelines also in other [private] resort managements.

My decision is to be requested in the event of any doubts, especially, if there is any question as to whether a bath or resort is to be regarded as a health resort.

9.   Jewish Self-Concentration

During the 1930's an increasing impoverishment of the Jews produced a migration from small towns to the major cities, where the migrants hoped for help from the larger Jewish communities. The inflow encountered negative attitudes among mayors, particularly in Frankfurt, but the SS and Police wanted no disturbance of the movement, since it furthered the goal of mass emigration. Later, the concentration of Jews in the cities was also functional for deportations. The SS-Major General referred to in the letter is Reinhard Heydrich, chief of the Security Police and the Security Service under Heinrich Himmler.

[Alexandria document EAP VIII–173–b–16–14/38, Microfilm T 175, Roll 409.]

The Security Service of the Reichsführer—SS/The Security Service Leader of the SS-Main District Fulda-Werra
to Security Service Sub-Districts: Hessen Darmstadt
                                                                    Kassel
                                                                    Koblenz
                                                                    Trier
                                                                    Wiesbaden
          as well as Security Service outpost Frankfurt a. M.
Frankfurt a. M., August 2, 1939

Subject: Migration of Jews to Cities
Previous: Nothing
The following communication of the Security Main Office is sent on for information:
   Notice is hereby given that in accordance with a decision of the SS-Major General nothing is to be undertaken against the migration of Jews to the cities.
   Rather it is intended that, with an additional decrease of the Jews in Germany, the concentration of Jews in the major cities will be furthered. A final regulation for the orderly migration of Jews to the major cities will follow in the future.
The Security Service Leader in the SS-Main District Fulda-Werra

                                   [signature illegible]
                                   SS-first lieutenant

10. The Ghettos of Poland

In the course of the first six years of the Nazi regime, the Jews in Germany were subjected to definition, expropriation, and the beginnings of concentration. After the German army occupied most of Poland in 1939, the scope of the destruction process was enlarged and its force intensified. A medieval phenomenon appeared in the newly conquered areas—ghettos, several of them fenced or walled, were established in all the major Polish cities. Completely constricted from the outside, the ghettos were left largely to their own devices for the maintenance of essential services within their borders. For an overall view of these Jewish ghetto governments, see Isaiah Trunk, "The Organizational Structure of the Jewish Councils in Eastern Europe," in *Yad Vashem Studies,* VII (1968), 147–164.

The two largest ghettos were Warsaw and Lodz. Warsaw had free enterprise involving both Jewish and German firms, controlled commodity exchanges with the outside world, deficit spending by the Jewish Council, as well as considerable food smuggling. The system allowed some families to hold on, but the death rate was so high that the local German general in Warsaw expressed his revulsion in blunt language.

The Lodz ghetto was a large workshop which employed about fifty thousand people, sometimes in three shifts, to fill orders for the German army. The average inventory of the raw material alone was about 50–60,-000,000 Reichsmark. (Report by Protective Police Command in Lodz, signed Keuck, January 30, 1942, German Federal Archives R 70 Polen/1.) The work was tightly organized and run by a large ghetto bureaucracy. Services, including health care, were also highly developed. When the ghetto was formed in 1940, it had

ninety-two physicians including specialists in gyne-
cology, urology, surgery, otolaryngology, stomatol-
ogy, ophthalmology, internal medicine, dermatology,
neurology, psychiatry, and venereology. It operated
three ambulances (two of them horse-drawn) and provided free insulin treatments as well as free care of
tuberculosis patients. All the same, there was sickness,
starvation, and death. Two tables from a lengthy ghetto
report show the number of deaths in 1941 by month and
by cause. It should be pointed out that the daily average
of deaths in 1941 (31.33) was doubled during the first six
months of 1942 (62.28).

Jews attempting to escape from ghettos were liable to
be shot without warning. The last item among the
documents which follow is a report of a shooting incident in Kutno.

[From the Archives of the Jewish Historical Institute of Poland, in Jüdisches
Historisches Institut Warschau, *Faschismus-Getto-Massenmord* (Berlin: Rütten &
Loening, 2d ed., 1961), pp. 152–156.]

Diary of Stanisław Różycki, containing a monthly budget, probably
fall 1941, of his "tolerably well situated" family in the Warsaw ghetto.

Income (Actual)		Expenses (Actual)	
Father's salary	235 Zł.	Rent	70 Zł.
Son's salary	120 Zł.	Bread	328 Zł.
Public assistance	—	Potatoes	115 Zł.
Side income	80 Zł.	Fats	56 Zł.
	435 Zł.	Allotments	80 Zł.
		Fees	11 Zł.
		Electricity, candles	28 Zł.
		Fuel	65 Zł.
		Drugs	45 Zł.
		Soap	9 Zł.
		Misc.	3 Zł.
			810 Zł.

[The family balanced its budget by selling a clothes closet for
400 Zł.]

[Alexandria document 75022/5, Microfilm T 501, Roll 214.]

EXCERPTS FROM MONTHLY REPORT FOR APRIL 16–MAY 15, 1941
BY CHIEF FIELD HEADQUARTERS IN WARSAW DISTRICT (SIGNED
VON UNRUH) TO MILITARY COMMANDER IN GENERAL
GOVERNMENT [AT THAT TIME COMPRISING MILITARY REGIONS OF
WARSAW, LUBLIN, AND KRAKOW],
MAY 20, 1941

The situation in the Jewish quarter is catastrophic. Dead bodies of those who collapsed from lack of strength are lying in the streets. Mortality, 80% undernourishment, has tripled since February. The only thing alloted to the Jews is 1½ pounds of bread a week. Potatoes for which the Jewish council has paid in advance of several million, have not been delivered. The large number of welfare agencies created by the Jewish council are in no position to arrest the frightful misery. The ghetto is growing into a social scandal, a breeder of illnesses and of the worst subhumanity. The treatment of the Jews in labor camps, where they are guarded solely by Poles, can only be described as bestial.

[YIVO Institute, Lodz Ghetto Collection document No. 58, pp. 22, 26.]

Monthly Deaths in 1941

	Number of Deaths			Daily Average			Monthly Rate in %		
	Men	Women	Total	Men	Women	Total	Men	Women	Total
January	805	419	1,224	25.97	13.52	39.48	1.14	0.50	0.80
February	668	395	1,063	23.86	14.11	37.96	0.96	0.48	0.70
March	659	370	1,029	21.26	11.94	33.19	0.96	0.45	0.68
April	572	379	951	19.07	12.63	31.70	0.85	0.46	0.64
May	604	395	999	19.48	12.74	32.23	0.91	0.48	0.68
June	548	382	930	18.27	12.73	31.00	0.84	0.47	0.64
July	578	319	897	18.65	10.29	28.94	0.90	0.39	0.62
August	601	375	976	19.39	12.10	31.48	0.94	0.46	0.67
September	439	326	765	14.63	10.87	25.50	0.69	0.41	0.53
October	364	280	644	11.74	9.03	20.77	0.55	0.33	0.42
November	519	409	928	17.30	13.63	30.93	0.74	0.45	0.57
December	599	432	1,031	19.32	13.94	33.26	0.85	0.47	0.63
Total, 1941	6,956	4,481	11,437	19.06	12.28	31.33	0.86	0.45	0.63

These comparative figures are based on the death register of Lodz for the year 1938 and on an estimate of 225,000 Jews in lodz for the same year.

Monthly	Jan.	Feb.	Mar.	April	May	Jun.	Jul.
Rate in %	0.10	0.08	0.09	0.09	0.09	0.09	0.07

	Aug.	Sep.	Oct.	Nov.	Dec.	Jan.–Dec.
	0.09	0.08	0.11	0.08	0.10	0.09

Deaths by Cause 1941 [monthly totals omitted]

Cause	Men	Women	Total	% of Total
Dysentery	155	89	244	2.13
Typhoid Fever	10	12	22	0.19
Spotted Fever	3	10	13	0.11
Diphtheria	3	5	8	0.07
Whooping Cough	3	2	5	0.04
Meningitis	2	2	4	0.03
Lung Tuberculosis	1,725	827	2,552	22.31
Other Tuberculosis	107	106	213	1.86
Other Lung Diseases	416	190	606	5.30
Heart Disease	1,873	1,348	3,221	28.16
Diseases of Nervous System	205	175	380	3.32
Diseases of Digestive System	445	295	740	6.47
Food Poisoning	11	14	25	0.22
Cancer and Tumors	40	99	139	1.22
Diseases of Old Age	244	261	505	4.41
Starvation	1,342	792	2,134	18.65
Freezing	9	6	15	0.13
Gunshot Wounds	27	13	40	0.35
Other	336	235	571	4.99
	6,956	4,481	11,437	100.00 [sic]

[German Federal Archives, Koblenz R 70 (Poland), Folder 1.]

Daily Order No. 59
by Higher SS and Police Leader in Army District XX/Chief
of the Order Police (signed Knofe),
June 27, 1941
1. Citations . . .

   d. Citation by Mr. Government President in Hohensalza:
   "On May 19, 1941 the 18-year old auxiliary policeman
   Eduard Schulz, Protective Police, Department Kutno,
   acted resolutely to frustrate the escape of 5 Jews from the
   ghetto. They ducked out in a drainage canal which was
   strongly secured by barbed wire and, without the alert-
   ness and determination of the guard, would have disappeared in the dense terrain. The pursuit was extended
   over a distance of more than 1500 yards with the result
   that the 5 Jews were shot to death.
   "Because of the vigilance, resolution, and good shooting of
   auxiliary policeman Schulz, the great danger of a spread
   of spotted fever and other epidemics to the German population was removed. I express my appreciation to Schulz
   for this conduct and sense of duty."
I join in this citation.

11. A Jewish Labor Camp

One of the first major labor projects involving Polish
Jews was the construction of a defense line in the Lublin district between the Bug and San rivers, facing the
Soviet occupation force to the east. The following report concerns a labor camp on the line at Belzec. The
author, an unofficial army observer, refers obliquely to

the fact that the project was directed by the SS and Police. He makes clear that the food was supplied to the inmates by the Jewish Council of Lublin.

[Alexandria document 75022/3a (appendix 290a), Microfilm T 501, Roll 213.]

Report by operations officer of Chief Field Headquarters 379 (Lublin)
September 23, 1940

Reference: Telephonic order to ascertain the truth of complaints about conditions of Jewish employment in the anti-tank ditch between Bug and San

On the occasion of a tour of the newly assigned local command posts, a stop was made on September 22 at the Jewish labor camp at Belzec on the way from Tomoszow.

The impressions gained on one Sunday are not sufficient to generalize about the whole 80-mile stretch.

If after this sampling, there is a desire to enlarge the inspection, explicit authorization should be given (also for change of overnight accommodations).

Since the organization of labor projects between the Bug and San is evidently completely outside the jurisdiction of the Armed Forces, clarification would seem to be necessary as to how far the Chief Field Headquarters may proceed in this matter.

Yesterday's orientation trip was personally undertaken by the operations officer of the Chief Field Headquarters.

The impressions gained stem from short, entirely unostentatious conversations with individual Jews without interpreters. Despite the Jewish jargon, communication was perfect. The people selected for conversation made their points in a precise, quiet manner, as answers to questions put to them. The result is as follows:

I.   *Work Routine*
     5:30   Waking

6   March to work
7–12   Work on the ditch
12–13   Lunch pause
13–17   Work on the ditch
18   Arrival in the camp

Thereafter stacking of tools and supper. There is no relief during work. The men work also Sundays—that is called voluntary.

II.   *Food Supply*. Still in the hands of the Jewish Council of Lublin

Breakfast: Bread and coffee
Lunch: Potatoes, mixed daily with
                        meat. The meal is brought to
                        the work site in kettles on peas-
                        ant carts.
Supper: Bread and coffee

Quality of Food Supply
No vegetables, no fat. Meat in the potatoes is a matter of accident. Potatoes often underdone.

Bread: One loaf per day per man
                        [weight unclear]

Impression made by the men varies according to age. Some of the younger men look vigorous, older ones mostly undernourished. There appear to be fewer complaints about the food than about quarters.

III.   *Quarters*
Allegedly very crowded, no straw. People lie on the hard floor. In order to sleep at all they lie down head and shoulder on the neighbor and so forth. When the weather becomes colder, there will be a shortage of blankets.

The greatest deprivation is felt to be the lack of any opportunity to wash, since the work schedule allows no time for that. This was emphasized several times. They stay for weeks and months without any change of clothes.

One would have to check in the camp itself to find out if these allegations are true.

IV. *Clothing*

The men work in their own clothes. Since they have been here for three months already, there are human figures in literal rags. Those who are clothed better are people who can afford to pay for their own things. They are exceptions.

V. *Pay*

The men receive only food. Payment in money does not take place, so that supplementary purchases of food or clothes are out of the question.

VI. *Hygienic Conditions*

So far as can be determined, dysentery prevails, though apparently not to an extraordinary extent. Also fever (perhaps typhus) occurs. Allegedly there is no medical care, though Jewish doctors in sufficient numbers must surely be available.

There are sanitation men (Jews), but their armband with the Red Cross seems to be their only qualification.

These conditions are commented on with strong indignation. Lately, men over 60 and the sick have been released.

In answer to a question about deaths, it was said that they occurred, and cautiously it was added: "also shootings," for example in the morning of yesterday, Sunday.

In answer to a question about the reason, there was only a shrug of shoulders.

For the Chief Field Headquarters 379

The First General Staff Officer [operations]

signed Braune-Krikau

Major in the General Staff

Certified correct

Eidam

Captain

12. Open-Air Killings in Russia

The organized killings of the Jews began on June 22, 1941, the day of the assault on the U.S.S.R. The invading army groups were accompanied by mobile units of the Security Police and Security Service, which carried out the shootings. The unit with Army Group North was Strike Group A, a force of 990 men organized into four strike commandos. By November the group was stretched out in a large region which included Kovno, Riga, Tallin, Staraya Russa, and Krasnogvardeisk. Strike Commando 3, in Kovno, covered parts of Lithuania and Latvia which were densely populated with Jews. Its summary report of December 1, 1941, is the first selection in the following pages.

In 1942 local commands of the Security Police and Security Service in cities and towns of the occupied U.S.S.R. systematically thinned out and obliterated the remaining Jewish communities. In White Russia they also killed Jews brought in from Germany. The second document is a report written by an SS sergeant in Minsk about the activities of his men in a wide area around the White Russian capital.

The third item refers to the destruction of the Janov ghetto at a time when the Germans were feeling the growing shortage of skilled Jewish labor, and the fourth is a survivor's account of shootings in the vicinity of Pinsk. Janov and Pinsk were Polish territory before the war. They were occupied by the Red Army from September 1939 to June 1941, and then overrrun in the German offensive. Under German rule they were in the northern portion of the "Reich Commissariat" Ukraine; since the war they have been in the southern section of the White Russian S.S.R.

[Photostats of documents derived from Soviet sources, in Institut für Zeitgeschichte, Munich, Fb 85/2.]

The Commander of Security Police and Security Service   Kovno, December 1, 1941
Strike Commando 3
Secret Reich Matter!

5 copies
4th copy

Recapitulation of Executions carried out in the area of Strike Commando 3 until December 1, 1941

Security Police tasks in Lithuania taken over by Strike Commando 3 on July 2, 1941.

(The area of Vilna was taken over on August 9, 1941, the area of Shavli on Oct. 2. Until these dates Vilna was worked over by Strike Commando 9 and Shavli by Strike Commando 2.)

Executions carried out by Lithuanian partisans upon my instructions and orders:

4.7.41	Kovno—Fort VII	416 Jewish men, 47 Jewish women	463
6.7.41	Kovno—Fort VII	Jews	2,514

Upon formation of a raiding party under the direction of SS First Lieutenant Hamann and 8–10 trustworthy men of Strike Commando 3, the following actions were carried out in cooperation with Lithuanian partisans:

7.7.41	Mariampole	Jews	32
8.7.41	"	14 Jews and 5 communist functionaries	19

Date	Place		Number
8.7.41	Cirkalinei	communist functionaries	6
9.7.41	Wendziogala	32 Jewish men, 2 Jewish women, 1 Lithuanian woman, 2 Lithuanian communists, 1 Russian communist	38
9.7.41	Kovno—Fort VII	21 Jewish men, 3 Jewish women	24
14.7.41	Mariampole	21 Jewish men, 1 Russian & 9 Lithuanian communists	31
17.7.41	Babtei	8 communist functionaries (6 of them Jews)	8
18.7.41	Mariampole	39 Jewish men, 14 Jewish women	53
19.7.41	Kovno—Fort VII	17 Jewish men, 2 Jewish women, 4 Lithuanian communists, 2 communist Lithuanian women, 1 German communist	26
21.7.41	Panevezys	59 Jewish men, 11 Jewish women, 1 Lithuanian woman, 1 Pole, 22 Lithuanian communists, 9 Russian communists	103
22.7.41	"	1 Jew	1
23.7.41	Kedsiniai	83 Jewish men, 12 Jewish women, 14 Russian communists, 15 Lithuanian communists, 1 Russian Chief Politruk [political officer, Rec Army]	125
25.7.41	Mariampole	90 Jewish men, 13 Jewish women	103
28.7.41	Panevezys	234 Jewish men, 15 Jewish women, 19 Russian communists, 20 Lithuanian communists	288
29.7.41	Rassiniai [sic]	254 Jewish men, 3 Lithuanian communists	257
30.7.41	Agriogala	27 Jewish men, 11 Lithuanian communists	38
31.7.41	Utena	235 Jewish men, 16 Jewish women, 4 Lithuanian communists, 1 two-time felony murderer	256
11–31.7.41	Wendziogala	13 Jews, 2 murderers	15

August:

Date	Location	Description	Number
1.8.41	Ukmerge	254 Jewish men, 42 Jewish women, 1 Political Commissar [Red Army], 2 Lithuanian NKVD agents, 1 mayor of Jonava who gave the order to set the city on fire	300
2.8.41	Kovno—Fort IV	170 Jewish men, 1 USA Jew, 1 USA Jewish woman, 33 Jewish women, 4 Lithuanian communists	209
4.8.41	Panevezys	362 Jewish men, 41 Jewish women, 5 Russian communists, 14 Lithuanian communists	422
5.8.41	Rasainiai	213 Jewish men, 66 Jewish women	279
7.8.41	Uteba	483 Jewish men, 87 Jewish women, 1 Lithuanian who robbed corpses of German soldiers	571
8.8.41	Ukmerge	620 Jewish men, 82 Jewish women	702
9.8.41	Kovno—Fort IV	484 Jewish men, 50 Jewish women	534
11.8.41	Panevezys	450 Jewish men, 48 Jewish women, 1 Lithuanian and 1 Russian communists	500
13.8.41	Alytus	617 Jewish men, 100 Jewish women, 1 criminal	719 [sic]
14.8.41	Jonava	497 Jewish men, 55 Jewish women	552
15. and 16.8.41	Rokiskis	3200 Jewish men, Jewish women, and Jewish children, 5 Lithuanian communists, 1 Pole, 1 partisan	3,207
9. to 16.8.41	Rasainiai	294 Jewish women, 4 Jewish children	298
27.6 to 14.8.41	Rokiskis	493 Jews, 432 Russians, 56 Lithuanians (all active communists)	981

Date	Location	Description	Number
18.8.41	Kovno—Fort IV	698 Jewish men, 402 Jewish women, 1 Polish woman, 711 members of the Jewish intelligentsia from the ghetto as reprisal for ar act of sabotage	1,812
19.8.41	Ukmerge	298 Jewish men, 255 Jewish women, 1 Politruk, 88 Jewish children, 1 Russian communist	645 [*sic*]
22.8.41	Dvinsk	3 Russian communists, 5 Latvians, including 1 murderer, 1 Russian guard soldier, 3 Poles, 3 Gypsy men, 1 Gypsy woman, 1 Gypsy child, 1 Jewish man, 1 Jewish woman, 1 Armenian man, 2 Politruks (prison inspection at Dvinsk)	
22.8.41	Aglona	Mental patients: 269 men, 227 women, 48 children	544
23.8.41	Panevezys	1312 Jewish men, 4602 Jewish women, 1609 Jewish children	7,523
18. to 25.8.41	Rasainiai District	466 Jewish men, 440 Jewish women, 1020 Jewish children	1,926
25.8.41	Obelisi	112 Jewish men, 627 Jewish women, 421 Jewish children	1,160
26.8.41	Seduva	230 Jewish men, 275 Jewish women, 159 Jewish children	664
26.8.41	Zarasai	767 Jewish men, 1113 Jewish women, 1 Lithuanian communist, 687 Jewish children, 1 Russian communist woman	2,569
26.8.41	Pasvalys	402 Jewish men, 738 Jewish women, 209 Jewish children	1,349
26.8.41	Kaisiadorys	All Jews (men, women, and children)	1,911
27.8.41	Prienai	" " " "	1,078
27.8.41	Dagda and Kraslawa	212 Jews, 4 Russian prisoners-of-war	216
27.8.41	Joniskis	47 Jewish men, 165 Jewish women, 143 Jewish children	355
28.8.41	Wilkia	76 Jewish men, 192 Jewish women, 134 Jewish children	402
28.8.41	Kedainiai	710 Jewish men, 767 Jewish women, 599 Jewish children	2,076
29.8.41	Rumsiskis and Ziezmariai	20 Jewish men, 567 Jewish women, 197 Jewish children	784

Date	Place				Total
29.8.41 to 13.8.41	Utena and Moletai	582 Jewish men, 1731 Jewish women, 1469 Jewish children			3,782
31.8.41	Alytus and vicinity	233 Jews			233

September:

Date	Place				Total
1.9.41	Mariampole	1763 Jewish men, 1812 Jewish women, 1404 Jewish children, 109 mental patients, 1 female German national who was married to a Jew, 1 Russian woman			5,090

Date	Place				Total
28.8. to 2.9.41	Darsuniskis	10 Jewish men,	69 J. women,	20 J. childr.	99
	Carliava	73 "	113 "	61 "	247
	Jonava	112 "	1200 "	244 "	1,556
	Petrasiunai	30 "	72 "	23 "	125
	Jesuas	26 "	72 "	46 "	144
	Ariogala	207 "	260 "	195 "	662
	Jasvainai	86 "	110 "	86 "	282
	Babtei	20 "	41 "	22 "	83
	Wenziogala	42 "	113 "	97 "	252
	Krakes	448 "	476 "	201 "	1,125
4.9.41	Pravenischkis	247 "	6 "	[unintelligible abbreviations]	253
4.9.41	Cekiske	22 Jewish men,	64 J. women,	60 "	146
	Seredsius	6 "	61 "	126 "	193
	Velinona	2 "	71 "	86 "	159
	Zapiskis	47 "	118 "	13 "	178
5.9.41	Ukmerge	1123	1849	1737	4,709

Date	Location	Jewish men, all	J. women, all	J. childr. all	Total
25.8. to 6.9.41	Cleaning up in Rasainiai in Georgenburg	16	412	415	843
9.9.41	Alytus	287	640	352	412
9.9.41	Butrimonys	67	370	303	1,279
10.9.41	Merkine	223	355	276	740
10.9.41	Varena	541	141	149	854
11.9.41	Leipalingis	60	70	25	831
11.9.41	Seirigai	229	384	340	155
12.9.41	Simnas	68	197	149	953
11. and 12.9.41	Uzusalis				414
	Punitive action against inhabitants who supplied Russian partisans and who in some cases were armed				43
26.9.41	Kovno—Fort IV				1,608
	412 Jewish men, 615 Jewish women, 581 Jewish children (sick people and suspected carriers of epidemics)				

October:

Date	Location				Total
2.10.41	Zagare				2,236
	633 Jewish men, 1107 Jewish women, 496 Jewish children (As these Jews were being led away, a mutiny began which was put down immediately, however. In the course of it, 150 Jews were shot right away, 7 partisans were wounded.)				
4.10.41	Kovno—Fort IX				1,845
	315 Jewish men, 712 Jewish women, 818 Jewish children (punitive action, because a German policeman was shot at in the ghetto)				
29.10.41	Kovno—Fort IX				9,200
	2007 Jewish men, 2920 Jewish women, 4273 Jewish children (cleansing the ghetto of superfluous Jews)				

November:

Date	Place				Total
3.11.41	Lazdijai	485 Jewish men,	511 J. women,	539 J. childr.	1,535
15.11.41	Wilkowiski	36 "	48 "	31 "	115
25.11.41	Kovno—Fort IX	1159	1600 "	175 "	2,934
29.11.41	"	(Settlers from Berlin, Munich and Frankfurt am Main)			
29.11.41	"	693 Jewish men,	1155 J. women,	152 J. childr.	2,000
		(Settlers from Vienna and Breslau)			
29.11.41	"	17 Jewish men, 1 Jewish woman who had offended against ghetto laws, 1 Reich German who had converted to Judaism and attended a rabbinical school, further 15 terrorists of the Kalinin Group			34

Detachment of
Strike Commando 3
in Dvinsk from
13.7. to
21.8.41 — 9012 Jewish men, women and children, 573 active communists — 9,585

Detachment of
Strike Commando 3
in Vilna:

Date	Place			Total
12.8. to 1.9.41	Vilna City	425 Jewish men, 19 Jewish women, 8 communist men, 9 communist women		461
2.9.41	" "	864 Jewish men, 2019 Jewish women, 817 Jewish children (special action because German soldiers were shot at by Jews)		3,700

Date	Place	Jewish men	J. women	J. childr.	Total
12.9.41	Vilna City	993 Jewish men,	1670 J. women,	771 J. childr.	3,334 [sic]
17.9.41	" "	337 "	687 "	247 " and 4 Lithuanian communists	1,271
20.9.41	Nemencing	128 Jewish men,	176 J. women,	99 J. childr.	403
22.9.41	Novo-Wilejka	468 "	495 "	196 "	1,159
24.9.41	Riesa	512	744	511	1,767
25.9.41	Jahiunai	215	229	131	575
27.9.41	Eysisky	989	1636	821	3,446
30.9.41	Traksi	366	483	597	1,446
4.10.41	Vilna City	432	1115	436	1,983
6.10.41	Semiliski	213	359	390	962
9.10.41	Svenciany	1169	1840	717	3,726
16.10.41	Vilna City	382	507	257	1,146
21.10.41	" "	718	1063	586	2,367
25.10.41	" "	–	1766	812	2,578
27.10.41	" "	946	184	73	1,203
30.10.41	" "	382	789	362	1,533
6.11.41	" "	340	749	252	1,341
19.11.41	" "	76	77	18	171
19.11.41	" "	6 prisoners-of-war, 8 Poles			14
20.11.41	" "	3 "			3
25.11.41	" "	9 Jewish men, 46 Jewish women, 8 Jewish children, 1 Pole for possessing weapons and other equipment			64

Detachment of
Strike Commando 3
in Minsk from
  28.9. to
17.10.41: Pleschnitza,
          Bicholin,
          Scak,
          Bober,
          Uzda

620 Jewish men, 1285 Jewish women, 1126 Jewish children
and 19 communists   3,050
                                             133,346 [*sic*]

Before Security Police tasks were assumed by Strike Commando 3, Jews liquidated solely by partisans in pogroms and executions.   4,000

                                           Total 137,346

Today I can confirm that Strike Commando 3 has reached the goal of solving the Jewish problem in Lithuania. The only remaining Jews are laborers and their families:

in Shavli ca. 4,500
in Kovno ca. 15,000
in Vilna   ca. 15,000

I wanted to put also the work Jews and their families to rest, but the civil administration (Reich Commissar) and the armed forces declared war on me and issued the prohibition: These Jews and their families must not be shot!

Lithuania could be freed of Jews only because a specially selected raiding party was set up under SS-1st Lieutenant Hamann who shared my aims in full and who knew how to cooperate with Lithuanian [anti-communist] partisans and the appropriate civil offices.

The implementation of such actions is in the first instance an organizational problem. The decision to free each district of Jews necessitated thorough preparation of each action as well as acquisition of information about local conditions. The Jews had to be collected in one or more towns and a ditch had to be dug at the right site for the right number. The marching distance from collecting points to the ditches averaged about 3 miles. The Jews were brought in groups of 500, separated by at least 1.2 miles, to the place of execution. The sort of difficulties and nerve-scraping work involved in all this is shown by an arbitrarily chosen example:

In Rokiskis 3208 people had to be transported 3 miles before they could be liquidated. To manage this job in a 24-hour period, more than 60 of the 80 available Lithuanian partisans had to be detailed to the cordon. The Lithuanians who were left were frequently being relieved while doing the work together with my men.

Vehicles are seldom available. Escapes, which were attempted here and there, were frustrated solely by my men at the risk of their lives. For example, 3 men of the Commando at Mariampole shot 38 escaping Jews and communist functionaries on a path in the woods, so that no one got away. Distances to and from actions were never less than 90–120 miles. Only careful planning enabled the Commando to carry out up to 5 actions a week and at the same time continue the work in Kovno without interruption.

Kovno itself, where trained Lithuanian partisans are available in sufficient numbers, was comparatively speaking a shooting paradise.

All officers and men of the Commando in Kovno participated in the major actions in the city. Only one intelligence official was excused because of illness.

I regard the Jewish actions of Strike Commando 3 as virtually completed. The remaining work Jews and Jewesses are urgently needed, and I can imagine that they will still be needed after the winter. I am of the opinion that the male work Jews should be sterilized immediately to prevent any procreation. A Jewess who nevertheless becomes pregnant is to be liquidated. . . .

[signed] Jäger
SS-Colonel

[From Czechoslovak Archives in Castle Zàsmuky near Kolin, originally printed by Dragopress in Prague in 1965 and reprinted in *Unsere Ehre heisst Treue* (Vienna, Frankfurt, Zurich: Europa Verlag, 1965).]

Report by Group Arlt   Minsk, August 3, 1942

The work of the men remaining here in Minsk continues to be just about the same. The Jewish transports arrived in Minsk at regular intervals and we serviced them. So already on June 18 and 19, 1942 we were busy again digging pits in the village terrain. On June 19, SS-Staff Sergeant Schröder, who had died in the local military hospital, was buried in the new cemetery of the commander's estate. My group was reinforced by men of the Security Service and took part as honor guards in the funeral.

On June 26, the Jewish transport which was awaited from the Reich arrived. On June 27, we started off with pretty much the whole Commando for an [anti-partisan] action in Baranowice. Success as always was negative. In the course of this action we cleared the Jewish ghetto in Slonim. About 4000 Jews were laid to rest that day.

On June 30, we returned to Minsk again. The following days were filled with repair work, cleaning of weapons, and weapons inspections.

On July 2, preparations were made once again—digging of pits—for the reception of the Jewish transport.

On July 10, we and the Latvian Commando were deployed against partisans in the woods of Koydanov. On that occasion we were able to dig up a munitions cache. A Latvian comrade was killed on that occasion. During the pursuit of the [partisan] band, four men were shot to death.

On July 12, the Latvian comrade was buried in the new cemetery.

On July 17, a transport arrived with Jews and was brought to the estate.

On July 21, 22, and 23, new pits are dug.

On July 24, another transport arrives here with 1000 Jews from the Reich.

From July 25 to 27, new pits are dug.

On July 28, major action in Minsk Russian ghetto; 6000 Jews are brought to the pits.

On July 29, 3,000 Jews are brought to the pits.

The following days were filled with cleaning weapons and repair again.

Furthermore my group furnishes daily the corporal of the guard and services the local jail. Inmates ca. 50 men.

By order of SS-1st Lieut. Störtz, SS-Corporal Albert Lorenz was transferred to Riga. He was sent off on July 4, 1942.

SS-Corporal Skowranek and SS-man Auer had leave from July 8 to August 1st. Both returned punctually.

SS-man Otto was released July 28 from the military hospital as healed, with recommended convalescence leave. Otto was sent by headquarters on convalescence leave from August 3 to September 9. He is thinking of being married during that leave.

SS-man Hering received leave to go home from August 3 to August 27.

The behavior of the men, on and off duty, is good and gives rise to no complaints.

Arlt
SS-Sergeant

[Alexandria document Wi/ID 1.97, Microfilm T 77, Roll 628.]

Armament Command in Luzk to
Armament Inspectorate of Ukraine
November 23, 1942

[The following is an excerpt from the war diary of the armament command's branch office in Brest-Litovsk. The office was dissolved at the end of October and its diary is enclosed in the main report of the Armament Command in Luzk.]

Captain Stumpf made his last official trip as director of the branch office to Kobryn and Pinsk, and inasmuch as there will no longer be any possibility for frequent visits and advice, he was going to review the state of production one more time and give instructions for another four weeks. Even as in Brest, everyone in Kobryn and Pinsk was perturbed, because the threatened action against the Jews was going to have a depressing effect on production. Although certain classes of Jews, such as craftsmen and skilled laborers, are to be saved so that arms production may be carried on, the director is afraid that in the course of such mass-actions, no exceptions whatever will be made. In Janov, for instance, the entire ghetto with all of its inmates was burned down.

[Testimony by Mrs. Rivka Yosselevscka. Uncorrected English transcript of the Eichmann trial (mimeographed), May 8, 1961, session 30, pp. L1-N1.]

[The witness was born in Zagrodski, a town containing some five hundred Jewish families, in the Pinsk district. Her father, owner of a leather goods shop, was considered a notable there. Mrs. Yosselevscka was married in 1934, and when the Ger-

mans arrived she had one child. The events she describes took
place in mid-August 1942.]
Attorney-General: Do you remember the Sabbath at the beginning of the Hebrew month of Ellul, 1942?
A. I remember that day very well. Jews were not allowed to
go to pray, yet they would risk their lives and go into a cellar
in the ghetto . . . the only Jews left in the ghetto would endan-
ger their very lives to go into the cellar to pray—very early,
before dawn. On that night, there was too much commotion
in the ghetto. There was always noise in the ghetto. Germans
would be coming in and leaving the ghetto during all hours of
the night. But the commotion and noise on that night was not
customary, and we felt something in the air.

We did not let our Father go into the cellar to hold prayers,
but he did not listen to us. He did go down to pray, into the
cellar. We saw that the place was full of Germans. They surrounded the ghetto. We went down and asked—there were
some of the police that we knew—and we asked what was
going on. Why so many Germans in the ghetto?
Presiding Judge: Who were these policemen?
Witness: White Russians. The policemen were White Russians
—those we asked. And we asked—why so many Germans in
the ghetto? They told us that there was a partisan woman
trying to get into the ghetto and mix with us. A group of
partisans, and if they succeed in mixing amongst us, they hope
not to be caught. This was not true. Our Father came up from
the cellar, after his prayer. He could not speak to us. He only
wished us "a good month." This was the first day of the
month. I remember very well—this was the first day of the
month of Ellul—the month of prayer and before the Jewish
New Year. We were told to leave the houses—to take with us
only the children. We were always used to leave the ghetto at
short order, because very often they would take us all out for
a roll-call. Then we would all appear. But we felt and realized
that this was not an ordinary roll-call, but something very
special. As if the Angel of Death was in charge. The place was
swarming with Germans. Some four to five Germans to every
Jew.

Attorney-General: Then all of you were driven out, and were taken to this square—weren't you?

Witness: No, we were left standing in the ghetto. They began saying that he who wishes to save his life could do so with money, jewels and valuable things. This would be ransom, and he would be spared. Thus we were held until the late afternoon, before evening came.

Presiding Judge: And did the Jews hand over jewels and so on?

Witness: We did not. We had nothing to hand over. They already took all we had before.

Presiding Judge: I see.

Attorney-General: Yes. And what happened towards sunrise?

Witness, Yosselevscka: And thus the children screamed. They wanted food, water. This was not the first time. But we took nothing with us. We had no food and no water, and we did not know the reason. The children were hungry and thirsty. We were held this way for 24 hours while they were searching the houses all the time—searching for valuables.

In the meantime, the gates of the ghetto were opened. A large truck appeared and all of us were put onto the truck—either thrown, or went up himself.

Attorney-General: Did they count the Jews?

A. Yes—they were counted. They entered the ghetto again, and searched for every missing person. We were tortured until late in the evening.

Q. Now—they filled up this truck. And what happened to the people for whom there was no room in the truck?

A. Those for whom there was no room in the truck were ordered to run after the truck.

Q. And you ran with your daughter?

A. I had my daughter in my arms and ran after the truck. There were mothers who had two or three children and held them in their arms—running after the truck. We ran all the way. There were those who fell—we were not allowed to help them rise. They were shot—right there—wherever they fell. All my family was amongst them. When we all reached the destination, the people from the truck were already down and

they were undressed—all lined up. All my family was there—
undressed, lined up. The people from the truck, those who
arrived before us.

Q. Where was that?

A. This was some three kilometres from our village—the market-place.* There was a kind of hillock. At the foot of this little
hill, there was a dugout. We were ordered to stand at the top
of the hillock and the four devils shot us—each one of us
separately.

Q. Now these four—to what German unit did they belong?

A. They were SS men—the four of them. They were armed
to the teeth. They were real messengers of the Devil and the
Angel of Death.

Q. Please go on—what did you see?

A. When I came up to the place—we saw people naked lined
up. But we were still hoping that this was only torture. Maybe
there is Hope—hope of living. One could not leave the line,
but I wished to see—what are they doing on the hillock? Is
there anyone down below? I turned my head and saw that
some three or four rows were already killed—on the ground.
There were some twelve people amongst the dead. I also want
to mention that my child said while we were lined up in the
Ghetto, she said, "Mother, why did you make me wear the
Shabbat dress; we are being taken to be shot"; and when we
stood near the dug-out, near the grave, she said, "Mother, why
are we waiting, let us run!" Some of the young people tried to
run, but they were caught immediately, and they were shot
right there. It was difficult to hold on to the children. We took
all children not ours, and we carried—we were anxious to get
it all over—the suffering of the children was difficult; we all
trudged along to come nearer to the place and to come nearer
to the end of the torture of the children. The children were
taking leave of their parents and parents of their elder people.

Presiding Judge: How did you survive through all this?

Attorney-General: She will relate it.

Presiding Judge: Please will you direct the Witness.

Witness: We were driven; we were already undressed; the

*Interpreter's comment: The Prosecution corrects that the witness did not say
the 'market-place,' but the witness said 'to the place.'

clothes were removed and taken away; our father did not want to undress; he remained in his underwear. We were driven up to the grave, this shallow. . . .

Attorney-General: And these garments were torn off his body, weren't they?

A: When it came to our turn, our father was beaten. We prayed, we begged with my father to undress, but he would not undress, he wanted to keep his underclothes. He did not want to stand naked.

Q: And then they tore them off?

A: Then they tore off the clothing off the old man and he was shot. I saw it with my own eyes. And then they took my mother, and she said, let us go before her; but they caught mother and shot her too; and then there was my grandmother, my father's mother, standing there; she was eighty years old and she had two children in her arms. And then there was my father's sister. She also had children in her arms and she was shot on the spot with the babies in her arms.

Q: And finally it was your turn.

A: And finally my turn came. There was my younger sister, and she wanted to leave; she prayed with the Germans; she asked to run, naked; she went up to the Germans with one of her friends; they were embracing each other; and she asked to be spared, standing there naked. He looked into her eyes and shot the two of them. They fell together in their embrace, the two young girls, my sister and her young friend. Then my second sister was shot and then my turn did come.

Q: Were you asked anything?

A.: We turned towards the grave and then he turned around and asked "Whom shall I shoot first?" We were already facing the grave. The German asked "Who do you want me to shoot first?" I did not answer. I felt him take the child from my arms. The child cried out and was shot immediately. And then he aimed at me. First he held on to my hair and turned my head around; I stayed standing; I heard a shot, but I continued to stand and then he turned my head again and he aimed the revolver at me and ordered me to watch and then turned my head around and shot at me. Then I fell to the ground into the pit amongst the bodies; but I felt nothing. The moment I did feel I felt a sort of heaviness and then I thought maybe I am not alive any more, but I feel something after I died. I thought I was dead, that this was the feeling which comes after death. Then I felt that I was choking; people falling over me. I tried to move and felt that I was alive and that I could rise. I was strangling. I heard the shots and I was praying for another bullet to put an end to my suffering, but I continued to move about. I felt that I was choking, strangling, but I tried to save myself, to find some air to breathe, and then I felt that I was climbing towards the top of the grave above the bodies. I rose, and I felt bodies pulling at me with their hands, biting at my legs, pulling me down, down. And yet with my last strength I came up on top of the grave, and when I did I did not know the place, so many bodies were lying all over, dead people; I wanted to see the end of this stretch of dead bodies but I could not. It was impossible. They were lying, all dying; suffering; not all of them dead, but in their last sufferings; naked; shot, but not dead. Children crying "Mother," "Father"; I could not stand on my feet.

Presiding Judge: Were the Germans still around?

Witness: No, the Germans were gone. There was nobody there. No-one standing up.

Attorney-General: And you were undressed and covered with blood?

Witness: I was naked, covered with blood, dirty from the other bodies, with the excrement from other bodies which was poured onto me.

Q.: What did you have in your head?

A.: When I was shot I was wounded in the head.

Q.: Was it in the back of the head?

Q.: I have a scar to this day from the shot by the Germans; and yet, somehow I did come out of the grave. This was something I thought I would never live to recount. I was searching among the dead for my little girl, and I cried for her—Merkele was her name—Merkele! There were children crying "Mother!" "Father!"—but they were all smeared with blood and one could not recognize the children. I cried for my daughter. From afar I saw two women standing. I went up to them. They did not know me, I did not know them, and then I said who I was, and then they said, "So you survived." And there was another woman crying "Pull me out from amongst the corpses, I am alive, help!" We were thinking how could we escape from the place. The cries of the woman, "Help, pull me out from the corpses!" We pulled her out. Her name was Mikla Rosenberg. We removed the corpses and the dying people who held onto her and continued to bite. She asked us to take her out, to free her, but we did not have the strength.

Attorney-General: It is very difficult to relate, I am sure, it is difficult to listen to, but we must proceed. Please tell us now: after that you hid?

A.: And thus we were there all night, fighting for our lives, listening to the cries and the screams and all of a sudden we saw Germans, mounted Germans. We did not notice them coming in because of the screamings and the shoutings from the bodies around us.

Q.: And then they rounded up the children and the others who had got out of the pit and shot them again?

A.: The Germans ordered that all the corpses be heaped together into one big heap and with shovels they were heaped together, all the corpses, amongst them many still alive, children running about the place. I saw them. I saw the children. They were running after me, hanging onto me. Then I sat down in the field and remained sitting with the children around me. The children who got up from the heap of corpses.

Q.: Then the Germans came again and rounded up the children?

Witness Rivka Yosselevscka: Then Germans came and were going around the place. We were ordered to collect all the children, but they did not approach me, and I sat there watching how they collected the children. They gave a few shots and the children were dead. They did not need many shots. The children were almost dead, and this Rosenberg woman pleaded with the Germans to be spared, but they shot her.

Attorney-General: Mrs. Yosselevscka, after they left the place, you went right next to the grave, didn't you?

A.: They all left—the Germans and the non-Jews from around the place. They removed the machine guns and they took the trucks. I saw that they all left, and the four of us, we went onto the grave, praying to fall into the grave, even alive, envying those who were dead already and thinking what to do now. I was praying for death to come. I was praying for the grave to be opened and to swallow me alive. Blood was spurting from the grave in many places, like a well of water, and whenever I pass a spring now, I remember the blood which spurted from the ground, from that grave. I was digging with my fingernails, trying to join the dead in that grave. I dug with my fingernails, but the grave would not open. I did not have enough strength. I cried out to my mother, to my father, "Why did they not kill me? What was my sin? I have no one to go to. I saw them all being killed. Why was I spared? Why was I not killed?"

And I remained there, stretched out on the grave, three days and three nights.

Q.: And then a shepherd went by?

A.: I saw no one. I heard no one. Not a farmer passed by. After three days, shepherds drove their herd onto the field, and they began throwing stones at me, but I did not move. At night, the herds were taken back and during the day they threw stones believing that either it was a dead woman or a mad woman. They wanted me to rise, to answer. But I did not move. The shepherds were throwing stones at me until I had to leave the place.

Q.: And then a farmer went by, and he took pity on you.

A.: I hid near the grave. A farmer passed by, after a number of weeks.

Q.: He took pity on you, he fed you, and he helped you join a group of Jews in the forest, and you spent the time until the summer of '44 with this group, until the Soviets came.

A.: I was with them until the very end.

Q.: And now you are married and you have two children?

A.: Yes.

Presiding Judge: Dr. Servatius, any questions?
Dr. Servatius: No, I have no questions.
Presiding Judge: Please, quiet in the courtroom. Some respect, please. Thank you, Mrs. Yosselevscka. You have completed your evidence.

13. The Roumanian Sector

One of Germany's allies on the eastern front was Roumania. Before 1940 the Roumanian-Soviet border was the Dniestr River. In June of that year the Soviet Union issued an ultimatum to the Roumanians which forced them to withdraw from the river and abandon the provinces of northern Bukovina and Bessarabia. Only one year later the Roumanians reoccupied their lost territories and, pushing on across the Dniestr, captured Odessa on the Black Sea. Odessa became the capital of a region called "Transnistria," which was to be under Roumanian jurisdiction for the next three years.

Before 1941 northern Bukovina and Bessarabia had about 300,000 Jews, Transnistria another 300,000. When war broke out, the two populations were marked for destruction. At the start, Strike Group D of the German Security Police swept over the area, killing many thousands. Then the Roumanians began to herd the Bukovina and Bessarabian Jews across the Dniestr. Strike Group D, still in Transnistria, declined the added burden of killing the seemingly endless columns and closed the Dniestr bridges. When the Roumanians took over Transnistria's administration on August 28, 1941, the flow of Jews resumed. Two documents reprinted here deal with the expulsions: one, a letter of complaint by Otto Ohlendorf, Strike Group D commander, about the Roumanians, the other a diary of a

Jewish deportee from Bukovina's capital Cernauti (Czernowitz in German, Chernovtsy in Russian). In all, about 185,000 deportees were to arrive in Transnistria; two-thirds of them were to die there in camps and so-called "colonies."

Odessa's prewar Jewish population was about 175,-000. Some 90,000 may have been left behind when the city fell after a siege on October 16, 1941. Most of these 90,000 were shot by the Roumanians that month. The third document in this series describes the initial occupation period from the perspective of a German intelligence officer in the city. During the following months most of the remaining Odessa Jews were deported to other districts in Transnistria. Nearly 20,000 were sent to autonomous ethnic German villages in the Berezovka district where they were shot by German personnel who may have been local ethnic German police. An anonymous eyewitness account of Berezovka killings, received by a Jewish rescue organization in Switzerland soon after they occurred, is the fourth item in this group of documents. For additional background information, see also Alexander Dallin's *Odessa, 1941–1944: A Case Study of Soviet Territory Under Foreign Rule*, RAND Corporation Research Memorandum RM–1875, ASTIA document number AD123552, February 14, 1957, Santa Monica, California, and Dora Litani's "The Destruction of the Jews in Odessa in the Light of Roumanian Documents," *Yad Vashem Studies* VI (1967), 135–154.

At the end of 1942 about 100,000 Jews were left in Transnistria, including the surviving deportees from Bukovina and Bessarabia and the surviving local Jews. The two communities were intermingled in towns or collective farms, each under a Jewish council *(Obshina)*. Life in many of these ghettos was a layer of corruption on a bedrock of hard existence. Thus, a survivor from Bershad: "Whoever owned a gold watch or money could buy himself loose from a work detail." (Deposition by Hermann Picker, 1959, Yad Vashem Oral History Depot, Tel Aviv, 868/88.) In Shargorod, the *Prominente*—those with connections or money—were also exempt. (Deposition by Benno Schieber, 1959, Yad Vashem, Tel Aviv, 959/91.) And in Kopaygorod, "Whoever did not possess anything or was not fit to beg, died of starvation." (Deposition by Baruch Rostoker, 1960, Yad Vashem, Tel Aviv, 1224/73.) By early 1943 the Roumanian government, increasingly conscious of a possible military defeat on the eastern front, became more benign in its treatment of the Jews and permitted a Jewish relief commission from Bucharest to visit the Jewish colonies in Transnistria. Excerpts from the report of the commission conclude this description of events under Roumanian control.

[Alexandria document 29222, Microfilm T 501, Roll 278.]

[The following report was part of eighteen pages of material enclosed on October 29, 1941, by Army Group South to the Chief of the German Army Mission to Roumania (Brigadier General Hauffe) for submission in "suitable form" to Marshal Antonescu.]

Copy

The Plenipotentiary of the Chief of Security Police and Security Service with the Commander of Army Group Rear Area South—SS Strike Group D (signed by an SS-colonel [Ohlendorf])
via Intelligence Officer, 11th Army to
11th Army Command
September 2, 1941

Conduct of Roumanian Occupation Troops . . .

The Roumanians in Bessarabia and Bukovina see *a solution of the Jewish question* in the following amongst other things: they gave to the rich Jews an opportunity to "buy themselves loose," while the poorer ones and those unable to work were herded together to be brought across the Dniestr into the German sphere of influence. During trips in the Dniestr area one could see endless columns of ragged Jews who were guarded by Roumanian soldiers and driven to the Dniestr bridges only to be chased back, since the SS Commandos and German troops did not allow them to cross. The purpose appears to have been to drive the Jews back and forth often enough so that they would collapse. The consequence was that at intervals, frail old men and women were lying in the mud, and that there was a real danger of epidemics.

Before the closing of the Dniestr bridges, the Roumanians had driven ca. 5000 Jews into the district east of the Dniestr which was considered a German sphere of influence until August 28, 1941. As reported previously, Commandos of the SS Strike Group D pushed 27,500 Jews at Mogilev-Podolski and Jampol back into Roumanian territory. . . .

[Yad Vashem Oral History Depot, Tel Aviv, document 1024/55.]

[Notes by Leopold Rauch covering his experiences from October 11, 1941, to November 8, 1941, and certified by Dr. Ball-Kaduri, December 23, 1959. Rauch is described as an engineer born in 1912 in Czernowitz. He died before the end of the war, and the notes were saved by his widow. The first part of this account deals with the Czernowitz ghetto which was formed on October 11, 1941. The excerpts which follow describe the deportations in November across the Dniestr to Mogilev.]

. . . The next morning, on the third of November, showers hit the windows and washed off the regulations pasted on the panes. As the scraps of paper were driven by the cold wind across the pavement, soldiers appeared in the apartments and declared all medical certificates worthless, every postponement annulled, any staying on prohibited. Other military in the streets used sticks to drive off waiting peasant carts. The peasants, not wishing to forgo the collection of fat fares, came back through the alleys and the ghetto streets were full of people chasing after the carts. In another hour the first column left. That Sunday we joined families who were our friends, so

that for the unknown duration of this forced transfer we
would at least be pressed against people who had washed
themselves. The kind of humanity that crawled out of their
holes that day! The poorest of the poor, everyone who had not
yet been evacuated, the whole of the poor Jewish people was
now leaving its home. The smallest handcarts were overloaded
with all kinds of belongings. This lowest level of the poor
Jewish masses, accustomed by misery and deprivations to use
even the least significant thing for some daily need, did not
leave behind as much as a rag. The scene repelled us; these
dirty people who were no longer conscious of how unkempt
they were filled us with nausea.

Supporting my wife, I walked beside the cart on this all too
familiar route until everyone halted towards noon, waiting for
an order to proceed. The guard was to be told by phone
whether the carts could be allowed or only hand luggage. This
daily comedy always produced large sums of money which
flowed into the pockets of the Roumanians in charge of the
column. The last segment of the way led through uncountable
tracks to the loading platform. We men supported the cart
which sank from one hole into the other almost tipping over.
On the ramp an officer used his whip on the Jews as soldiers
stood around grinning. Then they drove us to the cattle car.
A soldier, his eyes glittering through his crumpled face, said:
"Hand it over!" I had hardly taken the money out of my pocket
when he tore it all out of my hand and pushed me ahead. Like
cattle we were herded into the car. There was no time to sweep
it out; the luggage was thrown on top of the rubbish and
people were pushed in after it. Again bribes had to be paid lest
more than 43 persons be squeezed into the car. For those who
came after us, it was much more difficult to fight for room. The
peasants were forced by the soldiers to throw baggage into the
mud and left quickly. The sky was now only a square in the
sliding door. Outside, sticks still came down on people who
howled and cried—then all of us became numb. A transport
was ready.

For a few hours we still saw the silhouette of my native city;
then the locomotive jolted the cars several times throwing

together people and baggage as we moved to another track. We sat still during the dusk, transfixed, pondering, in thick, dusty, sweaty air, or stood at the sliding door staring at the tracks losing themselves in the night. A man, thick and heavy, stood in the middle and lighted a candle. Now a white strand of hair glistened on his temple; was he thinking about all he had lost? Was he thinking about all that would happen now? Would these thoughts help at all? Who could answer the question: "What now?" There was talk about a trip through Ataki into the Ukraine. It should be a favorable trip, someone said. There was hope that one would not have to remain in Bessarabian camps. It was also said that we would wind up under German administration. Some thought that on the other side of the Dniestr, German trucks were supposed to take expellees to their destination. Others had heard reports by previous deportees who upon arrival had immediately been mobilized by the Germans for work and who had been allowed to earn their bread (also that they were paying 30 kopeks for a 2.4-pound loaf). Some cried, because crying is easier than thinking or talking. The transport moved at 8:30 P.M. into the night. From time to time it halted for a few minutes. Men relieved themselves through cracks in the door; women dared to climb out of the car during the stops. In previous transports "warning shots" had "accidentally" killed people who had climbed out. . . .

It was impenetrable night when the train halted again. A voice filled with the sound of command came closer and then yelled into our car: "All watches and armbands are to be handed over immediately!" One could surmise quickly that some railroad man who felt himself unobserved had decided to play "government" for easy gain. Though fearful, we did not react, but now all the sliding doors were slammed shut so that we could not breathe. Our shouting and knocking was of no avail—the train went on. Aroused, suffocating, we did not know how much time had passed before we reached the next stop. An old man about to choke lay at the door and shouted for water. A soldier approached and demanded ten thousand Lei [$70]—he got them and disappeared. Finally another soldier came and promised the water, but wanted 50,000 Lei, saying jokingly that "over there" the Lei would be confiscated anyway. Bargaining did not help; the money had to be handed over and after a few minutes the soldier actually returned with a glass that he held out laughing stupidly to the trembling man who leaned over for it—only to watch the soldier pour it out on the ground.

The train moved again, the doors shut tight. At the next station, during a stop of a few minutes, a passing man accepted a tip to open the door and then climbed on himself. He smelled of alcohol and said he was going to Ataki; this is how we discovered the direction we were going in. He was in a mood for conversation and answered all questions with relish. He said that the train would halt in Lipnic for two hours in the morning, and that then we would have another 2½ hours to Ataki. In unvarnished language he described the agony we faced. The man with the candle stood without moving at his old spot and the dancing light fell on horror-stricken faces.

The visitor went on, apparently satisfied just to talk. Right after the train started moving, he left us, clambering on the side of the car to the next one. We were determined to consider everything an exaggeration; we were sure that he only wanted to torment us (a cheap pleasure with Jew-rabble), but we died a little and the strength which might have sustained us started to dissolve, even though we did not actually know that the indifferent words pouring out of that stinking alcoholic mouth were only naked truth. Fifteen minutes later, something unexpected happened. While we congregated at the open door to face the cold refreshing night air, the opposite door, against which baggage was heaped to the ceiling, suddenly flew open. Packs, valises and bales rolled out. Hands reached in and pulled them out in seconds; we turned, shouting, to save what had not already disappeared through the black hole. Already the robbers were enveloped in the night, as we heard the shrill cries of women recede in the distance.

That is how, one after the other, cars were unbolted in systematic thievery. As we rolled on, the train seemed to pick up speed and we tried somehow to close the doors again from the inside, even while we listened to the crying of the people who had lost their belongings. Now we understood the purpose of the visitor and his searching glances. . . .

. . . A man S. demanded the agreement of his wife that he kill her, himself and his old mother. She, a young vigorous woman, said a definite "no." Not very long afterwards, he prepared tea for his mother and himself and the two died an hour before daybreak. . . .

Dawn, a stop in Lipnic, continuation of the journey. About 9:30 A.M. (it was Tuesday, November 4), shivering, we saw the hilly region of the Dniestr approach closer and closer. Soon we could see soldiers on rises along the track, standing singly at short intervals, sticks in hand, watching the train pull in. Then the clanking and clattering of the wheels stopped. The train stood still and so did for a moment our heartbeat. There was the shrill sound of the locomotive followed by a guttural order. The Jews were to jump out like hares and within five minutes form into a column. Frantic crowding brought about blockages at the doors and the soldiers released the safety catches on their rifles. All along the train, baggage was dumped into a ditch, a yard wide, filled with water. The earth was soft under the footsteps, and beyond the puddles a mound of wet clay rose steeply 15 to 18 feet. Superhuman strength was now required to climb the hill. Everyone panted, dragging the baggage on all fours and clawing the watery mud. Most of the climbers collapsed wishing that a merciful God would let them die. They were beaten so long that they raised their bodies, crawling on, leaving behind their last piece of bread. Those who had died in the train were left there and no one knew where their bodies were subsequently disposed of. I don't know how I managed to go on, how I could drag some part of our things even while I abandoned our best clothes and the food in a hole full of water. That mountain was the end of all our hopes and all we had ever worked for. Bent over, wading in the mud to our knees, we were constantly being beaten. My coat was soaked with sweat. Only for the sake of my wife did I still totter with the baggage for a mile and a half. We moved, oblivious to the sticks landing on our backs, necks, and heads, clambering over people in the morass, between heaps of baggage.

I can still remember next to my feet the bodies of two women, one apparently dead, since her head was buried in the clay, the other on her back looking at the sky. She tried to raise her head, but strands of her white hair had been meshed by some shoe into the ground. The head fell back and her eyes became glassy and immobile. Only much later did her son learn about the end of his mother.

Then we had to show our chest to the military physician. We were driven on, weak, all tendons hurting. At a crossroads, a soldier selected with a look some of the men in the passing column. Beating them wildly, he diverted them into a side street. He noticed me and raised his stick when my wife began to shriek at the top of her voice. The beast was momentarily startled and I could escape straight ahead into the crowd. My sister-in-law, a few dozen steps in front of me, took in the situation and pointing to us, quickly pressed money into the hands of the soldier. Later we found out that the victims had been beaten to a pulp inside a synagogue and robbed of everything down to their shirt. Soon we saw a square which already held more than 1000 people lying around in mud, gasping for air and wiping away sweat and blood. Unable to move further, we too slumped down. From the hill on which we were lying, we shuddered to see only ruins, houses half burned and collapsed, heaps of brick and stones covered with earth from which household effects jutted out, and in the distance under the gray sky the outlines of black rubbish piles. . . .

Perhaps it was the hammering of my blood, but I imagined a giant guillotine in the dusk, and heard the crush of the blade which shook me. It did not rain anymore, but the mud clung to us like plaster. A few hundred steps farther, we lined up into a mass of humanity which became thicker and blacker, backing up and pushing forward, to be examined by the control commission and to exchange money at the rate of 40 Lei for one R.—those same Lei which at the counters of the Roumanian National Bank had been exchanged one for one. [R. or RKKS—Reichskreditkassenscheine—the currency of

Transnistria.] The darkness surprised us and we rested, empty of desire, surrounded by an indistinct roar of voices.

In the middle of the square, at its crest, a gaping hole had been torn by a shell. Through the crater one could see a subterranean passageway. It was easy to climb into the hole and slide down the stones about 6 feet. (At that moment this was the only opportunity to relieve oneself.) But soon the eyes, becoming accustomed to the darkness below, recoiled at what they saw. A few naked corpses thrown on top of one another and half rotted lay there, left over from a mass of dead. Such reminders turned up in all the rooms and cellars of the houses. I soon got to know the story of these victims. The naked human bodies were the end of the Jews from Edineti camp. . . .

[Alexandria document 29222, Microfilm T 501, Roll 278.]

Director, German Armed Forces Intelligence Office
in Roumania
(signed Rodler)
to
11th Army Intelligence Officer
German Army Mission in Roumania—Intelligence Officer
German Air Force Mission—Intelligence Officer
German Navy Mission—Intelligence Officer
Bucharest, November 4, 1941

The liaison officer from this office to the Roumanian intelligence service was in Odessa after the occupation of that city by the Roumanians and reports his observations as follows:

The impression to be gained as soon as one enters Odessa is completely different from any other experience in an occupied city of the east. One is struck first of all by the hundreds, even thousands of men of military age drifting in the streets in civilian clothes. According to the Roumanian General Staff, the Roumanians captured about 7,000 Russians in Odessa. Several times as many men are drifting around in the city as civilians. All these elements have doubtlessly served in the Red Army and they have either remained behind voluntarily or been left behind deliberately. It is not difficult to see a hostile attitude in the faces of these men. More than half of the inhabitants of the city are Jews (about 300,000) [*sic*]. During the first few days the Jewish elements were treated relatively well. There were no special excesses. Notwithstanding all that, the city had fires and small explosions night after night to the day of my arrival. Since Tuesday, October 21, the harbor area has been closed off, but a part of the population lives inside the closed-off zone. In the harbor area, considerable quantities of explosives, munitions, hand grenades, charges, capsules, etc. are lying around openly. Even if guards are posted, it is obviously not difficult to get hold of these things.

The entire harbor is completely intact and precisely this fact is in a certain sense weird. After all, it is known that until now the Russians have destroyed everything that could have been of use to the opponent before their departure. Within the city too—in contradistinction to Chisinau, Dorohoi, Cernauti, etc. —the buildings have not suffered from demolitions. The only destroyed objects are those which have been shot to pieces by German or Roumanian bombers or heavy artillery. In the harbor area, there is a relatively large motor pool. Brief inspection did reveal that most of the vehicles have been damaged. Also artillery is to be found at the harbor, including some 15 cm. heavy howitzers, anti-aircraft artillery, etc. The aiming devices are broken. Many trucks lie in the sea; in some cases one can see the upper half above water. At any rate, the depots in the harbor area contain quite a few supplies. One could see large quantities of rubber items. The tire depot was burned. A few tires swam in the sea.

Entry into the harbor is now forbidden to all persons, including the military in uniform. For entering the harbor, one needs a special permit made out by the harbor captain.

On October 17, 18, and 19, German truck columns are said to have driven up repeatedly to load up and remove supplies as they saw fit.

Plans have been discovered which show that Odessa has

catacombs more than 120 miles long. There are 160 known entrances, but apart from these, every patrician house has access to the catacombs through its cellar. According to reports gathered by the Roumanian intelligence service, the catacombs are filled with hundreds, perhaps thousands, of Red Army men and communists.

Until October 22, all military activity took place on Engel Street. Roumanian military headquarters was located in the former NKVD [Soviet secret police] building on that street. During the Bolshevik period all the neighboring houses were the homes of those favored by the Communist system. From the first day of the occupation, the Roumanian secret service submitted warnings, based on the material it had gathered, to headquarters. The reports said that without exception the buildings on Engel Street were mined. On Tuesday, October 21, following an alarming rumor, the Roumanian headquarters was evacuated temporarily. On the afternoon of October 22, at 3:30 P.M. two Communists are said to have appeared with the warning that the building would be blown up in the next half hour. This warning was disregarded because of the false alarm on the previous day. At 5:30 P.M. the building was actually blown up. At the moment of the explosion the following German officers were in the building: [Naval] Captain Schmidt, [Naval] Commander Reichert, Captain of Coast Artillery Kern and a Lieutenant of Coast Artillery, as well as two specialists [warrant officers]. All of them died. According to unconfirmed reports, 2 German officers of the armored branch were also in the building. As for the Roumanians, the commander of the 10th rifle division, Major General Glogoianu and his entire staff were in the building. Up to the moment of my departure, 46 bodies were found, among them 21 officers. Additional bodies will be discovered once the rooms on the ground floor are cleared. Estimated number of dead about 80. The clearing of the debris was remarkably efficient and fast. Already 10 minutes after the explosion, two large searchlights of the Roumanian anti-aircraft artillery were trained on the site. The neighboring buildings were evacuated after the catastrophe. This was all the more necessary, because of rumors that all the surrounding buildings would be blown up that same night.

There is absolutely no doubt that the detonation was set off electrically by remote control. During the morning hours of the 23rd, a complete telephone installation which was said to have been connected directly with the NKVD men in the catacombs was found in the immediate vicinity of the destroyed building under the bed of a Jew. The arrested Jew declared that partisan activities were being directed from the catacombs.

In reprisal for the assassination, mass-shootings were carried out during the night of the 22nd/23rd. During the morning of the 23rd, about 19,000 Jews were shot near the harbor in a square surrounded by a wooden fence. Their bodies were covered with gasoline and burned. The supervisor of the Roumanian telephone system told me that on Friday another 40,000 Jews were taken from Odessa to Dalnic. There they were driven into tank ditches and shot.

Rodler

[Yad Vashem document, File M 20.]

[Undated account (probably late 1942) by an eyewitness (not identified) of events in Transnistria, in the files of Dr. Adolf Silberschein, chief of a small Jewish rescue organization in Geneva, Switzerland.]

In the whole of the Berezowka district there is no Jewish woman who was not raped or beaten. Most of the women have venereal disease. Many of them were forced to live with Roumanian gendarmes in order to save their lives.

After the occupation of Odessa, the Roumanians evacuated a part of the Jewish population of the city to the Berezowka district where they were distributed to individual villages. In the fall of 1941, an SS detachment appeared in one of the villages and arrested all the Jews. They were arrayed in front of a ditch by the road and told to undress. Then the leader of the SS group declared that the Jews had released the war and that the assembled people had to pay for that. After this speech the grown-ups were shot and the children slain with rifle butts. The bodies were covered with gasoline and set on fire. Children who were still alive were tossed into the flames.

[Yad Vashem document, File M/20.]

OFFICIAL REPORT OF THE JEWISH COMMISSION ON ITS VISIT TO TRANSNISTRIA (SIGNED FRED SARAGA) JANUARY 31, 1943 [EXCERPTS]

Crasna (Mogilev District)

There are 995 Jews, including 100 from Dorohoi, 300 natives, and the remainder from Bukovina.

Social welfare facilities:

1 hospital with 14 beds and 1 physician.

Canteen and orphanage *do not exist.*

Bath is available, but out of commission.

General health is not bad. Cases of spotted fever did occur.

The native Jews are living 8-15 in a room. In November 1941 public workshops were erected in 18 sections of which the following are functioning: tailor shop, shoe shop, barber shop, carpentry shop, tinsmith, and mechanics' workshop. Workers in these shops have received sufficient food. Registers are properly kept and balances are sent to Mogilev.

We have audited the allocation for collective as well as individual welfare payments.

RKKS 1500.—were appropriated [by the commission] for a canteen which is to serve food *once* a day to 350 needy, and for the repair of the bath.

On the evening of January 6, 1943, the commission left Smerinca for Mogilev where it arrived at 6 A.M. next day.

That morning the commission was received by Engineer Jägendorf, President of the Jewish Committee of Mogilev, with whom it met for the first time and from whom it received an oral report about the local situation. Fourteen prominent Jews of Mogilev were also invited to supply requested information about this place and to transmit to the commission the complaints of the Jewish population.

It was emphasized that there had to be complete harmony between those who were destined to lead the community.

Between 3 P.M. and 4:30 P.M. visits were made to the orphanage No. 1, the hospital, and the iron shops with annexes.

The 3 orphanages of Mogilev contain ca. 900 children aged 2–16.

Most of the children are unclothed; we found all of them in bed (4–6 to a bed) under hygienic conditions which leave something to be desired. The hospital for infectious diseases has 63 patients of whom 27 have spotted typhus.

The administrator and the physician Dr. Druckmann have indicated to me that food was not sufficient and not nutritious, especially for convalescing patients. The iron shop is functioning fully and, together with the electric works and the nail factory, employs some 500 people.

On the books, the work is carried out on order of the Government of Transnistria.

According to Engineer Jägendorf, director of the enterprises, the numerous shops of the plant produce machines, tools, and parts which are needed by the army, or by industry and the economy in Transnistria.

The use of qualified workers and the training of a considerable number of apprentices, including even adults, have had very good results. . . .

On January 8 and 9, 1943, a regional conference took place in Mogilev with the participation of the representatives of the Jewish Committees of Mogilev, Shargorod, Murafa, Giurin, Kopaigorod, Crasna, Jaruga, Lucineti, Vindiceni, Tropova, Nemerci, Derebcin, Ozarineti and the residents of Mogilev.

The conference was attended by Mr. Juliu Mumuianu, delegate of the Cabinet, and Captain Joan Mihail [sic] of the gendarmerie, Inspectorate of Transnistria. Captain Mihail Z. Joan opened the meeting and, explaining its purpose, declared that it had been organized with the consent of the authorities. Then I followed with my prepared talk.

I began by indicating that this visit of the delegation from the Central Organization of the Jews in Roumania had been made possible only through the good will of the authorities for which we must all be grateful. I brought greetings from the Central Organization, from the Welfare Commission, and from the Jews in Old Roumania. Furthermore, I pointed out everything that had been done so far in the way of assistance to the Jews of Transnistria in that I enumerated the cash donation in the amount of more than 40,000,000 Lei, the drugs, tools, screws, wood for construction, window panes, and everything that is about to be sent.

In the same vein I spoke about the clothing campaign and its results, in that I mentioned the quantities that had been shipped to every location in the Mogilev district. I indicated the good will of the Central Organization of the Jews in Roumania and the efforts of the Jewish population which, with its limited means, was doing everything in its power. Then I explained at length how social welfare (canteens, hospitals, orphanages) should be organized or reorganized.

Furthermore, I went into the problem of labor organization so as to show what the Administration of Transnistria had decided on in this area, and warmly recommended to all who were present that they might encourage the masses to raise production and learn skills.

I paid special attention to the problem of Jewish emigration from Transnistria and the preparations which must be made to this end.

Finally I emphasized the necessity for complete mutual understanding and called on the leaders of the Jewish communities to instill the spirit of order and discipline in everyone, and to accommodate themselves to the instructions of the authorities, since all of the measures were being adopted for the benefit of the deportees. Attorney Ebercohn explained the legal provisions which allowed the Jews in Transnistria to dispose of their property in Old Roumania. He stated that in accordance with instructions of the Governor of Transnistria, powers of attorney made out by Jews had to be authorized by the *Primar* [town chief] or *Praetor* [district chief] whose signatures would then be given legal force by the Directorate of Local Administration in the Government [of Transnistria] in order to have validity in Old Roumania.

Mr. Juliu Mumuianu, delegate of the Cabinet, expressed the concern of the high authorities for the situation of the Jews in Transnistria, which he described as a historical fatality. He requested that the deportees take their place in productive labor, both for the sake of maintaining their health and life and that they may be better prepared for emigration. He said that he had supported the distribution of the *Gazeta Evreesca*, official organ of the Central Organization of the Jews in Roumania, amongst the Jewish deportees in Transnistria, and that eventually a special Transnistria page may be added for purposes which he will point out.

Dr. [Meier] Teich [chief of the Jewish Council in Shargorod] speaking for himself as well as for all those present with him, expressed his thanks to the representatives of the government for their interest in the Jews of Transnistria. He also thanked the Central Organization of the Jews in Roumania for everything it was doing for the Jews and closed with the remark that the Jews of Transnistria were absolutely convinced that their existence depended on Roumania's rule in this territory.

Captain Mihail Z. Joan concluded the meeting by repeating the suggestion that all Jews should accommodate themselves to the instructions of administrative offices and respect all their legal dispositions. . . .

14. German Army Propaganda

The Intelligence Office of the German Armed Forces (*Amt Ausland-Abwehr* under Admiral Wilhelm Canaris) prepared leaflets calling upon the Red Army to kill

Jews in its midst. In the field, German intelligence officers then discovered that the leaflets were a failure. The theme of the message was subsequently adjusted to allege that the Soviet Jews were not doing their part in the war, and so forth. The following are two examples of "before" and "after" evaluations.

[Alexandria document OKW-638, Microfilm T 77, Roll 1006.]

Office of Major Baun
to Intelligence Division I H East N. Berlin
August 2, 1942

Secret
Subject: Own Propaganda
Source: Prisoner-of-war; time: early July, 1942

At the beginning leaflets were not suited for a proper propagandistic effect on Red Army men. Only lately did they become considerably better. He mentions several cases in which propaganda had bad results, for example, German leaflets which called for the killing and murder of Jews. He considers an anti-Semitic tendency in leaflets to be correct, but views invitations to violence as misdirecting the primitive mind of the Russian soldier, who will infer from them that Germans are inclined towards violence and for that very reason will be afraid to surrender.
Signed by instruction
2nd Lieut. Tietze
[Notation:] To German Armed Forces Propaganda Office via Foreign Intelligence Division

Command Staff Walli I
to Intelligence Division I H East N. Berlin
for Foreign Intelligence
August 8, 1942

Subject: Propaganda
Source: Captured 1st Lieutenant

German leaflets which point out to Red Army men and officers that Jews are not fighting at the front, are not employed in heavy or the heaviest labor, and stay only where it is not dangerous, are being read with interest. In general, the contents are approved of.

Signed by a major
[Illegible signature, probably: Baun]

15. The Final Solution

When the Germans wanted to refer to the annihilation of European Jewry, they talked about the "final solution of the Jewish problem." Much is implied by that phrase. It means crossing a psychological threshold, scoring an administrative breakthrough, making no exceptions, and halting before no consequences. It was to be a historic act beyond measure: the target which Germany was now striking down would never again arise for yet another generation.

The idea of the final solution surfaced in a number of localities and offices during the middle of 1941. The documents reproduced here deal with this crystallization. The first is a letter from an SS-major in Poland to Adolf Eichmann. It reports discussions held in the office of Gauleiter Greiser, who administered the so-called Warthegau—Polish incorporated territory comprising Lodz and Poznan. The second item, an order from Göring to Heydrich, was the authorization to begin deportations in all the German-dominated areas of Europe. The third is the record of an interministerial conference called after some delays by Heydrich in reliance upon the authorization. Finally, some of Eichmann's recollections of the conference are included for a view of the setting in which it took place.

Many rungs separated Göring from Eichmann. Hermann Göring was the No. 2 man in Nazi Germany. His order was sent over Heinrich Himmler's head to the Chief of the Reich Security Main Office, Reinhard Heydrich. In that Main Office, Office IV was the headquarters of the Gestapo, IV B dealt with "sects," and IV B 4 with "Evacuations and Jews." Eichmann headed the Reich Security Main Office's IV B 4.

When the conference was held on January 20, 1942, a camp at Chelmno had already started operating with gas-vans for the Jews of Gauleiter Greiser's Warthegau. Since other camps were not yet in existence, the conferees were still thinking of deportations to Russia where Heydrich's own mobile units were shooting the Jews. It may be noted that the estimates of Jewish populations in the conference record include a number of countries that were not under German control (England, Ireland, Switzerland, Turkey, Spain, Portugal). The figures for two other regions (Ukraine and Southern France) are large overestimates.

During the conference, Heydrich made reference to an "Old People's Ghetto" for Jews over sixty-five and invalided and decorated Jewish war veterans. It was officially decreed on February 16, 1942, by Heydrich in his capacity as *Reichsprotektor* of Bohemia and Moravia. The ghetto, which was located in the Czech town of Theresienstadt, became also a transit point for the Czech Jews on their way to the death camp in Auschwitz. Most of those who did not go on to Auschwitz died in the ghetto.

Although the conferees were concerned with a European-wide "solution," they devoted a great deal of attention to the perennial theme of the *Mischlinge* and the Jews in mixed marriage. This topic was on the agenda of a number of subsequent "final solution" conferences;

but while the Germans managed to kill five million Jews, that particular problem was never solved.

[*Biuletyn* Glowney Komisji Badania Zbrodni Hitlerowskich W Polsce (Warsaw, Wydawnictwo Prawnicze) XII, 1960, pp. 27F–29F.]

L Hö/S
[Higher SS and Police Leader in Warthegau/SS-Major Rolf-Heinz Höppner]
to
Reich Security Main Office
Office IV B 4
Attention SS-Lt. Col. Eichmann
Berlin
July 16, 1941

Dear Comrade Eichmann,
    Enclosed is a memorandum on the results of various discussions held locally in the office of the Reich Governor. I would be grateful to have your reactions sometime. These things sound in part fantastic, but in my view are thoroughly feasible.
1 enclosure
L Hö/S   Poznan July 16, 1941
                    Memorandum
Subject: Solution of the Jewish question
    During discussions in the office of the Reich Governor various groups broached the solution of the Jewish question in Warthe province. The following solution is being proposed.
    1. All the Jews of Warthe province will be taken to a camp for 300,000 Jews which will be erected in barracks form as close as possible to the coal precincts and which will contain barracks-like installations for economic enterprises, tailor shops, shoe manufacturing plants, etc.
    2. All Jews of Warthe province will be brought into this camp. Jews capable of labor may be constituted into labor columns as needed and drawn from the camp.
    3. In my view, a camp of this type may be guarded by

SS-Brig. Gen. Albert with substantially fewer police forces than are required now. Furthermore, the danger of epidemics, which always exists in the Lodz and other ghettos for the surrounding population, will be minimized.

4. This winter there is a danger that not all of the Jews can be fed anymore. One should weigh honestly, if the most humane solution might not be to finish off those of the Jews who are not employable by means of some quick-working device. At any rate, that would be more pleasant than to let them starve to death.

5. For the rest, the proposal was made that in this camp all the Jewish women, from whom one could still expect children, should be sterilized so that the Jewish problem may actually be solved completely with this generation.

6. The Reich Governor has not yet expressed an opinion in this matter. There is an impression that Government President Übelhör does not wish to see the ghetto in Lodz disappear since he [his office] seems to profit quite well with it. As an example of how one can profit from the Jews, I was told that the Reich Labor Ministry pays 6 Reichsmark from a special fund for each employed Jew, but that the Jew costs only 80 Pfennige.

[Nuremberg document PS-710.]

REICH MARSHAL OF GREATER GERMAN REICH GORING TO CHIEF OF
SECURITY POLICE AND SECURITY SERVICE HEYDRICH
BERLIN, JULY [31], 1941

Complementing the task already assigned to you in the decree of January 24, 1939, to undertake, by emigration or evacuation, a solution of the Jewish question as advantageous as possible under the conditions at the time, I hereby charge you with making all necessary organizational, functional, and material preparations for a complete solution of the Jewish question in the German sphere of influence in Europe.

In so far as the jurisdiction of other central agencies may

be touched thereby, they are to be involved.

I charge you furthermore with submitting to me in the near future an overall plan of the organizational, functional, and material measures to be taken in preparing for the implementation of the aspired final solution of the Jewish question.

[Nuremberg document NG-2586.]

Secret Reich Matter
Conference Protocol
30 copies
16th copy

I. The following participated in the conference of January 20, 1942, in Berlin, Am Grossen Wannsee 56–58, on the final solution of the Jewish question:

Gauleiter Dr. Meyer and Reich Office Director Dr. Leibbrandt	Reich Ministry for the Occupied Eastern Territories
Undersecretary Dr. Stuckart	Reich Ministry of the Interior
Undersecretary Dr. Neumann	[Office of] Plenipotentiary of the Four Year Plan
Undersecretary Dr. Freisler	Reich Justice Ministry
Undersecretary Dr. Bühler	Office of Governor General [of Poland]
Assistant Secretary Luther	Foreign Office
SS [Senior]-Colonel Klopfer	Party Chancellery
Ministerial Director Kritzinger	Reich Chancellery
SS-Major General Hofmann	Race and Resettlement Main Office
SS-Major General Müller	Reich Security Main Office
SS-Lt. Colonel Eichmann	Reich Security Main Office
SS [Senior]-Colonel Dr. Schoengarth, Commanding Officer of Security Police and Security Service in General Government [Poland]	Security Police and Security Service

SS-Major Dr. Lange, Commander of Security Police and Security Service for General Commissariat Latvia, as deputy of Commanding Officer of Security Police and Security Service for Reich Commissariat Ostland [Baltic states and White Russia]

Security Police and Security Service

II. Chief of Security Police and Security Service, SS-Lieutenant General Heydrich, opened the meeting by informing everyone that the Reich Marshal [Göring] had placed him in charge of preparations for the final solution of the Jewish question, and that the invitations to this conference had been issued to obtain clarity in fundamental questions. The Reich Marshal's wish to have a draft submitted to him on the organizational, functional, and material considerations aimed at a final solution of the European Jewish question requires that all of the central agencies, which are directly concerned with these problems, first join together with a view to parallelizing their lines of action.

The implementation of the final solution of the Jewish question is to be guided centrally without regard to geographic boundaries from the office of the Reichsführer-SS and Chief of the German Police (Chief of Security Police and Security Service).

The Chief of Security Police and Security Service then reviewed briefly the battle fought thus far against these opponents. The principal stages constituted
a) Forcing the Jews out of individual sectors of life [*Lebensgebiete*] of the German people
b) Forcing the Jews out of the living space [*Lebensraum*] of the German people

In pursuance of this endeavor, a systematic and concentrated effort was made to accelerate Jewish emigration from Reich territory as the only temporary solution possibility.

On instructions of the Reich Marshal, a Reich Central Office

for Jewish Emigration was established in January, 1939, and its direction was entrusted to the Chief of the Security Police and Security Service. In particular the office had the task of
  a) taking every step to *prepare* for a larger volume of Jewish emigration,
  b) *steering* the flow of emigration,
  c) expediting emigration in *individual* cases.
The goal of the task was to cleanse the German living space of Jews in a legal manner.

The disadvantages brought forth by such forcing of emigration were clear to every agency. In the meantime, however, they had to be accepted for the lack of any other solution possibility.

The migration work in the ensuing period was not only a German problem, but also one that concerned the offices of the countries of destination and immigration. Financial difficulties, such as increasingly demanding regulations on the part of various foreign governments for money to be shown by the immigrant or to be paid by him on landing, insufficient berths on ships, constantly increasing immigration restrictions and suspensions—all this placed extraordinary burdens on emigration efforts. In spite of these difficulties, some 537,000 Jews were moved out from the day of the seizure of power to October 31, 1941. Of this total

from January 30, 1933 out of the Old Reich ... ca. 360,000

from March 15, 1938 out of Austria .... ca. 147,000

from March 15, 1939 out of the Protectorate
    Bohemia and Moravia .... ca. 30,000

The emigration was financed by the Jews (or Jewish political organizations) themselves. In order to avoid having a residue of proletarianized Jews, the Jews with means had to finance the departure of the Jews without means; an appropriate assessment and emigration tax were used to finance the payments of debts owed by the poor Jews in the course of their emigration.

In addition to this levy in Reichsmark, foreign currencies

were required for showing or payment on landing. In order to spare German foreign currency reserves, the Jewish financial institutions abroad were called upon by Jewish organizations at home to take care of the collection of an appropriate foreign currency pile. In this manner about $9,500,000 were made available through these foreign Jews as gifts to October 30, 1941.

Meanwhile, in view of the dangers of emigration in time of war and in view of the possibilities in the east, the Reichsführer-SS and Chief of the German Police [Himmler] has forbidden the emigration of Jews.

III. In lieu of emigration, the evacuation of the Jews to the east has emerged, after an appropriate prior authorization by the Führer [Hitler], as a further solution possibility.

While these actions are to be regarded solely as temporary measures, practical experiences are already being gathered here which will be of great importance during the coming final solution of the Jewish question.

Around 11 million Jews are involved in this final solution of the Jewish question. They are distributed as follows among individual countries:

Country	Number
A. Old Reich	131,800
Austria	43,700
Eastern Territories [Poland]	420,000
General Government [Poland]	2,284,000
Bialystok [Poland]	400,000
Protectorate of Bohemia and Moravia	74,200
Estonia—free of Jews	
Latvia	3,500
Lithuania	34,000
Belgium	43,000
Denmark	5,600
France/occupied territory	165,000
unoccupied territory	700,000
Greece	69,000

Netherlands	160,000
Norway	1,300

B.

Bulgaria	48,000
England	330,000
Finland	2,300
Ireland	4,000
Italy, including Sardinia	58,000
Albania	200
Croatia	40,000
Portugal	3,000
Roumania, including Bessarabia	342,000
Sweden	8,000
Switzerland	18,000
Serbia	10,000
Slovakia	88,000
Spain	6,000
Turkey (European portion)	55,500
Hungary	742,800
USSR	5,000,000

Ukraine 2,994,684
White Russia, excluding
Bialystok 446,484

Total: over 11,000,000

So far as the Jews of the various foreign countries are concerned, the numbers listed include only Jews by religion, since definitions of Jews according to racial principles are in part still lacking there. Given prevailing attitudes and conceptions, the treatment of the problem in individual countries will encounter certain difficulties, especially in Hungary and Roumania. For example, even today a Jew in Roumania can buy for cash appropriate documents officially certifying him in a foreign nationality.

The pervasive influence of Jewry in the USSR is known. The European area contains some 5 million, the Asian barely a half million Jews.

The occupational distribution of Jewry in the European area of the USSR was approximately as follows:

agriculture	9.1%
urban workers	14.8%
trade	20.0%
state employees	23.4%
private professions—	32.7%
medical, press, theater,	
and so forth	

In the course of the final solution, the Jews should be brought under appropriate direction in a suitable manner to the east for labor utilization. Separated by sex, the Jews capable of work will be led into these areas in large labor columns to build roads, whereby doubtless a large part will fall away through natural reduction.

The inevitable final remainder which doubtless constitutes the toughest element will have to be dealt with appropriately, since it represents a natural selection which upon liberation is to be regarded as a germ cell of a new Jewish development. (See the lesson of history.)

In the course of the practical implementation of the final solution, Europe will be combed from west to east. If only because of the apartment shortage and other socio-political necessities, the Reich area—including the Protectorate of Bohemia and Moravia—will have to be placed ahead of the line.

For the moment, the evacuated Jews will be brought bit by bit to so-called transit ghettos from where they will be transported farther to the east.

SS-Lieutenant General Heydrich pointed out further that an important prerequisite for the evacuation in general was the exact specification of the category of persons liable to be involved.

It is intended not to evacuate Jews over 65, but to transfer them to an old people's ghetto (the plan calls for Theresienstadt).

In addition to these age groups—some 30% of the 280,000 Jews who lived in the Old Reich and Austria on October 1,

1941, are over 65—the old people's ghetto will receive badly invalided Jewish war veterans and Jews with war decorations (Iron Cross First Class). Many intercessions will be eliminated in one blow by means of this purposeful solution.

The start of major individual evacuation operations will depend in large measure on military developments. With regard to the treatment of the final solution in European areas occupied or influenced by us, it was proposed that the appropriate specialists of the Foreign Office get together with the experts having jurisdiction in these matters within the Security Police and Security Service.

In Slovakia and Croatia the situation is no longer all that difficult, since the essential key questions there have already been resolved. Meanwhile, the Roumanian government has already appointed a plenipotentiary for Jewish affairs. To settle the matter in Hungary, it will be necessary before long to impose upon the Hungarian government an adviser on Jewish questions.

Regarding a start of preparations in Italy, SS-Lieutenant General Heydrich considers it appropriate to contact Police Chief [Himmler].

In occupied and unoccupied France, the seizure of Jews for evacuation should in all probability proceed without major difficulty.

Assistant Secretary Luther [Foreign Office] then pointed out that with a deeply penetrating treatment of these problems in some countries, such as the nordic states, difficulties would emerge and that meanwhile it would therefore be best to hold these countries in abeyance. In view of the insignificant number of Jews involved there, the postponement would not amount to a substantial restriction. On the other hand, the Foreign Office sees no major difficulties in southeastern and western Europe.

SS-Major General Hofmann intends to dispatch a specialist of the Race and Resettlement Office for general orientation to Hungary as soon as the Chief of Security Police and Security Service is about to tackle the situation over there. It was decided that temporarily the specialist of the Race and Resettlement Office—who is not to become active—should be officially attached as an assistant to the Police Attaché.

IV. The Nuremberg laws should constitute the basis, so to speak, of the final solution project, while a solution of the mixed marriage and mixed parentage questions is a prerequisite for the complete purification of the problem.

The Chief of the Security Police and Security Service addressed himself to a letter of the Chief of the Reich Chancellery, and speaking theoretically for the moment, dealt with the following points:

1. Treatment of *Mischlinge* of the 1st degree

In view of the final solution of the Jewish question *Mischlinge* of the first degree are placed into the same position as Jews.

To be excepted from this treatment will be

a) *Mischlinge* of the 1st degree married to Germans, if this marriage produced offspring (*Mischlinge* of the 2nd degree).

These *Mischlinge* of the 2nd degree are in the main placed into the same position as Germans.

b) *Mischlinge* of the 1st degree who in some (vital) area have been accorded exceptional treatment by the higher authorities of the party or state. Each individual case has to be examined anew, whereby one must not exclude an unfavorable decision for the *Mischling*.

Prerequisite for an exemption must always be basic merits of the *Mischling* himself (not merits of the German parent or marital partner).

To avoid any progeny and to clean up the *Mischling* problem once and for all, the *Mischlinge* of the 1st degree who are to be exempted from evacuation must be sterilized. Sterilization is voluntary, but it is a prerequisite for remaining in the Reich. The sterilized "*Mischling*" is then liberated from all the constricting ordinances to which he has heretofore been subjected.

2. Treatment of *Mischlinge* of the 2nd degree

In principle, the *Mischlinge* of the 2nd degree will be treated as Germans, with the exception of the following cases in which *Mischlinge* of the 2nd degree will be placed into the same position as Jews:

 a) The descent of the *Mischling* of the 2nd degree from a bastard marriage (both parts *Mischlinge*).

 b) Racially exceptionally poor appearance of the *Mischling* of the 2nd degree, so that for external reasons alone he has to be considered a Jew.

 c) A particularly unfavorable appraisal from a police and political viewpoint which indicates that the *Mischling* of the 2nd degree feels and behaves like a Jew.

Even these considerations, however, should not apply if the *Mischling* of the 2nd degree is married to a German.

 3. Marriages between full Jews and Germans

In individual cases, it must be decided whether the Jewish partner is to be evacuated or whether, considering the effect of such a measure on the German relatives, he is to be transferred to an old people's ghetto.

 4. Marriages between *Mischlinge* of the 1st degree and Germans

 a) Without children:

 If there are no children, the *Mischling* of the 1st degree is to be evacuated, or transferred to an old people's ghetto (same treatment as in the case of marriages between full Jews and Germans, point 3).

 b) With children:

 If there are children (*Mischlinge* of the 2nd degree) and they are placed into the same position as Jews, they will be evacuated along with the [parent who is a] *Mischling* of the 1st degree, or transferred to a ghetto. Insofar as these children are placed into the same position as Germans (the regular case) they are to be exempted from evacuation, and so will [the parent who is a] *Mischling* of the 1st degree.

 5. Marriages between *Mischlinge* of the 1st degree and *Mischlinge* of the 2nd degree or Jews

In the case of these marriages, all the elements (including the children) are to be treated as Jews and hence evacuated, or transferred to an old people's ghetto.

6. Marriages between *Mischlinge* of the 1st degree and *Mischlinge* of the 2nd degree

Both partners, without regard to children, are to be evacuated, or placed into an old people's ghetto, since racially the children, if any, regularly reveal a stronger Jewish blood component than do *Mischlinge* of the 2nd degree.

SS-Major General Hofmann is of the view that one will have to make widespread use of sterilization, especially since the *Mischlinge*, faced with the choice of being evacuated or sterilized, would rather submit to sterilization.

Undersecretary Dr. Stuckart [Interior Ministry] stated that in this form the practical implementation of the possibilities just mentioned for cleaning up the mixed marriage and mixed parentage problem would entail an endless administrative task. In order to be sure, however, of taking into account also the biological facts, Undersecretary Dr. Stuckart proposed to proceed with compulsory sterilization.

To simplify the *Mischling* problem, one should further think about the possibility of enabling the lawmaker to say in so many words: "These marriages are dissolved."

As for the effect of the evacuation of the Jews on economic life, Undersecretary Neumann [Four Year Plan] declared that at the moment Jews employed in important war work could not be evacuated until replacements became available.

SS-Lieutenant General Heydrich pointed to the fact that in accordance with directives authorized by him for current evacuations, these Jews were not being evacuated anyhow.

Undersecretary Dr. Bühler stated that the General Government [of Poland] would welcome the start of the final solution of this question in its territory, since the transport problem was no overriding factor there and the course of the action would not be hindered by considerations of work utilization. Jews should be removed from the domain of the General Government as fast as possible, because it is precisely here that the Jew constitutes a substantial danger as carrier of epidemics and also because his continued black market activities create constant disorder in the economic structure of the country. Moreover, the majority of the

2½ million Jews involved were not capable of work.

Undersecretary Dr. Bühler stated further that the Chief of the Security Police and Security Service was in charge of the final solution of the Jewish question in the General Government and that his work was being supported by the offices of the General Government. He only had one favor to ask: that the Jewish question in this territory be solved as rapidly as possible.

Finally there was a discussion of the various types of solution possibilities, with both Gauleiter Dr. Meyer and Undersecretary Dr. Bühler expressing the view that they could carry out certain preparatory measures in their territories on their own, provided, however, that any disturbance of the [non-Jewish] population had to be avoided.

The conference was closed with a plea of the Chief of Security Police and Security Service for the cooperation of all the participants in the implementation of the solution tasks.

[Testimony by Adolf Eichmann, uncorrected English transcript of the Eichmann trial (mimeographed), June 23, 1961, session 78, pp. Z1, Aa1, Bb1; June 26, 1961, session 79, p. B1; July 24, 1961, session 107, pp. E1, F1, G1.]

Dr. Servatius: . . . Will the Witness explain what do you know in connection to the initiative to call this conference?

Accused: Without any doubt, the main reason for the convening of the conference was Heydrich's intention to extend the scope of his influence.

Dr. Servatius: Was he afraid of any difficulties? Did he have reason to be afraid.

Accused: Experience up to then showed that all those questions were usually dealt with by various authorities and if it were, there was no co-ordinated activity and, therefore, actions were delayed considerably as there were all sorts of activities carried out within various offices. And, in a nutshell, one may point out that in the deliberations which were held so far they wouldn't see the wood for the trees, and they wouldn't arrive at any definite solution or any co-ordination solution. This is

one of the reasons why Heydrich convened the Wannsee Conference, why he actually convened it on his own initiative in order to imprint his own will and that of the Reichsführer SS.
Dr. Servatius: The witness I believe already declared here in Court that you prepared Heydrich's speech. Or this may be collected from the appendix to the Sassen report.
Presiding Judge: Yes.
Dr. Servatius: Are you ready to repeat once again your explanation how it came about that you were asked to prepare this speech?
Accused: Yes. I was instructed to collect material which Heydrich thought relevant for his speech which he was about to hold. That means to say that it should have been a general survey of all the operations that had been carried out in the course of the last years in the realm of the emigration of Jews. It had to be a survey of the results and the difficulties of the operations in question. These prepared remarks that I drew for Heydrich's speech can be seen on the seven pages of the document in front of us, but it struck me that certain points which I prepared were [not] prepared by me. They are not the fruit of my pencil, so to speak, but simply expressed by Heydrich without taking heed of what I had prepared. Because very often as I had seen from experience he would speak very freely, without always taking care of the prepared points. And here on page 6 the last passage, according to which Jews were earmarked for special labor effort and they were to be sent, within the framework of the final solution, to the eastern territories and, as I said, this was to conform with the framework set for the labour effort in the east. The labour columns were to be formed and a separation was to be carried out between the sexes so that the Jews fit for work would be brought within the framework of this plan and would be employed in the construction of the roads. This particular passage could not have possibly stemmed from me and the remarks couldn't possibly been ascribed to what I wrote because this particular passage actually constituted a turning point in the policy towards the Jews and this policy appears for the first time in the Wannsee conference.

Presiding Judge: I believe there is a written translation into the Hebrew of this document.

Court Interpreter: I do not have it before me.

Accused: May I further point out, your Honours, to complete the picture, that the second function which was bestowed upon me was the function of keeping minutes of the meeting together with a secretary.

Dr. Servatius: Do the minutes describe the contents of the deliberations correctly?

Accused: These minutes to which I was referring were rendering the salient points quite clearly. But so far as the particulars were concerned, I have to point out that this was not a verbatim report because certain colloquialisms were then couched by me in official language and certain official terms had to be introduced. Later on it had been revised three or four times by Heydrich. It came back through official channels to us through the channel of Mueller and then again we had to elaborate on it until it assumed its final form. . . .

Dr. Servatius: What is not reflected in the protocol is the spirit which reigned at this conference. Can you report or comment regarding the spirit and attitude at this conference?

Accused: Yes, the climate of this conference was characterized as it were by a relaxed attitude of Heydrich who had actually more than anybody else expected considerable stumbling blocks and difficulties.

Q. It is important how these things found expression on the part of the other participants.

A. It was an atmosphere not only of agreement on the part of the participants, but more than that, one could feel an agreement which had assumed a form which had not been expected. Unflinching in his determination to participate fully in the functions with regard to the final solution of the Jewish problem and particularly outstanding in the enthusiastic and unexpected form of agreement was the State secretary, Buhler [Bühler], and even more than Buhler, Stuckart had evinced boundless enthusiasm. He was usually hesitating, and reserved, reticent and furtive, but all of a sudden he gave expression to boundless enthusiasm, with which he joined the others with regard to the final solution of the Jewish question.

Q. The witness saw before the calling of this conference the preparations in the East for the extermination? He saw the steps taken there?

A. Yes, sir.

Q. Did the participants at this conference know anything about the way for the final solution?

A. I have to assume that the things were known to the participants of the Wannsee Conference because after all the War against Russia had been going on already about six months. As we saw in some various relevant documents, the operational groups were already acting in the Russian war theater and all those key personalities in the Reich Government must have known about the state of affairs at that time.

Q. How long did this conference go on and what happened after the conference was over?

A. The conference itself took only a very short period of time. I can't recall exactly how long it lasted, but it seems to me that I would not be mistaken in saying that it didn't take longer than an hour or an hour and a half. Of course, the gentlemen who participated in it would later on be standing in small groups to discuss the ins and outs of the agenda and also of certain work to be undertaken afterwards. After the conference had been a[d]journed, Heydrich and Mueller still remained and I was also permitted to remain and then in this restricted get-together, Heydrich gave expression to his great satisfaction I already referred to before. . . .

Presiding Judge: . . . Now in connection with the Wannsee conference, you answered my colleague Dr. Raveh that this part of the meeting, which is not mentioned in the protocol, the discussion was about the means of extermination, systems of killing.

A: Yes.

Q. Who discussed this subject?

A: I do not remember it in detail, Your Honour. I do not remember the circumstances of this conversation. But I do know that these gentlemen were standing together, or sitting together, and were discussing the subject quite bluntly, quite differently from the language which I had to use later in the record. During the conversation they minced no words about it at all. I might say furthermore, Your Honour, that I would not have remembered this unless I had later remembered that I told myself—Look here, I told myself, even this guy Stuckart, who was known as one of these uncles who was a great stickler for legalities, he too uses language which is not at all in accordance with paragraphs of the law. This incident remained engraved in my memory and recalled the entire subject to my mind.

Q: What did he say about this subject?

A: In detail I do not—

Q: Not details in general, what did he say about this theme?

A: I cannot remember it in detail Your Honour, but they spoke about methods for killing, about liquidation, about extermination. I was busy with my records. I had to make the preparations for taking down the minutes. I could not perk up my ears and listen to everything that was said. But it filtered through the small room and I caught fragments of this conversation. It was a small room so from time to time I heard a word or two.

Q: I believed that this was the official part of the meeting, of the conference.

A: The official part did not take too long.

Q: Was this in the official part of the conference, or not? It was my belief that this was in the official conference because this should have been included in the protocol of the meeting, although nothing is mentioned.

A: Well of course, it was in the official part, Your Honour. But again this official part had two subdivisions. The first part where everyone was quiet and listened to the various lectures, and then in the second part, everyone spoke out of turn and people would go around, butlers, agitants, and would give out liquor. Well, I don't want to say that there was an atmosphere of drunkardness there. It was an official atmosphere, but nevertheless it was not one of these stiff, formal, official affairs where everyone spoke in turn. But people just talked at cross vertices.

Q: And were these also recorded by the short-hand typists?
Accused: Yes, yes—they were taken down.
Presiding Judge: And you were ordered by someone not to include it in the memorandum of the meeting—in the official Protocol of this meeting, weren't you?
Accused: Yes, that's how it was. The stenographer was sitting next to me and I was to see to it that everything would be taken down; then she deciphered this and then Heydrich gave me his instructions as to what should be included in the record and what should be excluded. Then I showed it to Heydrich and he polished it up and proof-read it and that's how it was kept.
Q. And that which was said about this very important theme, you cannot remember at all—is this what you say?
A. Well, the most important thing here was. . . .
Q. I did not say, *the* most important—I said it was an important theme, and important enough to be excluded from the record.
A. Well, no. The significant part from Heydrich's point-of-view, was to nail-down the Secretaries of State, to commit them most bindingly, to catch them by their words; and therefore, it was quite the contrary—the important part did go into the record and the less significant ones were excluded. It was, I would say, that Heydrich wanted to cover himself, wanted to be sure that each and every one of these Secretaries of State would be nailed-down—and these matters, therefore, were put down.
Q. That means to say that the methods of killing—the systems of extermination—was not an important theme?
A. Ah! the means of killing. . . .
Q. *That* is what we are speaking about—the means of killing.
A. No, no—this of course was not put into the record—no, no!
Q. Did they discuss killing by poison gas?
A. No, with gas—no.
Q. But, how then?
A. It was . . . this business with the engine, they spoke about this; they spoke about shooting, but not about gas.
Q. Later, the Protocol goes on to say, in the same passage, that Gauleiter Mayer and Secretary of State Dr. Bühler (?) believed

and were of the opinion, that certain preparations, for implementation in various districts, be made at the same time; certain preparatory work in connection with the "final solution" should be made immediately, in the discussed areas, but unrest amongst the population should be avoided. Can you remember this?

A. What did you mean, Your Honour—I did not understand it.

Q. You did not understand? All right—I will read it out to you once again: Dr. Mayer and Dr. Bühler—that their opinion was that preparatory work should begin immediately for the "final solution" in the various areas, but at the same time to avoid unrest and anxiety on the part of the population.

A. Ah, yes. . . .

Q. To which preparatory work does this refer?

A. I cannot imagine anything, but. . . .

Q. Don't imagine! My question is—and I put it to you, as the Attorney-General put it to you before and all the time—what can you remember? This was a turning point, in fact.

A. I was there and I witnessed the preparatory work, with these two little houses in the Lublin area.

Q. Which two little huts in the Lublin area? I'm asking you this question about the Conference.

A. Well, I had seen the preparatory work before—in fact, but I don't really know. They spoke about the matter, at the meeting, of not creating any anxiety and perplexity amongst the local population, so all I thought was being discussed, was this same kind of business.

Q. And did you report what you saw to this Conference?

A. At the Wannsee Conference? No, I never uttered a syllable; I was not authorized to open my mouth. No, I had no permission.

Q. So, who was it, who brought the technical details to the Conference?

Accused: Well, no-one discussed the technical details. That is to say, Heydrich opened the meeting and then everyone spoke about it. Well, I mean maybe Büller [Bühler] spoke about it or possible Krueger—I suppose he would have—he was the senior SS and Police Commander in the Government General. In a way he was the head of the entire business, in charge of it. Globocnik was subordinated to this man Krueger. Krueger, as the boss, must have known it in detail.

Presiding Judge: But Krueger did not take part at the Wannsee Conference, according to the list of participants.

A. Yes, but earlier he visited Heydrich and extracted from him an invitation for Büller [Bühler] to take part at the meeting. And then, one spoke about it in detail. Heydrich and Krueger discussed it and for that reason I had to issue special invitations for Krueger and Büller [Bühler].

Q. You told the Court that you do not consider yourself an anti-Semite and that you never were an anti-Semite.

A. An anti-Semite I never was—no.

16. A Railroad Timetable

About three million Jews were transported to their deaths in trains. The requests for trains were made by the Reich Security Main Office, and schedules were decided centrally for many transports in advance at railway conferences held in various cities such as Berlin, Frankfurt, or Vienna. Territorially, the German railways in the Reich operated out of three General Management Directorates: East (Berlin), West (Essen), and South (Munich). From here orders were sent to all the Reich Railway Directorates on the routes. The telegram below deals with "special trains" of five kinds: Vd is the designation for ethnic Germans, Rm for Roumanians, Po for Poles, Pj for Polish Jews, Da ("David"?) for Jews generally. Lp stands for an empty train.

It will be noted that for Jews there are three destinations in the timetable: Auschwitz, Treblinka, and Theresienstadt. Auschwitz was a death camp near Katowice which received Jews from all parts of Europe.

It was also the final stop for non-Jewish transports (a Polish group is included here), but non-Jews were employed there as slave labor in industries and were not subject to gassing. Treblinka was a pure killing center northeast of Warsaw. Only Jews were sent to Treblinka, and most of the victims came from nearby ghettos such as Warsaw and Bialystok. Theresienstadt was the "Old People's Ghetto" mentioned in the Final Solution conference of January 20, 1942.

There are very few railway documents in archives or institutes, and the copy below comes from the Reich Traffic Directorate in Minsk which noted on it in ink: "We are not involved." Soviet authorities found the document and transmitted a copy, with several other finds from the Minsk station, to West Germany.

[Institut für Zeitgeschichte, Munich, document Fb 85/2.]

German Reich Railways   Berlin, Jan 13, 1943
General Management Directorate East
PW 113 Bfsv
                          Telegraphic Letter!
To
Reich Railway Directorates
Berlin, Breslau, Dresden, Erfurt, Frankfurt, Halle (S), Karlsruhe, Königsberg (Pr), Linz, Mainz, Oppeln, East in Frankfurt (O), Posen, Vienna,
General Directorate of East Railway in Krakow,
Reichsprotektor, Group Railways in Prague
General Traffic Directorate Warsaw,
Reich Traffic Directorate Minsk
copies to
General Management/Directorate South, Munich
General Management/Directorate West, Essen
— Special, 3 copies each —
Subject: Special trains for resettlers during the period from
            January 20 to February 28, 1943

We enclose a compilation of the special trains (Vd, Rm, Po, Pj, and Da) agreed upon in Berlin on January 15, 1943 for the period from January 20, 1943 to February 28, 1943 and a circulatory plan for cars to be used in these trains.

Train formation is noted for each recirculation and *attention is to be paid* to these instructions. After each full trip, cars are to be well cleaned, if need be fumigated, and upon completion of the program prepared for further use. Number and kinds of cars are to be determined upon dispatch of the last train and are to be reported to me by telephone with confirmation on service cards.

                                        Signed Dr. Jacobi

[in handwriting]
33 Bfp 5 Bfsv   Minsk Feb. 9, 1943
1) we are not involved
2) [illegible] Bfsv

General Management Directorate East—Berlin
PW 113 Bfsv of
Jan 16, 1943

Compilation
of special trains agreed upon in Berlin, January 15, 1943 for Vd, Rm, Po, Pj, and Da resettlers in the period from January 20 to February 18, 1943, arranged according to departure date

1 Date	2 Train Number	3 From	4 Departs	5 To	6 Arrives	7 Circulation No.
20.1.	Vd 201	Kalisch	8.22	Ottersweier		106
	Da 101	Theresienstadt		Auschwitz		128
21.1.	Lp 102	Auschwitz		Theresienstadt		128
22.1.	Lp 202	Ottersweier		Andrzejow		106
23.1.	Da 103	Theresienstadt		Auschwitz		128
24.1.	Lp 104	Auschwitz		Theresienstadt		128
25.1.	Vd 203	Andrzejow		Linz		106
	Rm 1	Gleiwitz		Czernowitz		107
	Po 61	Zamocz	8.20	Berlin Whagen	17.30	126
26.1.	Da 105	Theresienstadt		Auschwitz		128
27.1.	Lp 204	Linz		Kalisch		106
	Lp 106	Auschwitz		Theresienstadt		128
28.1.	Lp 2	Czernowitz		Gleiwitz		107

1 Date	2 Train Number	3 From	4 Departs	5 To	6 Arrives	7 Circulation No.
29.1.	Da 13	Berlin Mob	17.20	Auschwitz	10.48	126
	Po 63	Zamocz	8.20	Berlin Whagen	17.30	127
	Da 107	Theresienstadt		Auschwitz		128
30.1.	Vd 205	Kalisch	8.22	Ottersweier		106
	Lp 108	Auschwitz		Theresienstadt		128
31.1.	Lp 14	Auschwitz		Zamocz		126
1.2.	Rm 3	Gleiwitz		Czernowitz		107
	Da 109	Theresienstadt		Auschwitz		128
2.2.	Da 15	Berlin Mob	17.20	Auschwitz	10.48	127
	Lp 110	Auschwitz		Myslowitz		128
3.2.	Po 65	Zamocz	11.00	Auschwitz		126
4.2.	Lp 4	Czernowitz		Ratibor		107
	Lp 16	Auschwitz		Litzmannstadt [Lodz]		127
	Lp 66	Auschwitz		Myslowitz		126
5.2.	Pj 107	Bialystok	9.00	Auschwitz	7.57	121
6.2.	Pj 109	Bialystok	9.00	Auschwitz	7.57	122
7.2.	Pj 111	Bialystok	9.00	Auschwitz	7.57	123
	Lp 108	Auschwitz		Bialystok		121
8.2.	Rm 5	Ratibor		Czernowitz		107
	Lp 110	Auschwitz		Bialystok		122
	Lp 112	Auschwitz		Myslowitz		123
9.2.	Pj 127	Bialystok	9.00	Treblinka	12.10	121
	Lp 128	Treblinka	21.18	Bialystok	1.30	121

1 Date	2 Train Number	3 From	4 Departs	5 To	6 Arrives	7 Circulation No.
10.2.	Pj 129	Bialystok	9.00	Treblinka	12.10	122
	Lp 130	Treblinka	21.18	Bialystok	1.30	122
11.2.	Pj 131	Bialystok	9.00	Treblinka	12.10	121
	Lp 6	Czernowitz		Gleiwitz		107
	Lp 132	Treblinka	21.18	Bialystok	1.30	121
12.2.	Pj 133	Bialystok	9.00	Treblinka	12.10	122
	Lp 134	Treblinka	21.18	Grodno		122
13.2.	Pj 135	Bialystok	9.00	Treblinka	12.10	121
	Lp 136	Treblinka	21.18	Bialystok	1.30	121
14.2.	Pj 163	Grodno	5.40	Treblinka	12.10	122
	Lp 164	Treblinka		Scharfenwiese		122
15.2.	Rm 7	Gleiwitz		Czernowitz		107
16.2						
17.2						
18.2	Lp 8	Czernowitz		Gleiwitz		107

17. The Appeal of Fanny Steiner

The following letter was written by an old woman to
the mayor of Frankfurt after she had been told that a
transport of Frankfurt Jews had been sent to "Litz-
mannstadt," Nazi Germany's name for the city of Lodz
in Poland. Lodz was in incorporated territory, not—as
stated in the letter—in the General Government farther to the east; but transports did go there as Fanny
Steiner had heard. Mrs. Steiner's letter was found after
the war by the Commission for Research in the History
of the Frankfurt Jews. The Commission also discovered
her name on a list of Jews deported to the "Old People's
Ghetto" of Theresienstadt on August 8, 1942.

[City of Frankfurt am Main: F Hauptakte 2200/1, in: Kommission zur Erforschung der Geschichte der Frankfurter Juden, *Dokumente zur Geschichte der
Frankfurter Juden 1933–1945* (Frankfurt am Main: Verlag Waldemar Kramer,
1963), pp. 516–517.]

FANNY STEINER TO THE MAYOR OF FRANKFURT
OCTOBER 30, 1941

May I permit myself herewith to take advantage of your
well known kindness and humanity by troubling you with the
following. On October 19, 1941 about 1000 Frankfurt Jews
suddenly had to emigrate—I am told to Litzmannstadt-Lodz,
Poland, General Government. I was born on January 9, 1859
in Frankfurt/M—Heddernheim and I am Jewish. My ances-
tors, according to church records, have resided here for about
200 years and as can be shown have loyally and honestly eked
out their living. My brother Hermann Goldschmidt, Frank-
furt/M—Heddernheim, Habel Street 8, was a leather worker
for 50 years at the leather factory Bonames, and my late
brother Adolf Goldschmidt, Heddernheim, was employed, as
can be shown, for 40 years as a printer in the firm Osterrieth,

Mainzer Land Street. In short, they were everything but hagglers and usurers; instead they were honest artisans. My brother Hermann still lives in Heddernheim, Habel Street with his Aryan wife. His two children are baptized and raised as Christians.

My children too have been baptized since 1917. My son Willy spent four years in the World War and received various decorations. After that, he fought as a volunteer in 1920 in Upper Silesia. He was the founder of the aeronautical museum in Greiz, Thuringia, and as can be shown has conducted himself with extraordinary loyalty to nation and fatherland. In 1930, the War Ministry in Berlin, recognizing his meritorious service, gave him permission to take his photographic collection—consisting of material prepared in large part through his efforts—to foreign countries in order to give illustrated lectures for Germany.

My daughter Paula, at this point in Santiago de Chile, was a nurse for 35 years, most recently a head nurse in the Jewish Hospital in Hamburg, as well as director of children's homes in Bankensee near Hamburg. During the World War she cared for the wounded on the Western front over a period of years and received decorations for her services. My daughter Paula requested my immigration to Chile and I received permission from Chile to migrate there. I need only my visa for which I telegraphed today. As an 83 year old mother I should like to ask you most cordially and respectfully, Mr. State Counsellor, to direct the appropriate offices to postpone my expulsion to Poland long enough to permit my emigration to Chile, since the trip to the General Government would be my certain death. I rely on your kind assistance.

18. Special Accounts "W"

When the deportations began, the Reich Association of the Jews in Germany, seated in Berlin, maintained district offices and administered local Jewish community associations in various German cities. It was a puppet government which levied taxes and issued almost daily instructions at the behest of the Gestapo. At the end of 1941 it was also required to provide the funds necessary to defray the deportations costs, a large part of which were one-way fares payable to the German railways. To this end, the Gestapo directed the Reich Association to establish special accounts "W." The money to be deposited in the accounts was to be obtained by the Reich Association as "donations" from prospective Jewish deportees. The association's letter requesting the "donations" was signed by Dr. Paul Eppstein, chief of the Migration Division, and Dr. Arthur Lilienthal, chief of the Finance Division. Both men signed with the required middle name "Israel."

Special accounts "W" were based on the Gestapo notion that the Jews were to finance their own destruction. To be sure, the transactions violated the basic budgetary rule that receipts and expenditures of the Reich were to be entered as such by the Finance Ministry. Finance officials were disturbed because this measure (and similar ones in Vienna and Prague) constituted financing of a program outside the budgetary process. A memorandum written by the Finance Ministry's Jewish expert Maedel on December 14, 1942, deals with special accounts "W" in that spirit.

[Israel Police document 738.]

Copy

Reich Association of the Jews in Germany
Berlin-Charlottenburg, Kant St. 158
to
Jewish Community Associations,
District Offices of the Reich Association of the Jews in Germany
Berlin, December 3, 1941

Subject: Evacuations IV
       Cash Levy
       I/Dr. Li./Kl.—No 41/408/645

The following regulation is issued at the direction of our supervisory agency [Gestapo] for raising resources in connection with evacuation transports:

1. Every member of an evacuation transport should be induced to pay an appropriate portion of his liquid assets (not including securities) to the Reich Association. On that occasion it should be pointed out that the amount to be paid is not less than 25% of the liquid assets (not including securities).

2. This payment should be made as a donation the necessity for which might be made clear to the donor in a suitable manner. On that occasion it may be pointed out that the donations are intended primarily for the cash amounts which are to be taken along by the evacuation transports as well as for equipping the transport with food, tools, etc. Any additional amounts will serve the Reich Association in carrying out its tasks, especially welfare for its members.

3. Insofar as the responsibility for preparing the property list of a person assigned to an evacuation transport has been delegated by the local State Police office to the Community Association or District Office of the Reich Association, the cash levy is appropriately connected with the preparation of the property lists. So far as this is not case, the members of the transport have to be requested to make their donation immediately upon handing in their lists. If at all possible in the time allowed the request should be personal; otherwise it should be made by means of a circular letter addressed to the transport members. In the event of future transports, the appropriate local State Police office should be asked to hand over the transport lists in time sufficient to make possible the donation.

4. Insofar as the transfer of money from blocked accounts requires permission of currency control offices, appropri-

ate requests are to be made to the Superior Finance Presidents (Currency Control) who have jurisdiction in the matter. These release requests must be provided with an authorization signature by the appropriate State Police office. Requests of this kind will be processed by the currency control offices.

5. Those of the Community Associations and District Offices in whose territory evacuations are to be prepared have to set up a special account W in their banks. All receipts are to be deposited in special account W and all payments connected with evacuation transports must be made from special account W. So far as receipts may not suffice, especially for the first payments, requests are to be made to the Finance Administration of the Reich Association [of the Jews] for transfers of appropriate amounts to this account. Such requests, as well as requests for release of any sums in a special account W, are to be made as early as possible with approximate indications of probable expenditures and probable receipts.

   Every request for release of sums from special account W or for transfers to this account is to be accompanied with a statement of the current balance, which may be limited to the major categories of receipts and expenditures. Naturally, a detailed accounting is due on conclusion of the transports.

6. In the monthly report, receipts in special account W are to be entered as increases in the fund, and expenditures as decreases.

7. The instructions contained in this circular letter are effective at once; they apply also to evacuation transports already in preparation. Anything to the contrary in the circular "Evacuations III" is void.

Reich Association of the Jews in Germany
Signed Dr. Paul Israel Eppstein   Dr. Arthur
Israel Lilienthal

[German Federal Archives at Koblenz, document R 2/12222.]

Ministerial Councillor Maedel [Finance Ministry]
to Mayer [Finance Ministry]
  Kallenbach [Finance Ministry]
December 14, 1942

FINANCING THE SOLUTION OF THE JEWISH QUESTION
[Excerpt]

a) Old Reich

In its circular letter of December 3, 1941 the Reich Association called upon its members who are about to be moved to the east to donate at least 25% of their liquid assets to the Reich Association before being moved. According to the circular letter, the donations are intended for equipping the transports with tools and food. Disposition of the funds is in the hands of the Association's district offices which are accountable to the Association in Berlin. There is no doubt that also the costs of the transports as well as other expenses connected with the deportations are being met through these means. Although the State Police offices are not entitled to dispose of the accounts, one may deduce from occasional conversations with representatives of the Reich Security Main Office that in fact the State Police offices exercise considerable influence in the utilization of these funds (payment of transport costs, etc.). . . .

19. Watching Jewish Apartments

The contents of apartments left behind by deported Jews were considered Reich property. Confiscations at this stage were in the province of the Finance Ministry, which was anxious to make sure that nothing in the apartments would be disturbed at the last moment by persons having some inkling of impending deportations. The following letter is a request for cooperation by the Finance Office in Aachen to the Police president in the city. The police consisted of two branches: security police (state police—i.e., "Gestapo"—and criminal police) and order police (protective police in cities and gendarmerie in rural areas). The requested patrols involved the protective police.

[Alexandria document EAP VIII-173-b-16-14/31, Microfilm T 175, Roll 409.]

Copy

Finance Office, Aachen—City
to Police President—or deputy—in Aachen
July 15, 1942

Subject: Management and utilization of property falling to the Reich; here: securing property transfer

I am told by the Secret State Police—State Police Office Aachen—that the last remaining Jews who may be considered for removal under existing regulations will probably be moved on July 25, 1942 to Theresienstadt. The management and utilization of the property of these Jews will be my responsibility.

To guard the property in the interest of the Reich, everything must be done to avoid the possibility that unauthorized third persons lay their hands on movable belongings of the Jews before I can take them over. I request, therefore, that all appropriate steps be taken to guard the property of the Jews until the moment they are removed. Among other things it may be useful to have police officers watch the Jewish apartments several days in advance. The following houses are involved:

Alexander Street 95	Horst-Wessel Street 87
Emmich Street 39	König Street 22
Eupener Street 249	Promenaden Street 21
Förster Street 28	Frankenberger Street 20

Commando of Protective Police, Aachen
to Precincts 1, 2, 4, 5, and 6
July 21, 1942

Confidential:

[Enclosure of copies of above]

The above-mentioned Jewish apartments are to be watched with special care by the patrol force. The precinct leaders have to organize their patrols in such manner that these houses are under constant observation. The completed patrols are to be entered in the watch and patrol books. Controls are to be undertaken by precincts.

20. Jewish Firm Names

The elimination of the Jews from Germany was to be accompanied by the removal of all reminders of Jewish life in the country. One such reminder was a Jewish firm name. The trade associations sought to erase the Jewish names from all companies that had been "Aryanized." The letter below is an example from the files of Branch Group Private Bankers.

[Alexandria documents from the Dresdner Bank files, Microfilm T 83, Roll 97.]

The Director of Branch Group Private Bankers
to Owner, Bank Enterprise J. Löwenherz (Berlin)
April 29, 1942

Subject: Firm Names of de-Jewed Enterprises

Coming back to your letter of Aug. 30, 1941, I must ask you again to give up your Jewish firm name forthwith. What has been possible for all but two firms which are retaining their Jewish names should be possible also for you as one of these two firms. Your objection that your Jewish firm name has struck roots here and abroad is no longer acceptable. If you do not remove these last remnants of the Jewish past through an appropriate name change by July 1, 1942, I will be forced to request the Court of Registry to cancel immediately the post-ponement granted to you under §1 of the decree of March 27, 1941 (*Reich Legal Gazette* I, 177). Experiences with other banking houses have shown that there is not the slightest reason anymore for deferring a dictate rooted in a common political objective: the Aryanization of Jewish firm names.

Heil Hitler!
The Director of the Branch Group Private Bankers

21. Jewish Pensions

At the start of the deportations, the property of each deported Jew was confiscated on the basis of a finding that he was an "enemy" of the Reich. On November 25, 1941, a general confiscatory procedure was established in the Eleventh Ordinance to the Reich Citizenship Law (*Reich Legal Gazette* I, 722). The ordinance provided that Jewish property became Reich property as soon as its owner had crossed the border. Provision was also made for creditors and debtors, German creditors to be paid out of confiscated assets, German debtors to make their payments to the Reich. The Finance Ministry considered private pensions payable to Jews as Jewish claims which could be confiscated. German employers consequently scrutinized their pension contracts with care to determine their precise liabilities to Jewish pensioners. The following two letters were written by German banks after they had revoked pensions for emigrated and deported Jews.

[Alexandria document from bank file, Microfilm T 83, Roll 97.]

Deutsche Bank/Legal Division   Berlin W. 8
to Economic Group Private Banking—Central Association of German Banking and Bankers

June 29, 1942

Subject: Confiscation of pensions of former Jewish employees
by the Reich

   With reference to today's conversation of the undersigned
with your very honored Dr. Roer, we ask for clarification of
the following questions:
   In principle, pension claims arising from private employment are part of the Jewish property which has been confiscated for the benefit of the Reich in pursuance of individual
order or the Eleventh Ordinance to the Reich Citizenship
Law. Our bank has 2 categories of pensioners. First, all those
whom we have granted only a pension that we can freely
revoke any time, and then those who belong to the David
Hansemann pension fund; the latter have a legal claim for a
pension. Paragraph 8 of the statute of this pension fund reads
as follows:
   "Payment of the pension may be stopped:
      a) when the pensioner has been legally sentenced to a loss
         of civil rights because of a crime or an offense
      b) when a lien is placed on the pension
      c) when the pension is relinquished, pledged, or other-
         wise transferred to third persons, insofar as pensioner
         became an employee only after January 1, 1902."
   In the case of emigrated or evacuated Jews we have revoked
all of the pensions. In the first category this was possible because there was no legal claim, all the more since we have
reserved the right of revocation at any time. As for the members of the David Hansemann pension fund revocation is jus-
tified on the basis of §8 of the above-mentioned statute.
Sections b and c of §8 yield the conclusion that the pension
must benefit the employee himself. These stipulations must
therefore be applied also to seizures and confiscations which
are to ensue for the benefit of the Reich. The payment of
pensions rests on the idea of personal welfare. This basic idea
would be contradicted if we had to make pension payments to
a third party for years or decades.

Since several Superior Finance Presidents demand payments of the pensions from us despite our reference to §8 of the statute, we request that the matter become subject of a meeting in the Reich Finance Ministry. We should like to have the opportunity to take part in such a meeting.

> Heil Hitler
> Deutsche Bank
> [signature illegible]

Berliner Handels-Gesellschaft
Legal Division, Berlin
to
Economy Group Private Banking—Central Association of German Banks and Bankers
July 20, 1942
Your Sign: Dikt R/DW
　　　　　　 Diary No. 7113 J10

Reference: Pensions of former Jewish employees upon property confiscation

In reply to your kind letter of July 8, we should like to inform you that old age security of our former employees is provided for by the Old Age Security and Assistance Society (Assistance Society) for the Employees of the Berliner Handels-Gesellschaft at Berlin (e.V.), which grants to the former employees of our concern one-time or periodic assistance payments on the basis of its statutes. However, neither the statutes nor the fact of repeated or regular payments creates any legal claims for the members, so that a transfer of claims in accordance with §3 of the Eleventh Ordinance to the Reich Citizenship Law of Nov. 25, 1941 is out of the question.

The Assistance Society has in the meantime ceased payments of pensions to former Jewish employees who have emigrated or been shoved off. In one case, when the Superior Finance President of Berlin-Brandenburg demanded payment of a pension, we informed him of our practice with the remark that the stoppage ensued because there is no indication here that the pensioner in question is still alive. The Superior Finance President has taken no position in answer to this point.

Heil Hitler!
Berliner Handels-Gesellschaft
[signature illegible]

22. Last Annual Report from Vienna

The Jewish community of Austria was in a state of numerical decline when the Germans marched into the country on March 11, 1938. During the census of 1923 the Austrian republic had 201,513 Jews; by 1934 the count was 191,458, and over the next four years the downward trend continued. The Austrian Jews were highly urbanized (about 90 per cent of them lived in Vienna), and they had an exceptionally low birth rate. In 1938 their number increased when several thousand non-Jews, whose backgrounds included at least three Jewish grandparents, became Jews by definition. What happened during the next seven years is indicated by the following set of estimates:

	Total	Geographic Fate	Survived	Died
Defined as Jews (1938)	195,000			
Births (1938–45)	1,000			
Deaths in Austria		11,000		11,000
Emigration		130,000	115,000	15,000
Deportations		49,000	3,000	46,000
Remained (1945)		6,000	6,000	
	196,000	196,000	124,000	72,000

The emigration (fourth row), which was heaviest during the eighteen-month period between annexation and the outbreak of war, reached into all corners of the world, particularly the United States, Great Britain, Palestine, and Shanghai. The death toll (last column) includes about 15,000 emigrants caught in various countries overrun by the Germans in continental Europe, and some 46,000 of the deportees shipped out of Austria itself. The most complete account of Jewry's destruction in Austria is the article by Herbert Rosenkranz, "The Anschluss and the Tragedy of Austrian Jewry 1938–1945," in Josef Fraenkel, ed., *The Jews of Austria* (London: Vallentine Mitchell, 1967), pp. 479–546.

Throughout the time of Austria's incorporation in the German Reich, the chief of the Jewish community was Dr. Josef Löwenherz. He was a tireless administrator who carried out *every* assignment placed on his desk: emigration, care, and deportations. Of the 49,000 deportees, about two-thirds went to Poland, Minsk, and Riga, where they were not heard from again. The remaining third were shipped to Theresienstadt, the congested "Old People's Ghetto," in which space was created only by a very high death rate and the periodic departure of transports for the gas chambers in Auschwitz. Löwenherz did have an occasional word from Theresienstadt. For some time he carried on a bland correspondence through the regular mail with three men who lived in the same house inside the ghetto: Rabbi Dr. Benjamin Murmelstein, a former assistant who had compiled deportation lists in Vienna and who subsequently rose to become "Elder" in Theresienstadt; Rabbi Dr. Leo Baeck, former head of the Reich Association of Jews in Germany to whom Löwenherz sent birthday packages containing potatoes; and Dr. Heinrich Dessauer, another Viennese assistant who became chief of Theresienstadt's Interior Division. From Dessauer, Löwenherz received a note dated April 9, 1943, which said: "The work accomplished here is something to behold; the city pulsates in a rhythm of work and manifold activity." (The correspondence is in the Yad Vashem archives, document folder O 30/4.)

In January 1945 Löwenherz wrote his last annual report about his remnant community. It contains considerable material about a variety of problems which he had faced in the previous year, including two which involved new clientele. One was the arrival in nearby camps of Hungarian Jews being kept alive in pursuance of a complicated ransom deal between a Jewish rescue committee in Budapest and Heinrich Himmler. The other was the assignment of bombed-out people, including couples in mixed marriage and also "Aryan" households, to Jewish apartments where they were expected to double up with Jewish families. Heretofore it had been policy to set aside houses for Jews. Mixed couples classified as "privileged" were not subject to concentration in these houses. "Privileged" was any marriage in which there was a child with *"Mischling"* status, as well as any childless marriage, if the wife was Jewish and the husband "Aryan."

[Yad Vashem document O 30/5.]

EXCERPTS FROM THE ANNUAL REPORT OF THE DIRECTOR OF THE COUNCIL OF ELDERS OF THE JEWS IN VIENNA, SIGNED JOSEF ISRAEL LOWENHERZ, DATED JAN. 22, 1945

I. Population Changes

On January 1, 1944 the number of Jews registered with the Council of Elders in Vienna was 6,259
By December 31, 1944 the number was reduced by 460
to 5,799
The number of Jews in privileged mixed marriage is

	1,102	men
	2,286	women
Totaling	3,388	
In non-privileged mixed marriage	1,219	men
	139	women
Totaling	1,358	

In status as Jews [under definition decree], foreigners, and others   460   men
                                                                             593   women
                                            Totaling   1,053

Included in this addition is the small remaining number of Jews in the leadership of the Council of Elders of the Jews in Vienna, its agencies and other enterprises. The Jews in Vienna are divided into   men: 2,781
                                          women: 3,018

The Jews in Lower Austria [province surrounding Vienna] number   118

. . .

The number of the Jews was reduced [in 1944] by
                                            667
      of which death accounted for
                      226
      migration [deportations] 280
      delivery to camps and decisions of [party] offices on de-
      scent   161
There was an increase of   207
      of which new registration accounted for
                      203
      and births   4
so that the actual reduction was   460

. . .

II. *Labor Utilization*

On instruction of the Secret State Police/Secret State Police Main Directorate Vienna, the Population Division of the Jewish Council carried out a review of the Jews in privileged mixed marriage—without regard to whether these Jews were still married—so as to supplement last year's labor register. After this revision, the 5,799 Jews in Vienna included
                                            4,100
who were employed in labor of which
      2,021 were men
      2,079 women, hence   70.8%
of all the Jews living in Vienna.

. . .

IV. *Agencies and Institutions of the Council of Elders of the Jews in Vienna*

A. Hospital   Vienna, 2d District, Malzgasse 16

   Emergency Hospital   Vienna, 2d District, Malzgasse 7

B. Old Age Home   Vienna, 2d District, Malzgasse 7

C. Children's Hospital   Vienna, 2d District, Ferdinand Street 23

   Since Oct. 17, 1944   Vienna, 2d District, Mohapelgasse 3

D. Children's Home and   Vienna, 2d District, Mohapelgasse 3
   Dayschool

E. Community Kitchen   Vienna, 2d District, Kl. Pfarrgasse 8

F. Bath   Vienna, 2d District, Flossgasse 14

G. Poor People's Home   Vienna, 2d District, Gr. Mohrengasse 30

H. Clothes and   Vienna, 1st District, Lazenhof 2 and

   Furniture Depot   Vienna, 1st District, Fleischmarkt la

I. Relief Division   Vienna, 1st District, Seitenstetteng. 4

J. Library   Vienna, 1st District, Seitenstetteng. 4

K. Cemetery Administration   Vienna, 11th District, Simm.
   and Grounds   Hauptstr. 238

L. Technical Column and   Vienna, 1st District, Seitenstetteng. 4 and

   Workshop   Vienna, 2d District, Mohapelgasse 3

. . .

C. Children's Hospital

The number of patients on January 1, 1944, was   20
and rose by December 31, 1944, to   44
New admissions in the course of the year were
                                                       188
releases   150
deaths   14
The number of ambulatory treatments in the course of the
year 1944 was   3,429

The sudden increase of patients in the second half of the year was due in large measure to illnesses in the camps of the Hungarian Jews. During the air raid of Oct. 17, 1944, a bomb hit the house at Ferdinand Street 23, rendering the children's hospital entirely unusable. As an emergency a new hospital had to be set up overnight at Mohapelgasse 3. Naturally this hospital is beset with all the difficulties of a makeshift enterprise and it is also lacking space for all the sick children urgently in need of admission.

Accordingly, the Secret State Police/Secret State Police Main Directorate Vienna, and the City Construction Office authorized the repair of the children's hospital, and the Council of Elders of the Jews in Vienna handed the supervision of construction and carpentry to a competent architect against payment of a lump sum. . . .

E.   Community Kitchen

The community kitchen made available 43,892 meals during 1944. Since the community kitchen is intended primarily for Jews employed in labor, the leadership of the Council of Jewish Elders in Vienna ruled that lunch shall be served also in the evening, if the people involved are not able to leave their place of work during the lunch hour.

Persons employed in the scrap collection drive are handed their lunch at work.

The community kitchen was damaged in the air raid of November 5, 1944. However, repairs could be effected in the shortest time by the Technical Column of the Council of Elders and the kitchen could continue without interruption.

An air raid shelter was arranged in the cellar for visitors of the kitchen. Vegetables grown on the grounds of the cemetery are made available also to the community kitchen. . . .

Organizationally, major tasks faced the Council of Elders from the moment of the arrival of the first transports of Hungarian Jews in Vienna and Lower Austria and their subsequent allocation to labor camps. On instruction of the Secret State Police/State Police Main Directorate Vienna, the Council of Elders of the Jews in Vienna made itself available to the Commander of the Security Police and Security Service/Special Detachment Vienna, 2d District, Castellezgasse 35 and developed its increased activity in the following directions:

1.) the Council provided part of the meals for the transports in transit through Gänserndorf;

2.) assisted the Commander of Security Police and Security Service/Special Detachment and the Labor Office in taking over the transport at Strasshof and developing a register, and then allocated permanent help to the Special Detachment for maintaining the register and directing the accounts of the camp;

3.) established and administered a special account "U" at the main office of the Länderbank Wien A.G., and on instructions of the Commander of Security Police and Security Service/Special Detachment arranged for all transfers of money payable to the various camps, organizations, hospitals, drug stores, and suppliers;

4.) kept an accurate account of transactions and reported in part weekly and in part monthly to the Commander of Security Police and Security Service/Special Detachment on all deposits into and withdrawals from account "U," as well as on the delivery of Hungarian Jews to the hospital, the emergency hospital, and children's hospital, and their discharge from these institutions;

5.) arranged for the collection and burial of 373 bodies of Hungarian Jews until December 31, 1944. . . .

In 1944 the apartment allocation office of the Gauleiter in Vienna undertook to move families in mixed marriage and Aryans into Jewish apartments. The many difficulties which arose in consequence of this measure were pointed out by the Council of Elders orally and in writing to the Secret State Police/State Police Main Directorate Vienna as follows:

1.) Inasmuch as the Gau apartment allocation office declines in most cases to move bombed-out families in mixed marriages to other quarters, there is no practical possibility of quartering these people at all.

2.) In the event that Aryan bombed-out persons are directed to Jewish households, the official policy of separating Aryans and non-Aryans will be disturbed.

3.) The newly arrived Aryans resist the official requirement that Jewish apartments be marked with a star, giving rise to unpleasant explanations insofar as the Jewish person in charge of the household does not wish to contravene official regulations.

Accordingly the director of the Council of Elders has asked that available space in Jewish households be reserved for bombed-out Jews and that its disposal be left now as before to the Council of Elders acting in each case with the prior consent of the Secret State Police/Secret State Police Main Directorate Vienna. . . .

From January 1, 1944, to December 31, 1944, the 232 employees and volunteers in the Council of Elders were reduced to 225 through deaths and voluntary dissolutions of the work relationship. . . . The introduction of the 60-hour work week had no effect on the Council of Elders of the Jews in Vienna, since all of its divisions and institutions had previously adopted that work week, often exceeding these hours.

23. An Offer of Marmalade

On July 22, 1942, deportations began in the Warsaw ghetto. On that day about 380,000 people lived there; seven weeks later only 70,000 were left. It is this remnant which fought the famous Warsaw ghetto battle in the midst of the final roundup in April and May 1943. The massive summer deportations in 1942 were unopposed, and 310,000 ghetto inhabitants were transported from the railhead just outside the northern ghetto wall to the Treblinka death camp.

The overall direction of the operation was in the hands of the German SS and Police, but the actual seizure of the victims was largely the work of the Jewish ghetto police, the so-called Order Service. Its head, the churchgoing convert Jozef Szerynski, was apparently under suspension for graft at the time, and acting in his stead was Jakob Lejkin, variously spelled also Leikin or Laikin. On instructions of the SS, Lejkin posted notices in various apartment houses ordering the occupants to report to a hospital hurriedly cleared of patients on Stawki Street. Exempt for the moment were employees of German agencies and firms and those who were employable, the Jewish Council and its staff including the Jewish police, together with wives and children. Hospital patients not immediately dischargeable were also spared.

On July 29, Lejkin offered bread and marmalade to all Jews who presented themselves voluntarily during the next three days at the assembly point near the train. He then extended the offer for another three days. The extension, which has been reprinted in several document collections, is included also here as an illustration of the acuity of the situation. The Jewish underground subsequently struck down Szerynski and Lejkin, while the Germans were reported to have killed Lejkin's wife and baby.

Events in the ghetto were observed closely by the German Army District Commander in Warsaw, who reported on two aspects of the deportations which concerned him directly: reactions of the Polish population and the army's Jewish employees.

[Facsimile in: Jüdisches Historisches Institut Warschau, *Faschismus-Getto-Massenmord* (Berlin: Rütten & Loening, 2nd ed., 1961), p. 309. Italics in text.]

PROCLAMATION

TO THE INHABITANTS OF THE JEWISH DISTRICT

In accordance with official instructions of July 22, 1942 all persons not employed in institutions or enterprises will definitely be resettled.

Forcible removals are being continued uninterruptedly. I

call once more on all members of the population subject to resettlement to report voluntarily at the railway siding, and will extend for three days, including August 2, 3, and 4, 1942, *the distribution of 7 pounds of bread and 2 pounds of marmalade to every person who reports voluntarily.*

Families presenting themselves voluntarily *will not be separated.*

Assembly point for volunteers: Dzika 3-Stawki 27

The Director of the Order Service

Warsaw, August 1, 1942

[Alexandria document 75022/10, Microfilm T 501, Roll 216.]

EXCERPT FROM THE MONTHLY REPORT BY CHIEF FIELD HEADQUARTERS IN WARSAW (SIGNED BRIGADIER GENERAL ROSSUM), AUGUST 21, 1942. THE REPORT MARKED "SECRET" COVERED THE PERIOD JULY 16–AUGUST 15.

VIII. Civilian Population

1. Mood

At the moment the mood of the population in Warsaw is being strongly influenced by a curb on the black market. As a consequence black market prices have risen several fold so that an even larger part of the population is no longer able to buy butter, fat, or meat. Naturally this has an effect on the mood since the official ration has not been increased.

The major part of the population is reacting to the resettlement of the Jews with a degree of satisfaction. Relatively few people are offended by it. To be sure, atrocity stories, in part exaggerated, are circulating about the manner of the resettlement.

Workers who are employed by the armed forces or armament enterprises inside the ghetto have been concentrated in blocks which are closed off. The Chief Field Headquarters has assigned guards to individual blocks to supervise the Jews and maintain quiet and order in the enterprises. Jewish workers employed by armed forces agencies outside the ghetto are quartered in special barracks or buildings similarly as prisoners-of-war.

Armed forces offices other than [private] armament enterprises are employing

a) inside the ghetto, in 6 enterprises and 1 camp	ca. 8100 Jews
b) outside the ghetto, in 80 enterprises and 3 camps	1850 Jews
	ca. 9950 Jews

24. The Jewish Mood in Galicia

The district of Galicia was overrun by German troops in the initial thrust into Soviet-held Poland. A wave of killings by Security Police strike commandos covered the territory; then the civilian administration of the "General Government" took over control of the district, establishing ghettos in its cities and towns and mobilizing ghetto labor for war production. Most of the ghettos were short-lived, for already in the spring of 1942 the SS and Police in the district began the systematic deportation of Jews to the killing center Belzec. The freight cars were jammed as Galicia, a region densely populated with Jews, was drained of its Jewish communities. Lvov, third largest of the Polish ghettos, and towns which were almost entirely Jewish were engulfed and emptied. In one of the largest operations in Europe, 434,000 Jews were shipped to their deaths between April 1942 and June 1943.

Following are three excerpts from monthly reports covering mid-month to mid-month by the military command in Galicia to the military commander of the "General Government" in Poland (comprising the military regions of Warsaw, Krakow, Lublin, and Galicia).

The reports follow a standard format:
VII. Other
   1. Civilian Population
      A. Mood
         c. Jews.

[Alexandria document 75022/10, Microfilm T 501, Roll 216.]

Chief Field Headquarters 365/Operations Officer (signed Beuttel)
to Military Commander in General Government
August 17, 1942

In consequence of major actions which have temporarily been stopped in some parts of the district but which still continue in Lvov, the mood of the Jewish population is exceptionally depressed, yet astonishingly composed.

According to a statistic based on allocations of food rations, Lvov must have contained about 80,000 Jews before the current combing; it is assumed, however, that in fact there were 100,000. Since August 10, some 25,000 Jews were settled out of Lvov and another 15,000 will have to follow them before this action is closed.

Jewish workers, men and women, employed by the armed forces or in enterprises controlled by the armed forces, have been touched only very little by these actions, so that the enterprises can continue undisturbed, so far as this is at all possible given the current unrest among the Jews. This is without doubt a success of Chief Field Headquarters 365 which for months has been in close touch and has negotiated frequently with the SS and Police Leader in the district Galicia, instilling and maintaining in that office a noteworthy understanding of the problems of the armed forces. Until now it was also possible to make certain that families of Jewish employees were for the most part spared. To be sure, according to the latest information one must expect that at least in Lvov heavy inroads will be made into the Jewish families during the course of the current actions.

[Alexandria document 75022/10, Microfilm T 501, Roll 216.]

Chief Field Headquarters 365/Operations Officer (signed Beuttel)
to Military Commander in General Government
September 17, 1942

Jewish resettlements of major proportions took place in the district during the period reported on. Amongst others 40,000 Jewish resettlements were carried out in Lvov. It would be superfluous to describe scenes which occurred during these resettlements or the manner in which the Jews were concentrated for resettlement. All Jews of the Galician district are to be settled out by December 31, 1942. Replies to inquiries indicate that the vacancies in the labor force which will be created thereby, especially in the area of skilled labor, cannot be filled completely with Aryan workers. Political and economic considerations thus confront each other and it is to be assumed that if there is no resort to special measures, a lowering of production, especially in the area of skilled labor, will ensue during the first months of 1943. The Jews who are working for the armed forces have been quartered or are being quartered in barracks in Rawa Ruska, Stanislawow, Tarnopol, Drohobycz, Stryj, Sambor, and Zolkiew. In Lvov there has been no such quartering since the number of employed Jews is rather large (nearly 10,000) and all the more since their families have for the most part not been resettled as yet, and a separation from these family members would bring about a considerable decrease of productivity.

In the area of the Chief Field Headquarters a total of 14,202 Jews are employed by the armed forces and important war enterprises. They have been registered by the armed forces.

[Alexandria document 75026/12, Microfilm T 501, Roll 225.]

Chief Field Headquarters 365/Operations Officer (signed Beuttel)
to Military Commander in General Government
November 17, 1942

Meanwhile Jews have been quartered on a large scale in camps erected by the SS and Police Leader and the armed forces, and in many cases also at offices and enterprises. These measures, which brought about a separation of the workers from their families, naturally have a crushing effect on the psychic and hence also physical condition of the Jews in question. They say to themselves justifiably that although they themselves will enjoy temporary protection, the members of their families will probably become victims of coming actions. How right the Jews are in that assumption will be shown on the occasion of a major resettlement action which is in store for Lvov in the next few days. It is understandable that under such circumstances the productivity of the Jews drops sharply, that more and more of them collapse physically and mentally, and that there are also suicides.

25. The Jewish Artisans in Poland

The annihilation of Polish Jewry produced reverbera-tions in warehouses and plants dependent on Jewish labor. The loss of workers was felt acutely if it occurred in a sudden roundup, or if it involved artisans who were in short supply. An illustration of what could happen suddenly is provided by a letter from an army quarter-master protesting an incident at Radom early in August 1942. Indeed, the tactics of the SS and Police almost led to shooting between army personnel and Police raiders in the town of Przemysl (Israel Police documents 1113–1115). The Przemysl affair resulted in a decision at the highest level of the armed forces, on September 5, 1942, that military units and armament enterprises in the entire "General Government" (Krakow, Warsaw, Ra-dom, Lublin, and Lvov) were to "replace" their Jews immediately. The next document reveals that armaments firms nevertheless managed to enter into contracts with the SS and Police for the utilization of many thousands of Jews in enterprises such as steel and aircraft production. By mid-1944, however, the Jewish labor force was all but destroyed, as shown by a final report on the "Rationalization of the Artisan Trade in the General Government."

[Alexandria document 75022/9a, Microfilm T 501, Roll 216.]

Military Commander in General Government/Chief Quartermaster (Qu 1)
via Chief Field Headquarters, Krakow
to Liaison Officer with Military Commander in General Government
after dispatch to   Finance Officer
                    Armament Inspectorate
August 5, 1942
Tonight a large number of Jews were shipped out of Radom without prior notification of army offices.

Consequence [was] that today only half of the permanent Jewish labor force in the army food depot showed up for work and that additional Jews, needed to guard and load a herd of about 600 cattle, were unavailable. The cattle should be sent to the front tomorrow; in the next few days additional trainloads of cattle and flour are to be loaded for the front.

The seizure of workers without full timely replacement harms the supply of the front and lengthens the time needed for loading the railroad cars—is therefore directed at the prosecution of the war.

Help needed.

[Alexandria document EAP 161-b-12/364, Microfilm T 175, Roll 122.]

High Command of the Armed Forces
Armed Forces Command Staff/Quartermaster II (Administration)

Führer Headquarters
to Armed Forces District Commander in the General Government
September 5, 1942
In Reply to: Military Commander in General Government, Operations, No. 4271/21 Secret

Subject: Incident at Przemysl

Jews employed by the armed forces in the General Government for military auxiliary tasks and the armament economy are to be replaced immediately by Poles (non-Jews). Report implementation of this order.

  The Chief of the High Command of the Armed Forces
   signed Keitel

After dispatch:
Chief, Army Armament and Replacement Army
Economy Office via Liaison Officer
Armed Forces High Command—Staff for Special Purposes
Copies:
Reichsführer-SS and Chief of the German Police [Himmler], attention SS-Lieutenant General Wolff
Higher SS and Police Leader, General Government, Krakow —Government building

[Alexandria document Wi/ID 1.148, Microfilm T 77, Roll 619.]

War Diary, Armament Command in Krakow
Report for October 1–December 31, 1942
[Excerpt]

To cope with the urgent labor shortage in the armament enterprises, Jews have been employed. Already in April, the first experiment was made at the aircraft works in Mielec. Since it was a success, additional Jews were employed in the third quarter, and by the fourth quarter the question was settled to the extent most of the plants had their own Jewish

camps; that is, Stawola-Wola [Stahlwerke Braunschweig],
Rzeszow [aircraft motors], and Mielec [assembly plant for
Heinkel 111 aircraft] had more than 700 Jews each and other
works fewer. At first, the feeding and clothing of the Jews
posed major problems. With the close cooperation of the SS,
however, these questions too were gradually cleared up. Since
on the other hand a stay of the Jews in the plants was not
assured, negotiations have been taken up with the [Polish]
construction service so that it too may be employed in the
enterprises.

[Alexandria document 75027/4, Microfilm T 501, Roll 226.]

From the files of INFORMATION SERVICE OF GROUP TRADE IN
THE MAIN GROUP BUSINESS ECONOMY AND TRANSPORT IN THE
CENTRAL CHAMBER OF COMMERCE IN THE GENERAL GOVERNMENT
KRAKOW, APRIL 7, 1944

Not for publication, only for internal use of colleagues in main
offices and honorary offices, Group Trade
Copy [undated appendix]
1. The Rationalization of the Artisan Trade in the General
Government
　　Today's area of the General Government contained in *1939
ca. 235,000 artisan enterprises,* which declined by *October 1, 1943
to 73,000 (= 32% of the number in 1939)* because of the following circumstances:

a) gradual elimination of the Jews	ca. 115,000 enterprises
b) Aryan shops annihilated by the Bolsheviks in Galicia [1939–41]	ca. 15,000 "
c) liquidation by reason of with-drawal of Aryan owners for other labor utilization to the end of 1941	ca. 16,000 "
d) liquidations 1942–43	ca. 13,600 "
Total reduction of artisan shops	159,600 enterprises

In this manner the density of artisan enterprises had thinned by 1943 to ¼ of the density in the Reich, and it is to be noted that in consequence of these eliminations special lines of work particularly favored by the Jews have for the moment disappeared completely and cannot as yet be replaced everywhere.

The number of persons employed as artisans, which is to be estimated at ca. 600,000 for 1939, was reduced by October 1, 1943, to 195,000.

The largest part of the eliminated labor force consists of the Jews who numbered ca. 250,000, although they were not lost to war production all at once, since they were largely employed in major workshops for important war objectives. The volume of this Jewish labor declined, however, steadily and today it no longer constitutes a major economic factor.

[The report goes on to describe the assignment of Polish artisans to the Reich and to armaments enterprises within the "General Government."]

26. Pillaging

In the emptied ghettos of Poland, German soldiers and Polish citizens rummaged among the personal belongings left behind by the deported Jews.

[Alexandria document 75022/10, Microfilm T 501, Roll 216.]

Chief Field Headquarters 372 (Lublin)
to Commander, Army District of General Government
October 20, 1942
[Excerpt from monthly report covering September 16, 1942, to October 15, 1942]

On the occasion of the resettlement of the Jews from Czesto-

chowa, six members of the armed forces were indicted for
looting.

[Alexandria document Wi/ID 1.37, Microfilm T 77, Roll 619.]

Armament Command Radom War Diary
August 24, 1943

Major Hassler, together with Mr. Bretterklieber of Steyr-
Daimler-Puch, Inc., and the director of the housing office in
Radom, visited houses in the former Jewish district [ghetto];
it is determined, however, that they have been looted, ne-
glected, and damaged to an extent that their repair even in the
most rudimentary form for the quartering of Polish workers
would require amounts of money and materiel which cannot
be made available for such a purpose.

27. Deportations from Norway

On November 25, 1942, Eichmann's deputy, SS-Major
Günther, asked the commander of the German Security
Police in Oslo to take every advantage of the opportunity created by the German navy's unexpected offer
to provide transport by sea for the deportation of the
Jews of Norway (Israel Police document 1622). The
number of prospective victims was barely 2,000, some
1,200 of them in Oslo, 500 in Trondheim. Between 700
and 800 were shipped to the German port of Stettin,
then transported by land to Auschwitz. The major portion (532) left on November 26 on the *Donau;* a smaller
group of 158 followed on February 26 on the *Gotenland.*
About 900 were to reach safety by fleeing to neighboring Sweden.

Norway was ruled by a German civilian administrator (Terboven) and his native collaborator (Quisling), but the German military kept close watch on all developments. It commented on the roundup and its effects in a report at the end of the year. By that time the *Donau* Jews had already been "received" in Auschwitz.

[Alexandria document OKW-637, Microfilm T 77, Roll 1006.]

Armed Forces Commander Norway—Propaganda Group to High Command of the Armed Forces—Propaganda Division
December 30, 1942
[Excerpt]

The seizure and deportation to Poland of 532 Jews (302 men, 230 women and children) in the German troop ship *Donau*—to be followed early in January by another transport of 150 Jews who have been seized in the meantime—was the subject of talk which spread like wildfire in the Norwegian population. In the [Norwegian] National Socialist party, the anti-Jewish measure was received with such lack of understanding that, at a party meeting in Trondheim, Quisling addressed himself to the Jewish question once more, pointing out that Jewry was the originator of this war. The Swedish press, obviously informed in every detail from the Norwegian side, rendered the Jewish action into an international sensation. The arrest and transport of the Jews was described as a "manhunt" which "created dismay even in National Socialist circles and led to mass withdrawals from the party." The Germans were said to have fostered an impression that the action was purely Norwegian, but in reality the driving force is supposed to have been the Gestapo and SS-Major Wegener. The Swedish press asserts that the action was released upon a visit of SA-Chief Lutze in Oslo. . . .

The situation of the Norwegian theater has become very difficult because of the scarcity of coal. The Jewish action has increased nervous tension amongst the actors. . . .

[Israel Police document 1622.]

Concentration Camp Auschwitz
Headquarters/Division II
Auschwitz, December 1, 1942

Confirmation of Receipt

The receipt of 532 Jews from Norway is hereby confirmed.

The Camp Commander
[signed "on instruction" by SS-First Lieutenant—signature
illegible]

28. The Way It Was Done in the Netherlands

One of the most relentless operations was carried out in
occupied Holland. Here an efficient administrative apparatus rounded up every potential victim, then ago-
nized over the problem of reducing a hard core of Jews
in mixed marriages. The principal personalities of the
deportation machinery in the Netherlands were the
following:

Reich Commissar Seyss-Inquart
  Higher SS and Police Leader Rauter
    Commanding Officer of Security Police Harster
        Eichmann representative Zöpf
        Central Office for Jewish Emigration aus
        der Fünten
      Commander of Security Police, Amsterdam
      Lages

The Jewish community of Holland lost about 115,000
of its 140,000 people. For an overview of their history

under the Nazis, see Jacob Presser, *The Destruction of the Dutch Jews* (New York: Dutton, 1969). The following two letters, one by Harster, the other by Seyss-Inquart himself, reflect the spirit with which the Germans applied themselves to their task.

Harster's letter was written during the high tide of the deportations. The Jews were being funneled through three transit camps on their way to the east: Westerbork (1942–1945), which was a staging center for more than 100,000 Jewish deportees; 's Hertogenbosch (September 1942–June 1944), which was a stop for 12,-000; and Barneveld, a remote castle maintained from the end of 1942 to the end of 1943 for a few hundred "prominent" Jews. Buoyant, Harster anticipated no difficulties in the principal deportation city, Amsterdam, and suggested that most of the employees of the Jewish Council be moved out in the first roundup (they were in fact seized on June 20, 1943, and deported in September). He dwelt at somewhat greater length on the armament Jews, the Portuguese Jews, and the Jews in mixed marriages. In the armament industry, which needed its labor force, Jews were laid off gradually and diamond workers most gradually. A group of about 4,300 Portuguese Jews became an object of attention when they claimed in effect not to be Jews. Although members of the Jewish religion, these long-time residents of Holland asserted that over the centuries they had intermarried with the Christian population to such an extent that they could no longer be regarded as Jews by descent. The SS investigated the backgrounds of hundreds of these people, and one by one the Portuguese Jews were classified as eligible for deportation to Auschwitz or Theresienstadt until almost all of them were gone.

The full Jews in mixed marriages were manifestly linked to the Christian majority, and for this reason they and their children complicated Seyss-Inquart's life. Determined that there should be no further offspring in such marriages, he instituted a program of "voluntary sterilizations." The reward was freedom from wearing the star and the implied guarantee of immunity from deportation. More than 2,500 men and women were sterilized as a consequence of this policy. Since Seyss-Inquart was going further in this matter than agencies in Germany itself, he wrote a letter of justification to Party Chancellery Chief Bormann. The letter is reprinted here in full. One should only add that the Jews need not have subjected themselves to sterilization—the intermarried couples were left intact until the very end.

[Israel Police document 1356.]

The Commanding Officer of Security Police and Security Service in the Occupied
Dutch Territories B 4 [Jewish Affairs]
to
Central Office for Jewish Emigration in Amsterdam (2 copies)
Westerbork camp
Concentration camp Hertogenbosch
All field offices [of Security Police and Security Service]
May 5, 1943
Secret
Subject: Final Solution of the Jewish Question in the Netherlands
   On the basis of the latest instructions by SS-Major General Rauter and the discussions held with representatives of the Reich Security Main Office, the following actions are to be carried out during the next few months in the Jewish work:
1. *General Policy:*
    The Reichsführer-SS [Himmler] wishes that this year everything by way of Jews should be transported to the East so far as humanly possible.
2. *Next Trains to the East:*
    Inasmuch as a synthetic rubber plant, destroyed by bombs in the West, is to be built anew in Auschwitz, a maximum number of Jews from the West will be needed there, espe-

cially during May and June. It was agreed that Jews read-
ied for transport should be shipped out in several trains by
the first half of this month—in short, Westerbork camp is
to be emptied rapidly. The goal for May is 8000. Train
agreements will be made by the Commanding Officer,
Security Police and Security Service, The Hague, with the
Reich Security Main Office.

3. *Camp Hertogenbosch:*
Inasmuch as the Reich Security Main Office is demanding
another 15,000 Jews for June, preparations have to be
made as rapidly as possible so that the inmates of camp
Hertogenbosch may also be claimed.

4. *Amsterdam:*
The foregoing goal is covered by the intention of the SS-
Major General [Rauter] to order the evacuation of Jews
from the city of Amsterdam as soon as current political
opposition has been beaten down. Two phases are foreseen: the Jews are to be induced to report to concentration
camp Hertogenbosch voluntarily. The Central Office [for
Jewish Emigration] should have deliberations on whether
the evacuation should [then] advance section by section
(first south and west, then center or ghetto) or according
to other criteria, for example, alphabetically. During the
evacuation most of the [personnel of the] Jewish Council
would have to move first. No attention is to be paid to the
Jew economy (distribution of Jewish stores in sections of
the city).

5. *Armament Jews:*
It is absolutely necessary to insist on the promise of the
[Armed Forces] Armament Inspectorate etc. to reduce its
Jewish labor forces already during May. Insofar as armament enterprises are not transferred to Hertogenbosch,
the armament Jews and their families can immediately be
removed to Westerbork.

6. *Portuguese Jews:*
All Portuguese Jews (so far as there are no special reasons
for leaving them behind) are to be quartered in special
barracks of camp Westerbork, where they can be exam-

ned for their descent by SS-Major General Rauter and the leader of the [SS] Race and Resettlement Main Office.

7. *Barneveld:*
For the moment the final lists are to be examined for negative indications and the camp is to be inspected. An early transfer of all inmates to Theresienstadt should follow.

8. *A-B List:*
The Reichsführer-SS [Himmler] intends to set up a camp in Germany for ca. 10,000 Jews of French, Belgian, and Dutch nationalities whose connections abroad would make them suitable hostages. Eventually they might be allowed to emigrate in exchange for German returnees.

9. *Mixed Marriages:*
   a) Jewesses over 45 will be called up in groups to Amsterdam and freed from wearing the Jewish Star, so that word may get around that Jewish partners in mixed marriages are being allowed to remain if they can no longer have children.
   b) Jews in mixed marriages without children are to be transferred to a camp.
   c) For the remaining Jews and Jewesses the aspired goal is voluntary sterilization which is to be carried out in Amsterdam. In case of refusal, forced sterilization should follow in camp Hertogenbosch.
   d) Inquiries into the economic activities and professional commitments of male Jews in mixed marriages are to be made quickly. Report is to be submitted to the Reich Commissar [Seyss-Inquart].
   e) At the very least, all the mixed couples in which the husband is a Jew are to be concentrated without regard to sterilization. SS-Major General [Rauter] envisages some town in the east or southeast of the country for them, since he wants Amsterdam free of Jews for purposes of police control.

10. *Rewards per Head:*
If a large number of Jews are brought in, one might con-

sider as a reward also a grant of immunity [to former Dutch prisoners-of-war] from return to a prisoner-of-war camp. If need be, this matter is to be discussed with Armed Forces Commander, Netherlands.

11. *Foundlings:*

An attempt must be made to have all cases reported to Security Police. A special institution is foreseen for the reception of foundlings, where on the basis of available reports they can be certified as to their biological inheritance.

I request that all necessary preparations be made for these actions despite current political unrest. Detailed instructions will follow.

> signed Dr. Harster
> SS-Brigadier General
> and Brigadier General of Police

[Israel Police document 1439.]

Reich Commissar for the Occupied Netherlands Territories, The Hague
to Party Chancellery Chief Bormann
copies to General Commissars in Netherlands and
          Plenipotentiary Dr. Schröder
February 28, 1944

Dear Party Comrade Bormann:

We have cleaned up the Jewish question in the Netherlands, insofar as now we only have to carry out decisions that have already been formulated. The Jews have been eliminated from the body of the Dutch people and, insofar as they have not been transported to the East for labor, they are enclosed in a camp. We are dealing here first of all with some 1500 persons who have not been transported to the East for special reasons such as interventions by churches or by personalities who are close to us. In the main I have warded off the interference of the churches in the whole Jewish question in that I held back the Christian Jews in a closed camp where they can be visited weekly by clergy. About 8–9000 Jews have avoided transport by submerging [in hiding]. By and by they are being seized and sent to the East; at the moment, the rate of seizures is 5–600 a week. The Jewish property has been confiscated and is undergoing liquidation. With the exception of a few enterprises which have not yet been Aryanized, but which have been placed under trusteeship, the liquidation is finished and the property converted into financial papers of the Reich. I count on a yield of ca. 500 million Guilders [more than $250,000,000]. At some appropriate time the future utilization of this money is to be decided on in concert with the Reich Finance Minister; however, the Reich Finance Minister agrees in principle to the use of these funds for purposes in the Netherlands.

The question of Jews in mixed marriages is still open. Here we went further than the Reich and obliged also these Jews to wear the star. I had also ordered that the Jewish partner in a childless mixed marriage should likewise be brought to the East for labor. Our Security Police processed a few hundred such cases, but then received instructions from Berlin not to go on, so that a few thousand of these Jews have remained in the country. Finally, Berlin expressed the wish that the Jews in mixed marriages be concentrated in the Jewish camp Westerbork, to be employed here in labor for the moment. Herewith we raise the problem of mixed marriages. Since this matter is basic I turn to you. The following is to be considered with respect to marriages in which there are children: if one parent is brought to a concentration camp and then probably to labor in the East, the children will always be under the impression that we took the parent away from them. As a matter of fact, the offspring of mixed marriages are more troublesome than full Jews. In political trials, for example, we can determine that it is precisely these offspring who start or carry out most of the assassination attempts or sabotage. If we now introduced a measure that is sure to release the hatred of these people, then we will have a group in our midst with which we will hardly be able to deal in any way save separation. If, in short, there is a plan which is aimed at the removal of Jewish partners from mixed marriages with children, then the children of these marriages will sooner or later have to travel the same road. Hence I believe that it may be more appropriate not to start on this course, but to decide in each instance whether to remove the whole family or—with due regard to security police precautions—to permit the Jewish member to remain in the family. In the first case, the couple, complete with children, will have to be segregated, possibly like the Jews in Theresienstadt. But in that case one must remember that the offspring will get together to have more children, so that practically the Jewish problem will not be solved lest we take some opportunity to remove this whole society from the Reich's sphere of interest. We are [now] trying the other way in that we free the Jewish partner who is no longer able to have children, or who allows himself to be sterilized, from wearing the star and permit him to stay with his family. These Jews—at the moment there must be 4–5000 in the Netherlands —remain under a certain amount of security police control with respect to residence and employability. For example, they are not permitted to direct an enterprise which has employees or occupy a leading position in such an enterprise. There are quite a few volunteers for sterilization. I believe also that we have nothing to fear any more from these people, since their decision indicates a willingness to accept conditions as they are. The situation with the Jewish women is not so simple, since the surgical procedure is known to be difficult. All the same I believe in time this way will yield results, provided one does not decide on the radical method of removing the whole family. For the Netherlands then, I would consider the following for a conclusion of the Jewish problem:

1. The male Jewish partner in a mixed marriage—so far as he has not been freed from the star for reasons mentioned above—is taken for enclosed labor to Westerbork. This measure would signify no permanent separation, but action of a security police nature for the duration of exceptional conditions. These Jews will be employed accordingly and will also receive appropriate wages with which they can support their families who will remain behind. They will also receive a few days' leave about once in three months. One can proceed with

childless female partners in mixed marriages in the same way. We have here in the Netherlands 834 male Jews in childless mixed marriages, 2775 [male] Jews in mixed marriages with children, and 574 Jewesses in childless mixed marriages. Under certain circumstances these Jews can return to their families, for example, if they submit to sterilization, or if the reasons for separation become less weighty in some other way, or if other precautions are taken or conditions develop which make separation no longer seem necessary.

2. The Jewish women in mixed marriages with children— the number involved is 1448—should be freed from the star. The following considerations apply here: it is impossible to take these Jewish women from their families—the Reich Security Main Office agrees—if there are children under 14. On the other hand the women with children over 14 would in most cases have reached an age which would entitle them to request freedom from the star because it is hardly likely that they will have more children.

3. I am now going to carry out the Law for the Protection of Blood [prohibition of intermarriage and extramarital relations between Aryans and non-Aryans] in the Netherlands, and

4. make possible divorce in mixed marriages by reason of race difference.

These four measures together will constitute a final cleanup of the Jewish question in the Netherlands. Since this regulation could in a certain sense produce a precedent for the Reich, even while in the long run the regulation of mixed marriages in the Reich will also apply in the Netherlands, I am informing you, Mr. Party Director, of my intentions in the hope that I may have your reactions. I wrote in the same vein to the Reichsführer-SS [Himmler].

With best regards

Heil Hitler!
Your
Seyss-Inquart

29. France: Action Against Jewish Children

When France fell in 1940, most of the northern region and the whole Atlantic coast were placed under a German military commander. The French government under Marshal Pétain and Pierre Laval, with its seat in Vichy, continued to issue decrees for occupied as well as unoccupied territory, and retained its bureaucracy in both zones. In the area garrisoned by German troops, German authority was supreme, and there the German commander could override French measures at will. At times German offices in the occupied zone would also initiate action without French concurrence, but they could not always carry out their programs without French help.

The deportation of the Jews required French cooperation, because German military police and the forces of the Higher SS and Police Leader were insufficient for the task. The two zones contained 310,000 Jews, 165,000 of them in the north. A count in November 1940 had shown that the Seine *département* (Paris) had 149,734 Jews, of whom 85,664 were French nationals and 64,070 foreign and stateless persons, including refugees. On June 11, 1942, preliminary plans were made for the roundup of Jews between the ages of sixteen and forty. In subsequent discussions with the French government about the use of French police in Paris, Laval insisted on the exemption from all deportations of Jews with French nationality, while declaring his lack of interest in stateless Jewish children. Eichmann's representative in Paris, SS-Captain Dannecker, reported this news to the Reich Security Main Office on July 6 and, as he waited for clearance from Berlin to remove the children, went ahead with his preparations. A second message, reprinted below, followed on July 10. A week later, 4,051 children were in the hands of the police, and a few days thereafter Eichmann telephoned Paris that the children could be sent to Auschwitz. The Paris seizures of July 16–17, 1942, are described in Claude Lévy and Paul Tillard, *Betrayal at the Vel d'Hiv* (New York: Hill and Wang, 1969).

[Israel Police document 64.]

[Commanding Officer, Security Police and Security Service in France] IV J, Paris to Reich Security Main Officer IV B 4, Berlin
July 10, 1942
Urgent, to be submitted immediately!
Subject: Removing Jews from France
Previous: Discussion between SS-Lieutenant Colonel Eichmann and SS-Captain Dannecker on July 1, 1942 in Paris, my dispatch of July 6, 1942, IV J SA 225a.

French police will carry out the arrest of stateless Jews in Paris during July 16–18, 1942. It is to be expected that after the arrests about 4000 Jew-children will remain behind. For the moment French public welfare will care for these children. Inasmuch, however, as any lengthy togetherness of these Jew-children and non-Jewish children is undesirable, and since the "Union of the Jews in France" is not capable of accommodating in its own children's homes more than 400 children, I request an urgent decision by letter as to whether the children of the stateless Jews about to be deported may be removed also, starting with the 10th transport or so.

At the same time I request once more an urgent decision in the matter I raised in my dispatch of July 6, 1942.

By instruction
Dannecker

30. An Exemption

The organization of French Jewry during the occupation was the *Union Générale des Israélites de France* (UGIF). At the beginning of 1943, its employees numbered about two thousand, including some eight hundred in the north and twelve hundred in the south. The staff was composed of citizens as well as noncitizens of France, and in both of these categories there were salaried workers and unpaid volunteers. A position with the UGIF at this time afforded some protection from deportation and, as the following note reveals, the immunity could also cover relatives.

[Yad Vashem document O 9/5-la.]

Union Générale des Israélites de France
Director of the Liaison Office
signed Leo Israel Israelowicz
to Commanding Officer of Security Police and Security Service in the Area of the Military Commander in France—Paris Command
February 12, 1943
Subject: ANGEL, Tamas
    In the course of the action during the night between February 10 and 11, 1943, ANGEL, Tamas, residing at 79 Rue Sedaine, PARIS, and 72 years old, was arrested and brought to the Commissariat Rue de Chanzy.
    ANGEL, Tamas is the grandmother of our employee SICHEM, Suzanne, bearer of identification card 90, and they live together.
    The telephonic release order from your office to Commissariat was not carried out and the above named was transferred to DRANCY in spite of it.

In view of the fact that the granddaughter of the above named is an employee of the UGIF and with special reference to your release order, I ask for the liberation of Mrs. ANGEL, Tamas.

[Stamp in margin, with date, place, and signature added in ink:]

AGREED
Paris 12.2.43
Commanding Officer
Security Police and Security Service
in the Area of the Military Commander in France
Security Police and Security Service
Paris Command
[signature not legible]
SS-2d Lieutenant

31. Jewelry, Silver, Coins, Stamps

More than sixty thousand Jews were deported from France and tens of thousands fled from their homes to other countries or into hiding. The contents of the abandoned apartments were confiscated by a special Nazi party organization, the Rosenberg staff, for distribution to bombed-out Germans. The army looked down on these "invasions" of Jewish private property, asserting (in the words of a military police administration report, Alexandria document 75754, microfilm T 501, roll 184) that "The military administration has always represented the view that material gains scored by such invasions can never equal losses of moral reputation."

Two ordinances, however, were issued by the Military Commander (Heinrich von Stülpnagel) in 1942 and 1943 for the confiscation of property belonging to Jews who had held German, Czechoslovak, or Polish nationality. A commissioner, Ferdinand Niedermeyer, was charged with the administration of the decrees. Niedermeyer's interests overlapped to some extent with the Rosenberg staff, and so he concentrated on real estate, bank deposits, safe deposit boxes, and the like. An excerpt from his final report, drafted on February 28, 1945, in new quarters inside Germany, records some of the details of his unfinished work.

[Alexandria document 75753, Microfilm T 501, Roll 184.]

Report by FERDINAND NIEDERMEYER, ADMINISTRATOR OF PROPERTY FORFEITED TO THE REICH ON THE AREA OF THE MILITARY COMMANDER IN FRANCE DANSDORF, FEBRUARY 28, 1945 APPENDIX B TO REPORT

Jewelry, Silver, Coins, Stamp Collections

The procedure was as follows: most of the time items were taken from drawers; sometimes they were received by the Commissioner [Niedermeyer]. Receipt took place in the presence of the representative of the bank or of the Commissioner, the administrator of the warehouse, Mrs. Lampe, and the commissaire priseur Rostand. The latter immediately made a list, whereupon the items were packed in little packages, sealed by priseur Rostand and numbered 1 to 140 inclusively. They were then placed into the special drawer Niedermeyer at the Aero-Bank in Paris in the presence of a bank representative. Delivery always took place in the presence of Mrs. Lampe. The drawer was closed by means of an American combination system known only to bank employees as well as a lock for which Niedermeyer always had the key.

As a consequence of the events during August 1944 [the fall of Paris to the Allies] the packages listed below have remained in the Aero-Bank, Paris. There was unclarity about ownership and for that reason their sale was not permissible.

The remaining packages have been delivered—jewelry, silver, and coins to the Roges Co., Paris, and the stamp collections to the expert of the Reich Office Paper, Mr. Bibelje, Berlin, Jäger Street 82.

Package No.	Name		Estimated Value	
76	Klemperer, Oskar	R. 480	Frs.	6,040.—
92	Wölflin	R. 289	"	1,842.—
96	Balin, Leo	R. 626	"	142,017.—
97	Kahn, Richard	R. 491	"	113,905.—
100	Zimmer, Josef	R. 675	"	100.—
101	Kaatz, Hilde born Haas, wife of Polish Jew Kaatz	R. 716, 718	"	21,975.—
108	Hintz	R. 591	"	50,685.—
119	Duschnitz, Rudolf	R. 616	"	1,400.—
122	Meckler, Emil	R. 651	"	46,700.—
126	Scherman, Otto	R. 754	"	10,340.—
127	Silberstein, Evelina	R. 690	"	1,900.—
128	Kremer, Isaac	R. 815	"	5,035.—
129	Brunner, Hand and Francois	R. 841	"	185,000.—
130	Kahn, Hugo	R. 553	"	5,362.—
131	Wohl, Rubin	R. 908	"	10,000.—
132	Keller, Mendel	R. 911	"	11,000.—
133	Rabe, Rubinstein	R. 1159	"	15,000.—
134	Feist, Philippe	R. 371	"	37,500.—
135	Volweiler, Kurt	R. 274	"	6,000.—
136	Kahn, Sally	R. 531	"	28,300.—
138	Bornstein, Stanislas	R. 898	"	23,000.—
140	Unger, Hubert	R. 1281	"	176,225.—
		Total	Frs.	899,326.—

32. An Arrest in Rome

According to Italian Jewish community statistics presented by Massimo Adolfo Vitale at the Eichmann trial,

7,496 Jews were deported from Italy during the German occupation which began in September 1943. Almost all of the deportees went to Auschwitz, and 6,886 did not return. Some Jews were shot or committed suicide in Italy itself, so that the death toll may be put at about seven thousand—one in every six Italian Jews. The number of victims was not greater because many of the Jews lived in cities where the Germans depended heavily on the cooperation of the Italian population and police. In Milan, Turin, Venice, Siena, Bologna, Livorno, Ravenna, Pavia, Viterbo, Modena, and elsewhere, Jews were being seized one by one. Rome, Trieste, and Florence, where the Germans were active, suffered somewhat more heavily. The largest roundup, which involved German police and military units, took place in Rome on October 15–16, 1943. It is vividly described by Robert Katz, *Black Sabbath* (New York: Macmillan, 1969). After the transport left Rome with more than a thousand victims for the gas chambers in Auschwitz, Jews continued to be arrested in the city almost every day. In the Yad Vashem archives there is a metal box with nearly five hundred original arrest cards from the German Armed Forces Prison Regina Coeli. Three transports left Regina Coeli for Auschwitz on February 22, April 10, and May 20, 1944. Rome fell to the Allies on the following June 5. Below is a translation of one of the cards.

[Yad Vashem]

ARREST CARD FROM REGINA COELI PRISON (ENTRIES IN INK
UNDERLINED)

Rank:

Name: Anticoli   Profession: Laborer   Cell: 385

First Name: Glauco   Born 30.6.20   in Rome

Unit, Apartment: Rome, Via Ant. Rubino 4

(Open Citation, City, Street, Number)

Delivery		Release
on 14.4.44 at 12 o'clock	Deposited items:	on 20.5.44 at . . . o'clock
by SS-Sgt. Braun	1 belt, 1 cord	because of:
(Name, Rank)	1 briefcase with	transported away by SD
SD IV B	contents	
(Office)		
on account of: Jew		
		removed by:
		(Name, Rank)
		(Office)

Custody-Punishment
(Underline whichever
appropriate)

Notation of partial restitution (e.g. money) on
other side of card.
Deposited items re-   Receipt:
turned on . . . ,   Signature

Punishing Office: Signature   (Over)

[other side not filled in]

33. The Salonika Jews Are Destroyed

Greece collapsed under Axis attack in 1941. Its territory was divided among the Bulgarians, Italians, and Germans. The German share included the Macedonian city of Salonika and its environs, plus a detached strip adjacent to Turkey. While the Italians and Germans exercised complete power in their zones, they allowed a subordinate Greek government in Athens to carry on some of the everyday functions of administration. When Italy surrendered to the Allies in September 1943, the Germans occupied the Italian area in Greece, and a year later the Germans abandoned the whole of the Greek mainland.

In mid-April 1943 the Greek premier was Rhallis, the Greek governor general in Salonika was Simonidis, and Dr. Panos was an assistant to the governor general. The German military commander at the time was Major General Haarde, and German officials in the territory included his deputy for civil affairs Dr. Merten, the Foreign Office representative in Salonika Consul General Schönberg, the Commander of Security Police Paschleben, and the Eichmann representatives SS-Captains Wisliceny and Brunner. Two other personalities mentioned in the documents of this period were the Metropolitan of the Greek Orthodox Church and Rabbi Koretz, president of the Jewish community.

Before the war about 55,000 Jews—some five out of six in the country—lived in Salonika and the other Greek areas that were to be under German control in the spring of 1943. Many of the Salonika Jews were Sephardic and still spoke a variant of Spanish (Ladino). About 46,000 were deported from mid-March to August 1943. A reaction to the deportations by Rabbi Koretz, together with the stance of ranking Greek officials, is discussed in the following German memoranda.

[Alexandria document VII-173-b-16-14/26, Microfilm T 175, Roll 409.]

Copy

Special Commando of the Security Police for Jewish Affairs, Salonika-Aegean
signed: SS-Captain Wisliceny
to
[Military] Commander Salonika-Aegean
Attention War Administration Councillor Dr. Merten
To the German Consulate General, Salonika, Attention Consul General Dr. Schönberg
for information
April 15, 1943

Subject: Chief Rabbi Dr. Sewy Koretz

The arrested Chief Rabbi Dr. S. Koretz made the following comments during his interrogation about his call on [Greek] Premier Rallis [Rhallis]:

After his consultations with SS-Captains Wisliceny and Brunner on April 4, '43, it became clear to him that the resettlement of the Jews of Salonika would continue under all circumstances. He therefore hit upon the idea of persuading Greek offices to intervene. On Wednesday, April 7, '43, he found out that Premier Rallis [Rhallis] would visit Salonika on April 11. He therefore sought for a way to be received by the Premier. Consequently he turned to Dr. Panos who had looked him up for a discussion about the transfer of Jewish affairs. Panos agreed to transmit his wish to Governor General Simonidis. On Saturday, April 11, '43, Panos then notified him to come to the Metropolitan's Palace at 2:30 P.M. Furthermore, Koretz had had a telephone conversation with the Metropolitan who had turned to him in a religious matter. He had expressed the wish to see the Premier also to the Metropolitan. On Saturday, April 11, '43, after Dr. Panos had already communicated to him the invitation to participate in the audience, he was called personally by the Metropolitan who also requested him to appear at 2:30. The Metropolitan explained that he was speaking in the name of the Governor General. Koretz describes the progress of the conversation as follows: He was in the Palace of the Metropolitan by 2:30 where he waited in a hall on the ground floor together with the Bishop and the Chancellor of the University while the delegations waited in another room. Upon arrival of the Premier, the gentlemen left him and he had to wait until the end of the audiences. Then he was called. When he faced the Premier, he lost his composure and was able only to ask tearfully that Rallis [Rhallis] might appear before the German authorities, so that the 2000-year-old Jewish community of Salonika might not be liquidated. The Premier, however, replied only in a few irrelevant evasive words.

The description of the episode by Koretz could be true. Koretz was told that he had pushed through to Rallis [Rhallis] without the knowledge of the Governor General. He rejected that charge indignantly, insisting again and again that without the invitation of the Governor General he would never have gone to the audience.

signed Wisliceny
SS-Captain

German Consulate General, Salonika
Copy to
Plenipotentiary of the German Reich in Greece,
Minister Altenburg in Athens,
respectfully transmitted with request to take note.

A Greek witness reports that the Premier, who was visibly moved by the scene, replied to the Chief Rabbi that it was not in his power to contravene the resettlement of the Jews. He could only make recommendations to the occupying power. The Metropolitan then escorted the Chief Rabbi out, saying: "You see then that the Premier can do nothing in this matter."

The episode does not suffice in my view to proceed against the Archbishop or the Governor General or his assistant Dr. Panos, since they would claim in their defense that Chief Rabbi Koretz as chief executive of a recognized religious community in Greece could not have been refused a formal request to be received by the Premier. The occurrence does prove, however, that the participating Greek offices [in Salonika], which could have prevented its happening and which naturally foresaw that Koretz would attempt to move

the Premier into a position of opposing the resettlement measures, are in fact opposed to them. Presumably they also considered that in the event of the reappearance of the British in
Salonika (which at any rate seems possible to them) they
should have an alibi.

Because of the occurrence, which is viewed as an attempt at
countering a military order, the Commanding Officer, Salonika-Aegean, has removed Dr. Koretz from all of his offices and
has placed him with his family in a private house. He is to be
shipped out on one of the next transports, and as "prominent
Jew" will be held in Theresienstadt for possible exchange with
appropriate German prisoners.

Salonika, 16 April 1943
signature: Schönberg
(handwritten)

34. Paying for the Salonika Transports

After the deportation of the Salonika Jews, the German
Transport Ministry attempted to collect the bill for
their one-way dispatch to Auschwitz. The money was
due to the Greek State Railways, which was to pass on
the appropriate portions of the fare to other participating lines along the route (in Serbia, Croatia, and the
Reich itself). There were several possible sources of
collection. One was the military administration in
Salonika, which, according to the postwar testimony of
SS-Captain Wisliceny, held confiscated Jewish assets in
the amount of 280,000,000 drachma, or about 4,700,000
Reichsmark at the official rate of exchange. Although
the Security Police had originally referred the railway
to this source, the military administration declined payment. Another possibility was purchase of the drachma
by the German Finance Ministry, an avenue which
turned out to be impracticable, since drachma could be
obtained only if they were available in the German-

Greek clearing arrangement. Germany had employed clearing agreements with satellite and occupied states as a means of buying a maximum number of goods and services while exporting a minimum to these countries in turn. In the end, Germany was simply in debt, having in effect borrowed local currencies for purchases without replacing these currencies from sales. Inasmuch as the German Railway portion of the claim was in any case payable in Reichsmark, there were suggestions that the Finance Ministry be approached for the funds. Ultimately, this solution too was rejected, and it appears that no payment was made at all.

The following letter, one of the first in a long chain of correspondence, was signed by the chief of Section 17 (Military Tariffs and Travel Agreements) in the Railway Division E 1 (Traffic and Tariffs) of the Transport Ministry.

[German Federal Archives, Koblenz, Document folder R 2/14133.]

Ministry for Transport   17 TPA Or 29
signed: Dr. Rau
to High Command of the Army
March 1, 1944

In the spring of 1943 several trains with Jews from Greece were transported to Auschwitz [penciled in margin: Auschwitz?]. The special trains were ordered by the branch office of the Security Police and Security Service in Salonika. According to a statement made at the time on the telephone by the Reichsführer-SS and Chief of the German Police—Commando Security Police (Superior Government Councillor Huntsche [Hunsche]), the costs were to be borne from confiscated Jewish property which was at the disposal of the Military Commander—Aegean Area (Military Administration) in Salonika. The fare owed to the Greek State Railways as dispatcher of the trains, for the benefit of all participating railways, is 1,938,488 Reichsmark.

Repeated attempts were made to collect this amount from the above-mentioned office [the Military Commander], unfortunately without result so far. Now, on Feb. 1, '44 [the Army's] Field Railway Command 6, which has been primarily occupied with this situation, informed Reich Railway Directorate Dresden—which I deputized to carry out the negotiations —as follows:

"The Economic Attaché at the German Legation [in Athens], Mr. Höfinghoff, reported personally that payment of the transport costs of the Jewish special trains could not be made out of German-Greek clearing funds because there were no credits in this account. For the payment of ca. 1.9 million Reichsmark one would first have to obtain authorization from the Reich Finance Ministry. The Special Plenipotentiary of the Reich [in Greece] refused to request this authorization and indicated that the transport cost should be raised at the Reich Finance Ministry [directly]."

This suggestion obviously ignored the position of the Reichsführer-SS [Himmler] that the transport costs must be met from confiscated Jewish property.

I ask that this matter be cleared up with the Reichsführer-SS and Chief of the German Police/Command Security Police and possibly with the Reich Economy Minister and that care be taken to assure transmittal of the transport costs to the Directorate of the Greek State Railways. Kindly inform me about the progress of negotiations.

35. Memoir from Rhodes

The Dodecanese islands of Rhodes and Cos, close to Turkish shores, are now a part of Greece. They were Ottoman territory until the Tripolitanian War of 1911– 1912 when they were conquered by the Italians. Upon Italy's surrender in 1943, they were occupied by the 999th Division of the German army and held, despite British attempts to win footholds in the eastern Aegean, until the end of the European conflict.

Before the arrival of the Germans, the Jewish population on the Dodecanese was about 2,200. During July 1944, 1,950 Jews of Rhodes and 120 of Cos were deported to Auschwitz. In August the German division commander, Major General Klee, made a note of sentiments and feelings among the Greek, Turkish, and Italian inhabitants in his monthly report. Only the Italians, he said, had been somewhat critical; some of them had even characterized the Germans as barbaric.

Sixteen years after the event, the recollections of a surviving member of the Rhodes Jewish Council were recorded for the Yad Vashem Oral History Depot.

[Yad Vashem Oral History Depot, Tel Aviv, document 1745/67.]

DEPOSITION BY MAURICIUS SORIANO IN RHODES, SEPTEMBER 1961 [PHOTOGRAPHS OMITTED]

The Life of Jewry on Rhodes before World War II

The Greek island of Rhodes, with its 40,000 inhabitants, was Italian territory before World War II.

The population was mostly Greek. In addition, there were several thousand Turks who had remained from the time of the Turkish domination, as well as about 2,000 Jews of Greek and Turkish nationalities.

The Jewish population lived mainly in a Jewish quarter near the port in what is referred to as the old city today [refers to photographs]. The Jews involved themselves in retail and wholesale trade and maintained commercial relations with foreign countries from which they imported goods for the whole island. The economic situation was so good that one could hardly speak of poverty. They did business also in the new city, and employed members of other denominations (Greek Orthodox, Catholic, and Moslem). Only a few Jews lived in the villages of the island and they too did well.

The Jewish community was well organized. My father—today 81—was its chairman for many years. Our whole family was Zionist as I showed you on the basis of written documents in my home. In the old city, the community administered a small synagogue which was badly damaged by bombs in July 1944 and which is being rebuilt only now.

One of the most important sights on the island from prewar times is the Jewish cemetery which has had its present location only since 1937 when the authorities ordered it transferred from another area. All the graves were exhumed and the remains transferred to the newly designated place which is situated between the Christian and Moslem cemeteries. Only a few graves were unidentified and for those a common stone was erected. The rabbis are lying in a preferred spot [refers to photographs].

A large number of languages were spoken on the island especially by youth which had gone to school. In addition to these tongues—Greek, Turkish, Italian—the Jews spoke Judeo-Spanish [Ladino]. The Jewish intelligentsia spoke French in its contacts with foreigners.

At the beginning the war produced hardly any changes in our lives.

After the non-Italian population had been ordered in 1941 to hand in all radio receivers to the authorities, we did not even know much about the war. The lot of our coreligionists remained unknown to us. After all, since we were living on an island, we had no contact with the outside world.

Only after the termination of Italian rule and the arrival of the Germans, most horrible events transpired in short order.

The Bombings of July 1944

Heavy [Allied] bombings ensued in July 1944. The harbor, however, remained untouched; it was the Jewish quarter which was destroyed. Until today we do not know if this was done deliberately or not, but the harbor was definitely undamaged. In order to protect themselves from the repeated air raids, most of the Jews sought refuge outside the city in the nearby villages of Triando, Kremato, Mixi, and Kandli.

Measures of the Germans Against the Jews

Early in July 1944, when the Germans consolidated their hold on Rhodes, the first anti-Jewish ordinance was issued prohibiting Jews from living outside a radius of 33 miles [*sic* —Soriano evidently meant 3.3 miles] from the city. This zone enclosed only the five nearby villages. From other villages farther away, Jews had to move immediately on penalty of court martial. Now we could see that our situation was bad and already we were sorry that so few of our youths had left with the Italians. Those few had all fled against parental orders. They remained alive and escaped from the heavy suffering of Europe's Jewry. Most of them joined the partisans.

At 5 P.M. on July 19, 1944, a second order was brought out which required all Jewish men, 16 years or older, to report to the Gestapo at 8 A.M. the next day with identity and labor cards for registration. The Gestapo was quartered in the former Italian air building—today it houses the hotel school and is known as "Hotel Soleil." Unconsciously, but in defiance of history, Jewish tourists from Israel are staying precisely in this hotel. Next day all the men reported there. I allowed only my father, because of his advanced age, not to come along.

A commission, consisting of a Gestapo functionary and two noncommissioned officers accompanied by an interpreter, *Costa Ricanati*, examined our papers and questioned us about various details, only to take the documents from us in the end and incarcerate us on the ground floor of the building.

During the interrogation, I noticed that the interpreter, who represented himself as a Greek from Salonika, spoke remarkably fluent Judeo-Spanish [Ladino], so that as a director of the Jewish community I allowed myself to ask him how he had developed such exceptional language skills. He said that he was living in Salonika and that he had several Jewish friends. Since we had no proof that he was a Jew, we had to believe him, but doubt his statement to this very day.

We remained under lock and key without food or water until the next morning. At 9 A.M. Costa Ricanati arrived with the noncommissioned officers of the SS, and the directors of the Jewish community, *Mr. Franco R. Cohen* and I, were given the following order:

"You have to inform all families to report here by 4 P.M. tomorrow, with small baggage, food for 10 days, and all possessions of gold, jewelry, or valuables. You will be brought to a neighboring island where everyone will have to set up house and live off his savings." Without delay, the chairman of the community, Mr. Franco, was given a car. Accompanied by Costa Ricanati, he was to notify all Jewish families of the new decree. It was suggested that he speak convincingly to his coreligionists about taking along all their valuables. Costa Ricanati made a speech in Spanish: "My dear friends!?! It is in your own interest, if you do not wish to suffer, to take with you all your savings in money, jewelry, and gold, or you may die of hunger. Kindly don't reproach me afterwards that I did not tell you." He used all of his persuasiveness, gave out hope and illusions embedded in lies, did everything to place as many valuables as possible at the disposal of the Germans and to stuff his own pockets.

I must say that 90% of the people actually believed him when he told them that it was in their own interest, if they wanted to live, to take along everything they possessed. Under the circumstances, our panic became so great that we lost our ability to think and to react functionally.

After all the families had been brought together and locked up on the ground floor [sic], the chairman was ordered to hand over all the valuables. The commission threatened to shoot anyone who resisted its directive and refused to deliver his last possession. Even wrist watches had to be given up. Costa Ricanati was the one who delivered also this message: with all of his eloquence he demanded of everyone everything.

One can hardly imagine our panic now; I myself saw that our situation had become tragic and in my despair I offered Costa Ricanati one hundred pieces of gold if he could show me how I could get away. I made all sorts of proposals to him— whatever I could think of on the spot. Finally he asked me what nationality I had. I answered truthfully that I was Dodecanese and my wife a Turkish citizen. This latter information pleased him and he promised to do something for us.

At that time my wife and our two children were still living in a village outside the 33-mile [3.3-mile] perimeter to which I had sent them in spite of the prohibitions of the authorities. They also had all of our valuables with them. I did not completely trust Costa and wrote six slips of paper to my wife in which I urged her to go at once to the Turkish consul and ask his aid. I rolled the slips into little balls and threw them over the wall. Only one of these slips reached my wife; it was picked up by a passerby who had noticed my maneuver.

In honor of the Turkish consul, whose name I unfortunately do not remember, I must say that he intervened immediately with the German commission with which he conferred for a long time in behalf of all the Turkish citizens who were married to Dodecanese (there were 42).

I must add that during the [Allied] bombing of the island, the Turkish consul had lost two employees who were killed and that his wife had gone insane. To revenge himself, he did everything he could to harm the Germans [sic].

Since my wife was a Turkish citizen I too was liberated.

But this did not end my worries, for my parents were still interned by the Gestapo.

Now that I could move about freely and was required only to report daily to the Gestapo, I met with Costa Ricanati at an appointed place and gave him his dues. At the same time I promised him anything he might ask for the liberation of my parents. He replied with a blinking of the eyes which allowed me to attach my parents to the group containing the Turkish families. In all the Turkish consul removed 5 or 6 families from the Gestapo building, the only people to whose liberation Costa Ricanati made a contribution—albeit for money.

As I left the prison with my family, Costa walked over to me and hissed into my ear: "I expect you tonight at 9 P.M. in the hotel 'a l'Albergo delle Terme.' " Punctually I came and he waited for me at the door tearing from my hand the booty wrapped in a handkerchief. I gave a detailed list of the contents to the Maitre Apostolidis. This did not end the matter with my parents. Greeks had denounced them to the Gestapo with indications that my parents were really Dodecanese and had no right to recognition as Turkish nationals. Only through the help of an Italian doctor were they admitted as patients in the hospital and then we boarded the rented boat to Anatolia [Turkey]. Here too we had no luck. Even though the boat owners had been paid more than the fare, the boat was leaking and threatened to sink. Only after an unpleasant argument did we go back for repairs and then we finally made it.

We stayed in Turkey until the end of the war.

Deportations of the Jews from Rhodes

In the course of the next day, even as I was escaping from the Germans, all the interned Jews were brought to the harbor to be transported on three ships to Pireus and from there to the concentration camp Haidar. Then they were sent on to Poland and Germany.

Out of the 1950 deported Jews only 120 remained alive; all others perished.

Today 30 Jews (adults and children) live on Rhodes. They returned to the island after its liberation from the Germans.

No adults were saved on the island; amongst others Messrs. Franco perished. In their honor the grave of Lea Franco, who died before the war, was fitted out with a small flat plaque in memory of the deportees and all the family members who did not return [refers to photographs].

36. An Individual Survives in Yugoslavia

When Yugoslavia was overrun by Axis invaders in April 1941, its territory was dismembered. In the north the Germans created a new state, Croatia, which covered an expanse from the Drava River to the Adriatic Sea, but without the districts just north of Zagreb which were incorporated by Germany, and without a portion of Slovenia, some Adriatic ports, and islands off the Dalmatian coast which became Italian. Croatia was occupied by German and Italian troops; the Germans were stationed in Zagreb and Sarajevo, the Italians in the coastal area. In September 1943, German forces attacked the Italian divisions in Yugoslavia and seized the Italian-occupied zone of Croatia with all the adjacent areas which Italy had annexed, including the Slovenian city of Ljubljana and Dalmatian Spalato.

Meanwhile, the Croatian state maintained its own government, its own army, its own uniformed party formation (the *Ustasha*), and its own anti-Jewish laws. Goaded by the Germans in Zagreb, blunted by the Italians on the coast, the Croatian regime struck out vehemently, but also erratically, at the thirty thousand Jews within its borders. The ultimate fate of Croatian Jewry may thus be discerned in five principal outcomes: deportation to Auschwitz, death in Croatia (especially in forced labor camps), exemption from destructive measures by reason of mixed marriage or some other privileged position, escape to Italian- or Hungarian-held territory, and survival in hiding or with partisans in various parts of Yugoslavia.

The following deposition deals with an experience in hiding. The account is not only a description of local conditions but a self-portrait as well.

[Yad Vashem Oral History Depot, Tel Aviv, document 530/32.]

DEPOSITION BY MRS. MITZI ABELES, 1958

I was born on July 13, 1895 in Vinkovci, Yugoslavia. My maiden name was Mitzi Rosenberg. In April 1941, when the German Army occupied Yugoslavia, I was living in Zagreb, Gjorgjiceva 21. Our apartment contained also the office of my husband's business which was known under the name of Drvoexport (timber export).

From the end of April 1941, we Zagreb Jews had to wear the Jewish star. A few months thereafter I was forced to leave my apartment, because the next house, Gjorgjiceva 23, had become the collecting point of Jewish property and Ustasha were constantly standing guard there. Since it was dangerous to pass Ustasha with a Jewish star, I left my home. I want to add that my husband was no longer in Zagreb at that time; he was a prisoner-of-war in Germany, having fought against Germany in the Yugoslav Army. My daughter, who was [omission in text] years old, was also no longer with me; I had sent her, immediately after the arrival of the Germans, to Italy. I managed to do this in the following manner: During the very first moment of the German occupation, the supervision of the Jews in Zagreb was in the hands of the Croatian director of Jewish affairs in the local police. This man was in charge of the file of the Zagreb Jews and later the file was used for arrests and deportations to Auschwitz as well as confiscations of Jewish property. With this man I was able to have an understanding right at the beginning, and for a princely sum he gave my daughter a permit which allowed her to travel to the Italian border at *Rijeka-Fiume.* There she crossed the border with a false passport. By the way, false passports were very common in those days. We Zagreb Jews were terribly afraid and we had only one desire: to flee as quickly as possible to a foreign country. The director of the Jewish division in the police responded to our money and pleas also with another favor: he simply permitted my address, as well as the address of my cousin and aunt at Vlaska 72, to disappear from the list and the file. If the collecting point had not been opened in the next house, I would have been able to remain at home in relative security for another few weeks or months.

On account of the Ustasha, I had to leave my apartment without preparation during the first arrests of Jews and I left behind everything except my jewelry. I moved to my relatives at Vlaska 72 which was no longer in the files either. There I remained until August 8, 1942. That day agents of the state visited my cousin and her husband *Lina* and *Ladislav Stern.* It happened in the middle of the night. The agents arrested my relatives who later perished in Auschwitz. I saved myself by accident. The agents had knocked on the door and asked me what my name was. I gave them a fictitious purely Croatian name and they brushed me aside, probably taking me for a maid. I jumped in my nightshirt one flight into the rear courtyard and hid all night in the wooden shack of the building. The house superintendent's wife knew I was there. Next morning I left with clothes lent to me by the superintendent's wife and during the next few weeks I moved like a hunted animal, spending each night in a different place with friends. Finally an acquaintance arranged for my hiding in the apartment of a non-Jewish whore. This "lady," who behaved very decently toward me, had come from *Spalato*, Dalmatia. Her name was *Derencinova*. That was toward the end of September 1942. After a while this lady found out that the superintendent's wife knew about me and was about to denounce both me and my host. She then saw to it that I could travel to *Trnje*, a village outside Zagreb, where a peasant woman hid and maintained me under the condition, to be sure, that I stay at all times in the attic. Only at night was I allowed to come down to relieve myself and gather up food for another day. The attic was very cold and I developed bad rheumatism there. The police entered the house several times during searches and I escaped them narrowly. Once I had time only to cover my hair with a rag and to throw myself under the bedcovers. The agents were already coming up the stairs and the peasant woman declared with false calm that I was her sick mother. On another occasion I climbed out of the window and hid behind the smokestack until the agents were gone. In my poor condition I felt these experiences as physical strain and nervous tension. In February 1943 the peasant woman gave me to understand that I could no longer remain with her. Sick as I was, I therefore moved to one of her acquaintances in *Sestinski Dol*. He was a railway employee whose route was *Zagreb-Spalato* and in July 1943 he enabled me to get to Spalato. This city, the former Yugoslav Split, was now under Italian rule and the Jews there were relatively safe.

Split (Spalato) is bombed. I flee to Lagosta and Taranto.

I remained in Spalato until September 10, 1943. From there I fled by boat to the island of Lagosta. During my stay in Spalato, on September 2, 1943, the Italians had capitulated to the Allies. Since Italy was now joining the Allies, the Germans occupied most of Italy and marched into Dalmatia. Spalato was bombed heavily. I lived there with relatives who had a small baby. During the bombing I held the infant in my arms. The apartment was hit by a bomb and the mother (with whom I was related) died under it. The father of the child was missing afterward; his body could not be found. The child and I were not scratched. I succeeded in sending the baby to Zagreb to his Christian grandparents. The names of my relatives were *Zdenka* and *Zwonko Kollmann.*

After this tragedy, the Germans moved into the city. On that day I stood helplessly on the beach not knowing where to turn. Suddenly I saw a small fishing vessel crowded with a group of people. One of the persons on board motioned me to join them. It turned out to be an acquaintance of mine. Just at the moment when German troops were entering the city he offered me the opportunity to cross to the island of Lagosta which was reported to be still unoccupied by the Germans.

The trip was torture. We spent four days in this nutshell at sea. Since we had neither food nor water, older people lost consciousness in the sun. At Lagosta some of the men went into the village. They found a military radio transmission station which the Italians had abandoned. One of the men, who was a professional operator of such equipment, reported to Bari that the island was unoccupied and that we were a small refugee group from Spalato who were trying to get to Bari. We stayed on Lagosta for 14 days. Then on a moonless night we crossed, constantly afraid of German aircraft. When we reached Bari, we encountered the Jewish Brigade from Palestine. They took us to their messhall and I recuperated in their camp. We were all completely unkempt, and physically as well as psychologically in poor condition.

37. Compiling Lists of Slovak Jews

Slovakia became a separate state when Czechoslovak Bohemia and Moravia were occupied by Germany in March 1939. The new Slovak entity was a German creation, and it became a satellite in war and destruction.

The Jewish population in the Slovak census of December 1940 was 88,951. Deportations took place in two waves during 1942–1943 and 1944–1945. Complete figures for the transports were given to the tribunal in the Eichmann trial by Dr. Bedrich Steiner, who had been a statistical expert in the Jewish central organization of Slovakia. His total for the first phase is 57,837, of whom 18,746 were sent to Auschwitz, 4,501 to Lublin, and 34,590 to the small town of Opole (a railhead some twenty-five miles west of the city of Lublin in the Pulawy district), from where they were distributed to work camps or pushed directly into the gas chambers of one of the death centers nearby. All but a few of these 57,837 perished in Poland. While the deportations were still in progress, several thousand Jews escaped (or were expelled) to Hungary, others went into hiding, still other thousands became inmates of the labor camps Novaky, Sered, and Vyhne, and the remainder were privileged at home.

After an uprising of Slovaks in August, September, and October 1944, the deportations were resumed. This time, according to Dr. Steiner, 12,306 were moved out, including 7,936 whose destination was Auschwitz and 4,370 who were routed to Sachsenhausen concentration camp and Theresienstadt. Probably half of the deportees in the second wave were killed. Finally, several hundred Jews died in the upheaval of 1944 when they were shot by the SS on the spot.

The Slovak government which delivered more than seventy thousand of its Jews to the Germans was composed in part of the following personalities:

President	Monsignor Jozef Tiso
Prime Minister	Vojtech Tuka
Interior Minister	Šaňo Mach
Chief, Presidium of Interior Ministry	Dr. Izidor Koso
Director, Central Economy Office (an agency concerned with Jewish affairs)	Augustín Morávek

The official Jewish body in Slovakia was the Central Jewish Organization *(Ústredňa Židov).* Its first head *(starosta)* was Heinrich Schwartz, a member of the religious Orthodox faction. He was replaced in 1941 by a Social Democrat and former principal of an Orthodox Jewish school, Arpád Sebestyén, who remained in charge until December 1943. The last *starosta* was a Zionist, Oskar Neumann. Within the *Ústredňa Židov* various divisions were responsible for finance, education, training, labor, and "special tasks."

The following selections deal with the compilation of transport lists. The first, a small excerpt from a book by Oskar Neumann, contains a Slovak joke about Sebestyén. The next two are reports by the *Ústredňa Židov's* Division of Special Tasks, which was headed by an engineer, Karel Hochberg. He is believed to have been killed as a collaborator by Slovak insurgents in 1944.

[(Jirmejahu) Oskar Neumann, *Im Schatten des Todes* (Tel Aviv: Olamenu, 1956), p. 91.]

Morávek requested the *starosta* to report. The latter appeared (as he always did in actuality) with hand straight up in the Slovak Fascist salute and the greeting "On Guard!"

"Mr. *starosta*," Morávek said in a cold official voice, "the Slovak government has sentenced all of the Jews to hang until dead. The Jewish Central Office itself has to carry out the sentence immediately."

The *starosta* straightened up. "Yes, Sir! Allow me one question: The ropes have to be ordered by the Jewish Central Office itself?"

[Yad Vashem document M-5(18) 7]

ÚSTREDŇA ŽIDOV
Division for Special Tasks
Engineer Hochberg—Group I/East
Žilina [crossed out]   Nováky   June 12, 1942
Activity Report VI

In accordance with telephoned instructions, I reported with my group in Nováky on Tuesday, June 9, 1942. The camp is stable, a labor installation, and this facilitated our administrative work, insofar as we had at our disposal three good typewriters and some experienced clerical personnel. Given these circumstances we began the registration at 10 in the morning and finished a complete transport of 1000 persons by 6:30 in the evening.

This time my group consisted of Kriváček, Kolisch, Quitt, and Salzer (East) and the representatives assigned to us by the central organization: Rakovsky and Aftergut (Nováky).

After the expert [Dr. Zábrecky] gave instructions that the remaining portion in the camp should be processed separately on the next day for [transport to the camp in] Žilina, I charged Kriváček and Salzer with the registrations which should encompass ca. 200–300 persons.

Administratively, this transport was the best which we have put together out of the ca. 13,000 persons registered so far, and this success is to be ascribed especially to the fact that even while we were engaged in the registration, we set aside everyone who had a half-way well founded claim and included him in a remainder transport which is to leave Nováky in a few days for Žilina. The best proof of this is that not one name was struck off the list and that the transport, complete with 1000 persons, left Nováky on Tuesday at 11:30 P.M., passing Žilina at 12:30 P.M. Wednesday where the Žilina community provided lunch and food for the trip. Among other things, we reclaimed in Nováky in all 88 persons who will be released in accordance with camp tradition only after a few days. On this occasion, Wednesday night, we also regrouped concentration camp inmates consisting mostly of skilled laborers and their dependents into labor camp inmates. The reclamation division [of the Ústredňa Židov] was not present.

Categories [in the transport]

A	men capable of work, 14 to 60 years old	172
K	children over 14	278
F	women over 14	414
—	old men over 60	136
	Total	1,000

I have made a written report to the SS-Sergeant as well as to the expert Dr. Zábrecky. For the first time since our work began we have raised the age limit from 60.

On Friday Dr. Frank Julius reported in the camp.

In accordance with instructions I have to report in Žilina where the 16th and 17th transports are being processed on the 12th.

The following districts were assigned to Nováky: Prievidza, Bánovce, Zlat. Moravce, Topolčany, Hnušta, Zvolen, Revuca, Brezno n/Hr. Kokava, Nová Baňa and Žarnovica.

ÚSTREDŇA ŽIDOV
Division for Special Tasks
Engineer Hochberg—Group I "East"
Žilina [crossed out] Nováky
June 14, 1942
Activity Report No. IX

Yesterday noon I was ordered by Lieut. Dohnánsky to travel with him immediately by car to Nováky to determine the final count there and expedite the transport as a supplement to the XIX Žilina transport. A part of the registration had already been carried out by our Nováky representative Rakovsky, so that the final count was 280. The transport was checked out for last night to Žilina.

That same evening, yesterday, Saturday, I returned to Žilina, where preparations were being made for the 19th transport due to leave June 14. At the instigation of camp commander Polhara I received instructions to have my colleague Aftergut sent back to the central organization immediately for his incorrect conduct. I have already telephoned H. škpt. Rosenzweig about this. Although I tried to rescind his recall, I did not succeed.

The Žilina camp was inspected yesterday by SS-Captain Baron Dieter von Wisliceny. My work was verified by our division chairman engineer Hochberg, who then went on to camp Poprad.

Only today will I be able to divide the Nováky transport into categories and look at the Žilina lists of names. Categories:

		Nováky:	Žilina:
A	capable of work	136	96
K	children	55	172
F	women	88	185
—	old men and women	22	248
		301	701

38. Slovak Jewish Camouflage

Between 1942 and 1944 thousands of Jews attempted to assume an identity that would shield them from deportation. They tried to acquire a foreign passport, a Slovak name, or a baptismal certificate. By the end of 1944 the bearers of such papers were all in dire jeopardy, as even Jews in mixed marriages were caught in the roundups and moved out on the last trains.

The following instances are taken from the files of the SS Security Service in Vienna, which collected the information from the Security Service in the Slovak capital of Bratislava.

[Alexandria document EAP 173-g-12-18/38, Microfilm T 175, Roll 523.]

Consulate of the Republic of Paraguay in Berne
to
Mr. Henrik Kohlmann and Family
Bratislava, Zamocka 74
Slovakia

Berne, December 22, 1942

Dear Mr. Kohlmann,
   Herewith we are honored to inform you that on the basis of efforts by your relatives, you as well as your wife and children have obtained Paraguayan nationality.
   Enclosed is your family passport and we request that you confirm the receipt of this document by return mail.

> Cordially yours
> [signature not legible]
> Consul

[Alexandria document EAP 173-g-12-18/38, Microfilm T 175, Roll 523.]

SS Security Service, Bratislava
to SS Security Service Directorate, Vienna
attention SS-Captain Herrmann
August 20, 1942

Subject: Slovakization of Names by Jews
Previous: Nothing

   The Jewish owner of the timber enterprise "Slovakia," Herz, requested Slovakization of his name to Herec at the Interior Ministry. The request is being considered by a director Rybarik in the Interior Ministry and a Dr. Galvanek. Rybarik declared that when a Jew has been granted exceptional status, there is no legal ground for denying a request for Slovakization of his name.

[Alexandria document EAP 173-g-12-18/38, Microfilm T 175, Roll 523.]

REPORT BY SS SECURITY SERVICE IN SLOVAKIA, OCTOBER 10, 1942
SUBJECT: JEWS

It is generally known that most of the remaining Jews in Slovakia have already been baptized. When these baptized Jews discover that they are to be removed or that they are to go to a concentration camp—and they discover it always in time—they simply give their minor children to the nuns. The children are being accepted by the two nunneries in Žilina, that is the cloister of the St. Vincent and the cloister of the teaching nuns OSF. The Jewish parents themselves disappear, that is hide, in order not to be removed. The nunneries therefore exist for the purpose of preserving Jewish children. All Žilina smiles with the thought that in these cloisters nothing but Jewish children are being preserved. It is clear that the nuns are not working for charity or for love of neighbor—they are being paid very well.

During the month of October, all the churches in Žilina have rosary services, which are being attended like all services in provocative and demonstrative manner by baptized Jews. People laugh at this sudden piety and they do not believe that it is truthful or honest.

[Alexandria document EAP 173-g-12-18/38, Microfilm T 175, Roll 523.]

Diocese of Urad and Nitra
to Higher SS and Police Leader in Slovakia
December 1, 1944
Excellency!
Dear SS-Lieutenant General:
We hope your Excellency will not be offended if we submit the following plea:

In the course of various security measures, the concentration of non-Aryan persons in Nitra has affected also those who are living in mixed marriages with Aryans. It is a question of a few families which have assimilated themselves to their Christian environment, which educated their children as Christians, and which have hardly anything in common with Jewry.

Since this decree is having a harsh effect on Christian families and Christian children, we extend our fervent plea to your Excellency to kindly pause before this measure and to make an exception for those non-Aryans who are living in mixed marriages with Aryan persons.

We allow ourselves to submit this plea, for as we are informed such exceptions are made also in the Reich.

Accept, Excellency, the assurance of our highest consideration,

Respectfully,

Archbishop of Nitra

[various signatures]

[Notation in top margin: "Draft reply!" "Pastoral letter!"
The word "hardly" underlined
At the bottom additional notations including:
   "for the moment, not to be answered" (December 31)]

39. Prime Minister Tuka's Father Confessor

During the seizures of 1942, the Slovak government, strongly Catholic, spared thousands of baptized Jews. It was then subjected to repeated demands from the German Legation for the deportation of the remaining Jewish population, while it also faced questions from the Slovak clergy about the unbaptized Jews whom it had already abandoned to what was at best an unknown fate. The two cross-pressures are reflected in conversations between the German envoy, Minister Hans Ludin, and Slovak Prime Minister Tuka in 1943. The talks were summarized in a dispatch by Ludin to the Foreign Office in Berlin.

[Israel Police document 1016.]

German Legation in Bratislava, Slovakia
(signed by Minister Hans Ludin) to
Foreign Office in Berlin
April 13, 1943

The Slovak bishops dispatched a pastoral letter to the Catholic clergy with instructions to read it in all the churches on March 21. The text in translation is enclosed.

So far as can be determined to date, the public reaction has varied, frequently taking on a form not intended by the letter. Apparently in a few places, the clergy refused to proceed with the reading, while in other churches the pastoral message was weakened by comments in the sermons which were obviously designed to calm the public. In general one may ascertain that the effect has been negative in political as well as in clerical circles. After all, the basic anti-Semitic attitudes of the Slovak people, which we know from experience, as also the anti-Semitic propaganda which we have directed and consistently carried out during the last years, have created a soil which no longer seems receptive to that kind of venting by the ranking clergy.

As I learned from reliable sources, these considerations were already raised in a lively manner during the composition of the letter. The text provoked opposition among some of the bishops and that resistance is said to have become so strong that finally it was agreed to deprive the document of its highly official character. Accordingly it was printed, not (as is customary) in the episcopal press, but in the Catholic press chancellery. Seal, signature, and official numeration were omitted. Those of the clergy who refused to perform the reading in the church then seized upon these circumstances to point out that the official marks were missing and that therefore it was solely a circular letter whose public reading could not be regarded as obligatory.

Further, I am confidentially informed by Catholic circles that the letter did not have an ecclesiastical-dogmatic objective, but an outright political one. It was supposed to have been prepared by the Slovak Minister in the Vatican, Sidor, in cooperation with certain political circles of the Vatican in Slovakia. There is, however, no confirmation of that presumption.

Prime Minister Dr. Tuka let me know that he approached a bishop through Ministerial Councillor Dr. Koso about the pastoral letter. The bishop is said to have explained that the Slovak bishops had received reports of the following atrocities committed by the Germans against the Jews:

In the Ukraine Jews were shot en masse, and at that not only men, but also women and children. Before the execution they had been forced to dig their own graves. Those of the Jews who were not buried were boiled into soap. In one case a mother was shot or stabbed and her baby was tossed live into the grave.

Furthermore, Prime Minister Dr. Tuka let me know that the "naive Slovak clergy" would believe such atrocity fairy tales and he would be grateful to counter these fairy tales of atrocities with a description from the German side of conditions in the Jewish camps. In addition he considers that from a propagandistic view it might be specially valuable if a Slovak delegation, which should appropriately be composed of a legislator, a journalist, and perhaps also a Catholic clergyman, could visit a German camp for Jews.

If such an inspection might be organizationally feasible, I would certainly welcome its implementation.

As for the basic attitude of the Slovak government in the Jewish question as well as the basic resolution of certain governmental elements to pursue the resettlement of the Jews, the pastoral letter, according to my observations, changed nothing. To the contrary, it may be observed that also those personalities, who until now were very reserved in the matter of Jewish resettlement, stand ready to continue the action. Trustworthy sources have informed me, for example, that during the last cabinet meeting, which took place after the reading of the pastoral letter, General Catlos and especially also Minister Medricky spoke out for an intensified Jewish resettlement.

Recently Prime Minister Dr. Tuka told me that the papal Pronuntius Monsignor Burzio had appeared before him in order to protest verbally against the continuation of the resettlement of the Jews. However, Dr. Tuka declined even to accept the protest, pointing immediately to the purely political nature of this affair which did not touch the interests of the Holy See. The Pronuntius thereupon refrained from presenting the protest, but appealed to the Catholic-Christian conscience of the Prime Minister. Dr. Tuka thereupon replied that in this matter there was for him a higher authority than the Pope, namely Tuka's own father confessor. The confessor had asked him if in conscience he could justify the Jewish resettlement as being in the interest of his nation. When Mr. Tuka answered this question affirmatively, the father confessor is supposed not to have raised any objection against these measures.

I have instructed our propaganda offices to carry on the anti-Semitic propaganda purposefully, but to take no position vis-à-vis the pastoral letter or in the question of the Jewish resettlement itself. Similarly I avoided also now any kind of pressure on the Slovak government in questions of Jewish resettlement. This stance of mine has so far proved to be correct, since the application of pressure would have hindered the Slovak government more than it would have helped in this area. Basically I am naturally in favor of the most rapid and complete resettlement of the Jews from Slovakia.

40. Hungary's Reluctance

The last major deportation country in the German sphere of influence was Hungary. Hungary's alliance with Germany was opportunistic. It began with Hungarian territorial gains at the expense of Czechoslovakia, Roumania, and Yugoslavia. By mid-1941 Hungary was called upon to deliver supplies to Germany and dispatch divisions to the Russian front. As the tides of war turned, Hungary became a reluctant ally, hesitating in the war effort and holding on to its 750,000 Jews.

Hungarian Jewry was heavily involved in commerce as well as industry and, though subject to discriminations, continued to be active in these sectors while a short distance to the north the Slovak and Polish Jews were dying. In the course of negotiations between the Hungarian National Bank and a German Foreign Office trade representative, the Hungarians went so far as to refuse a German demand for the ouster of Jewish businessmen because these men were needed to maintain Hungarian links with countries outside the Axis fold. The discussion was the subject of a report by the Budapest representative of the *Südosteuropa-Gesellschaft e.V. Vienna* (soeg) which carried out economic intelligence in southeastern Europe.

In April 1943, German pressure was intensified. Hitler and Foreign Minister Ribbentrop, in a meeting with Hungarian Regent Horthy, bluntly demanded the destruction of Hungarian Jewry. Horthy was shaken, but still did not comply with Germany's wish.

[Alexandria document RWM/16/245p, Microfilm T 71, Roll 63.]

Confidential report by soeg representative in Budapest
(Franz Jung)
July 31, 1942
distributed to "smallest circle and Minister Clodius"
[Excerpt]

In the talk between Barany (Hungarian National Bank) and
Clodius, B. pointed out explicitly that an elimination of Jewry
and Jewish capital from the Hungarian economy had to be
viewed as an impossibility and that the Hungarian National
Bank had to stand or fall on this question. So long as there was
an independent Hungarian government, no responsible Hungarian political figure could act upon German initiative to
bring about the complete elimination of Jewish capital. For
the independence of Hungarian currency it was vital to maintain further Hungarian exports to countries free of German
influence, and if need be to throttle such exports to Germany.
Dr. Clodius then threatened to block transit [of Hungarian
goods through German-dominated territory].

[Nuremberg document D-736.]

Secret Reich Matter
Notes of discussion between the Führer and Hungarian Regent Horthy in Klessheim castle on April 17, 1943, in the
morning.
Salzburg, April 18, 1943 (signed) Schmidt
The discussion, which was carried on conversationally, began with the Führer's explanation of the bombing raids that
the British had carried out during the previous night over
German territory and in the course of which two British aircraft turned up also over Salzburg where they could be heard
quite clearly, causing an air raid alarm. The Führer told
Horthy that up to now 51 British planes had been brought
down and then offered some general remarks about British air
attack tactics. To cite an example, documents were found

wherein British pilots had been instructed prior to the attack on Frankfurt that no special emphasis was to be placed on industrial targets and that bombs might calmly be dropped on residential areas. This kind of conception has generated protest in the British air force. The attacks themselves were annoying, but without consequence. The kinds of losses inflicted on the enemy during air raids were more significant than normal losses in other combat operations, since air operations always caused the death of the most valiant and brave, while on land or at sea losses represented more or less an average between the brave and the less brave. For the rest, Germany was postponing its counteroffensive until the new aircraft models, which are far superior to all other machines, will be available in large numbers, and within 2 or 3 months Germany would be in a position to defend itself in such manner that the British would no longer be able to accomplish very much.

To hold out during such trials unity on the home front was essential. Furthermore, draconic measures were being taken against asocial elements such as thieves or saboteurs and especially against crimes committed during blackouts. In Germany all these crimes were being punished ruthlessly by death. As a result nothing was being stolen anymore during air raids. Besides, 99% of the crimes were being committed by foreign workers. Horthy remarked that also Hungary was taking energetic measures against these things, but that curiously the crimes still had not receded in Hungary. The Führer replied that one had to be very careful lest the asocial elements grow to the point where they could smother the government, as had happened in the [First] World War, and then nothing could be done anymore. At that time the criminal rabble had been treated with too much leniency so that the good elements were being killed at the front line while the bad ones were preserved until they gradually became preponderant.

The Führer then described German rationing which was being carried out with complete orderliness. There was no black market in Germany and the peasants were willingly delivering their assigned quotas. Produce which was made available to the government in excess of these quotas was purchased by government offices at considerably higher prices

—as much as double—so that also peasants could have the opportunity to make some money. Horthy remarked that these problems were very difficult for Hungary. Until now he had been unable to master the black market. The Führer replied that the Jews were at fault. They had regarded hoarding and profiteering as one of their main activities also during the [First] World War, just as in England at this time convictions for violations of rationing ordinances and the like involved mainly Jews. To Horthy's question what he should do with the Jews now that he had removed pretty much all of their sources of livelihood—he could not after all kill them—the Reich Foreign Minister replied that the Jews either had to be annihilated or brought into concentration camps. There was no other possibility. Upon Horthy's remark that Germany had it easier in this respect, since it had not possessed so many Jews, the Führer quoted statistics which showed that certain professions had been Judaized to an extraordinary degree. Horthy replied that he had certainly not known that.

In this connection, the Führer mentioned Nuremberg which had not tolerated Jews for 400 years, while Fürth accepted them. The consequence was that Nuremberg flourished and Fürth declined. The Jews weren't even worth anything as organizers. Contrary to fears which he (the Führer) had repeatedly heard in Germany, everything was functioning as before without the Jews. Wherever Jews had been left to their own devices, as for example in Poland, there was cruel misery and demoralization. They happened to be pure parasites. These conditions had been cleared up completely in Poland. If the Jews did not want to work there, they were being shot. If they couldn't work, they had to perish. They had to be treated like tuberculosis germs which could infect a healthy body. That was not cruel if one remembered how even innocent creatures like hares and deer were being killed in order to prevent damage. Why should these beasts who wanted to bring us Bolshevism be spared more? Nations which could not defend themselves against the Jews perished. One of the most famous examples was the downfall of a people who once were so proud, the Persians, and who now had to continue their miserable existence as Armenians. . . .

41. Postcards from Waldsee

On March 19, 1944, German troops entered Hungary, and almost immediately the "final solution" was set into motion. An SS commando headed by Eichmann himself coordinated and supervised the concentration process. On May 15, 1944, after less than two months of intensive preparation, the deportations began. By mid-July only the Jews of Budapest and the Jewish labor companies in the Hungarian army remained; some 440,-000 had been shipped out and 400,000 of them were dead in Auschwitz.

When the Hungarian operation was launched, the Germans could no longer count on secrecy. Europe was filled with the silence of the millions who had already disappeared. Occasionally there were stories, signals, and reports of gas. The rumor flow was picked up by Jewish rescue organizations in neutral countries, Jewish councils in the ghettos, and ordinary victims in their homes.

From about the middle of 1942, a Jewish rescue committee in Bratislava was accurately charting the destinations of transports. In September 1943 it identified the character of all the functioning death camps in a letter to Switzerland. The Bratislava committee, which was headed by Rabbi Weissmandel and Gisi Fleischmann, was also in touch with Jewish leaders in Hungary, but here the news was shut off. The Hungarian Jewish Council could not cope with the subject of Auschwitz. What transpired in the council at the onset of the deportations is recounted by one of its members, [Philipp von] Freudiger, in testimony at the Eichmann trial. Parenthetically it may be pointed out that the disbelief in Budapest was duplicated in many small towns. See, for instance, Elie Wiesel's description of Sighet in his *Night* (New York: Hill and Wang, 1960).

[Yad Vashem document file M20.]

Report by Gisi Fleischmann (Bratislava) received by Dr. Adolf Silberschein in Geneva, September 5, 1943 [Excerpt]

We know today that Sobibor, Malkyne-Treblinki, Belzec, and Auschwitz are annihilation camps. In the camps themselves small work parties are being maintained to create the impression that they are [ordinary] camps.

[Testimony by Pinchas (Philipp von) Freudiger, uncorrected English transcript of the Eichmann trial (mimeographed), May 25, 1961, session 52, pp. L1-01.]

Mr. Bach: Now, Mr. Freudiger, when actually was it clear to you that these transports went to Auschwitz?
A. That the people were being sent to Auschwitz, in fact, I perhaps knew even before the trains arrived at Auschwitz because I received a letter from Rabbi Weissmandel. A few days before the 15th of May on the 10th or 11th, I received a letter wherein he wrote that to our regret and sorrow this is the lot and fate decided upon for those Jews. But this really first concerned the Jews from the provinces and he wrote to me saying that there were negotiations between the railway authorities, the Hungarian railway authorities and the Slovakian authorities regarding the transfer of 300,000 Jews through Slovakia. Three hundred thousand is the figure which keeps cropping-up all the time; this was the number of the Jewish population.

I read this letter and told my colleagues in the Central Committee about the contents of this letter. They did not believe; they said that it was impossible: "How can they send the Jews from Hungary, outside Hungary?" I argued and said—
Q. With whom did you speak about this?

A. —"Here, I have a letter from Rabbi Weissmandel," but they refused to believe.

Q. With whom did you speak?

A. I kept on saying that we must try to verify if there is truth in that letter. This was some four days before the deportations began. Dr. Stocki (?) who had personal relations with a Hungarian politician who was the Finance Minister of the Hungarian Cabinet, went to see him privately—formally, Jews were not received any more—and he said, the Minister of Finance, that this was impossible. There was no Cabinet Meeting and no decision was ever taken, and would *never* be taken by the Hungarian Government that Hungarians be deported across the border. He returned on the same day and I had to keep quiet because the Hungarian Government assured us that there would be no deportation; but on the following morning, we had contact with the railway authorities, because we were supplying clothes to the railway authorities and through those connections, I learnt that there was a deportation of Jews through the Bratislava station.

Then, there was again a meeting of the Jewish Council and I reported what I had heard. There was a Department for Jewish Affairs in the Ministry of the Interior; we tried to contact this department—the General Director's secretary said that they would not be able to speak to him because he was, at that moment, at a meeting being held with the railway authorities. This was exactly one day before the deportations on the 14th May and the deportations began on the 15th.

Q. Mr. Freudiger, when did you first learn details about the fate of the Jews who were sent to Auschwitz? About what was happening to them there?

A. The S.S. officers with Krumey repeatedly promised that they were being sent to work in Germany. Any question we posed—he had an excuse. We asked: "how can they send the old and the children, an entire family—we could understand that in Kistarcsa—this is understandable, but if they are all sent"—the answer was: that this was the German system, to send whole families, because "then the work is more productive; there is no longing for a man's family." We negotiated for a week or a fortnight. We already knew that they were being deported to Auschwitz, because Weissmandel wrote describing the route which led to Auschwitz.

Mr Bach: Mr Freudiger, before we get to what Krumey told you, I want to ask you when you first learned from a Jewish source what was happening to the Jews in Auschwitz.

Judge Halevi: Did you mean the Hungarian Jews or in general?

Mr Bach: My question was about Hungary.

Witness Freudiger: I was always in correspondence with Rabbi Weissmandel—I got a letter nearly every week. This was at the end of May or early in June. . . . Once I received a letter with a report about Auschwitz—I believe the Court already heard about this report: the Slovaks who escaped . . . I received the mail which had been brought by the Slovakian courier. I had quite a number of letters from various people, and from Rabbi Weissmandel. I started to read the report, I kept on reading, studying it; and I asked myself: "Is this really possible, is it credible?" I refused to believe it—it was a letter about the extermination . . . I see before me the report. It says that up to now 1,000,450 Jews have been exterminated in Poland and other countries, and a further 300,000. . . . And other figures —more numbers. . . . The last sentence says: "Now they are preparing to start with the Jews of Hungary."

Q. Mr Freudiger, you told us about conversations you had with Krumey, about the fate of the Jews taken out of Hungary. Would you tell the Court something about certain postcards which reached Hungarian Jews at that time from the deportees?

A. Yes. Until this report had been received, we knew they were sent to Auschwitz but we did not know what Auschwitz meant. Krumey always said they were being sent to work. After a fortnight, when the first transports had already been sent—sometimes trains left every day—we received through our liaison officers, who used to go to Schwannenberg almost every day (we had liaison officers to do the routine work), quite a number of postcards written by deported Jews. The postcards were dated, and bore the message: "We are working here. Regards . . ."—or: "We feel well; we are working. Regards to. . . ." Nearly all the postcards were in the same style.

Q. What was always the address of the sender—Walze [Wald-see] . . . ?

A. At the top of the postcard there was written 'Walze' and a date—there was no address.

Q. Did you try to establish where this Walze was?

A. I went to Krumey after receiving the postcards and asked him where Walze was. He said in the centre of Germany—Thüringen. We searched the map but could not find it, and thought maybe this was such a small place; and the deception continued for three or four weeks, until they realised that it was not worthwhile any longer.

Presiding Judge: Was there a stamp on the postcards?

Witness Freudiger: No, they were not stamped. They said that the Command brought the mail by special bag. Two weeks later I came across a postcard with an erasure. (The postcards were written in pencil.) The word 'Walze' had been rubbed out. As a textile manufacturer I always kept a magnifying glass handy on my desk, and I noticed that the letters "—itz" were visible on the postcard: someone, instead of writing "Walze," had written "Auschwitz," and then erased it—the last letters, "itz," were visible. I took the postcard to Krumey and said: "Our people are in Auschwitz, not in Walze." He said: "How can you say such a thing?" I gave him the postcard and the magnifying glass and said: "Please take a look." He examined it and said: "Freudiger, I know you are a sensible man—you should not be too observant." Then the postcards stopped coming—in fact, there were no people to write those postcards any more.

Mr Bach: Was it clear to you that these postcards were actually written in handwriting which could be identified by the relatives?

Witness Freudiger: Yes, yes—of course.

Mr. Bach: Now, Mr. Freudiger, this report—this Auschwitz report which you received through Rabbi Weissmandel. Did you bring the contents of this document to the attention . . .

Presiding Judge: Was it through Rabbi Weissmandel or drafted by him?

Mr. Bach: Rabbi Weissmandel merely transmitted a report composed by these two refugees from Auschwitz.

Mr. Freudiger, did you bring this to the attention of the Judenrat people?

Witness Freudiger: Yes. On the following morning, I took the report not only to the Judenrat, the Jewish Committee, because our hands were quite tied. We had people working for us near the Judenrat and reported to them all I learned from this report. We decided to make the report known. We sent the report to the Nuntius, to other men of the clergy, and up to Horthy.

Q. Did you sent it abroad too, and if so, to which countries?

A. Yes. We sent the report to Switzerland. Moshe Krauss sent the report to Switzerland.

Presiding Judge: When was that? When did you distribute the report?

Witness Freudiger: This was in June.

Mr. Bach: Mr. Freudiger, in this period, do you know anything about attempts to escape Hungary in that period, flee from Hungary illegally?

A. Yes. At first, and especially in Budapest, we had no connections with the ghettos in the provinces because we were not permitted to travel. We had no telephone. But there were always indirect contacts.

There were people who started, individuals who started to escape. First the refugees from Poland and Slovakia, who were in Hungary. Some of them returned to Slovakia, and the Polish refugees started fleeing to Rumania, in spite of the fact that a day or two after Hungary was conquered, there was a law promulgated in Rumania that he who enters Rumania illegally will be sentenced to death.

Q. Mr. Freudiger, do you know anything about the attitude of the S.S. Sonderkommando toward such attempts at escaping?

A. Yes. Wherever they could, they caught the people, punished them, and they were driven back.

Q. Do you know, perhaps, of a specific incident which happened in this connection?

A. Yes. This was strange. I read that it was as though the S.S. men enabled people to escape and instructed the frontier po-

lice to close their eyes when Jews escaped.
Presiding Judge and *Mr. Bach:* Who said that?
Witness Freudiger: I read it in *Life.*
Mr. Bach: I merely asked you, what did you yourself know about this?
A. In fact, I know that a family, related to my family, Dr. Solomon Stern's family and Joseph Stern's family, a group of eleven people, and the family of Rabbi Cselevine (phon.) here in Jerusalem—they wanted to escape to Rumania. They were caught and taken to S.S. headquarters. On the following day, they were transported—there were no deportations at the time from Budapest—they were not punished, not imprisoned, but they were sent to a place where deportations took place, and they were deported together with the Jews of Komoran. I had a postcard from those people, which they threw out of the train. Someone picked up the postcard. There was my address and the postcard was delivered. But until I received the postcard and a picture of the children—the children were already ashes.
Q. Could you identify the postcard?
A. He writes here that they are being taken to Komoran.
Q. Now the children in this picture—are these the children of that same family?
A. There were two children—more—there were four children in all.
Q. And this is the very postcard which was thrown from the train window then?
A. Yes.
Q. Who wrote these letters here on top?
A. One of the people who wrote the postcard.
Mr. Bach: I should like to present this postcard in evidence.
Presiding Judge: Can you read what it says here on the card?
Witness Freudiger: Yes, I can, of course.
   "We are on the train. We are crossing through Budapest to Komoran."
Presiding Judge: Where is Komoran?
Witness Freudiger: Komoran?
Presiding Judge: This place—where is it?

Witness Freudiger: This is some 60 or 70 kilometers west of Budapest.

"We are now traveling through Budapest to Komoran. S.O.S."

And then signatures: "Mrs. Strassberg, Mrs. J. Stern, Mrs. Solomon Stern, and children."

Presiding Judge: Those were acquaintances of yours?

Witness Freudiger: Yes. My personal friends.

Presiding Judge: And how did you say the postcard got to you?

Witness Freudiger: My address is on this postcard, and someone delivered the card to my house. I found it in my home. The date is June 15, and I received it a week later.

Presiding Judge: In other words, you do not know how it reached that man who brought it to you.

Witness Freudiger: No, no. I don't know if it was handed to someone or if someone just found it, or maybe a railway officer. There were some righteous people at the time.

Mr. Bach: Were these people captured near the border or before they got to the border?

Witness Freudiger: I believe, that during their escape. . . .

(Interpreter's comment: Somebody is screaming in Hungarian from the audience, apparently at the witness but it is not clear what he is saying. It is all in Hungarian. He is being hustled out by policemen. The Presiding Judge asks for quiet in the Courtroom. There is quite a commotion in the audience. The Presiding Judge says that if there is no quiet in the Courtroom he might stop and interrupt the session.)

Presiding Judge: I wish to have quiet in the Courtroom. This is the last time I ask for this. You will have a chance later to discuss this incident among yourselves.

Mr. Bach: Later perhaps if we submit this postcard, maybe the witness can have it back later.

Presiding Judge: Yes, certainly you may make a photostatic copy and the witness can have it back.

(Interpreter's comment: Another person in the audience is screaming in Yiddish now.)

Presiding Judge: Take the man out and I am stopping the session.

(Interpreter's comment: The Court has ordered a recess in the meeting because there were two of these incidents where people screamed from the audience.)

42. A Ransom Attempt

A few days after the beginning of the Hungarian deportations, a Jewish delegate from Budapest arrived in Istanbul, Turkey, with a Gestapo offer to release the remaining one million Jews under German control in return for ten thousand trucks. The emissary, Joel Brand, was a member of the Jewish rescue committee in Hungary, and as further authorization he carried a letter signed on May 16, 1944, by Court Councillor Stern, chairman of the Jewish Council, and Philipp von Freudiger.

Brand had been talking to Eichmann in Budapest, and the proposal he was transmitting to the Allies had been considered by some of the highest strata in the SS and Foreign Office in Berlin. Under the terms of the offer, the Germans were prepared to free the first 100,-000 Jews for a thousand trucks, another 100,000 for the next thousand, and so on. Meanwhile, the killings would continue.

Both Germans and Jews were waiting for a reply. The Germans promised to use the vehicles only on the eastern front, and they were actually thinking of motorizing the Eighth SS-Cavalry Division *Florian Geyer* and the Twenty-second SS-Volunteer Cavalry Division *Maria Theresia*, both assigned to Hungary. The Jewish rescue committee was anxious for some move or sign of Allied acceptance which would give pause to the Germans or at least slow them down. The British, the first Allied power to receive word of the ransom attempt, summarized their attitude in a memorandum of June 5,

1944, to the United States. The Germans, in the mean-
time, went on with their killings. For Brand's own
story, see Alex Weisberg, *Desperate Mission* (New York:
Criterion Books, 1958). American policy is discussed by
Arthur D. Morse, *While Six Million Died* (New York:
Random House, 1967), and by Henry L. Feingold, *The
Politics of Rescue* (New Brunswick: Rutgers University
Press, 1970).

[Department of State, *Foreign Relations of the United States*, 1944, I, 1056–1058.
Footnotes have been renumbered.]

The British Embassy to the Department of State
AIDE-MEMOIRE

Attached to this *Aide-Mémoire* is the text of a telegram received by the Foreign Office from the High Commissioner,
Jerusalem.[1] His Majesty's Ambassador is instructed to inform
the United States Government of the proposal set out in that
telegram and to put before them the reactions of His Majesty's
Government which are as follows:

(*a*) Assuming suggestion was put forward by Gestapo in
form conveyed to us, then it seems to be sheer case of blackmail or political warfare. Implied suggestion that we should
accept responsibility for maintenance of additional million
persons is equivalent to asking the Allies to suspend essential
military operations.

(*b*) We could not bargain over any scheme with Gestapo and
agree to trade lives against military and economic concessions
calculated to stave off Germany's defeat. Demand that we
should in effect raise blockade is totally inadvisable [*unaccept-
able*]; to give Germany 10,000 lorries would bring important
access of military strength to the enemy, and German stipula-
tion of Spain and Portugal as sole exodus seems clearly designed to embarrass Allied military operations.

(*c*) Once committed to this kind of blackmail coupled with

[1]Copy of cipher telegram 683, not printed; it reported proposal described
in telegram 950, May 25, 4 p.m., from Ankara, p. 1050.

raising of blockade, which seems inseparably connected with it, the Allies would be driven to even further lengths.

(*d*) It would appear that selection of persons, if exchange were agreed, is to be in Hitler's hands. On this we think should be borne in mind that immense numbers of Allies are held by the Germans under terrible conditions and that to arrange any exchange on a basis to be determined by Hitler, leaving Allied internees and prisoners in German hands, would lay Governments open to extremely serious protest.

(*e*) While however refusing to deal with this scheme and channels through which it has come, we realize importance of not opposing a mere negation to any genuine proposals involving rescue of any Jews and other victims which merit serious consideration by Allied Governments. Whole record of United States Government and His Majesty's Government over refugees is a proof of their active sympathy with victims of Nazi terror. Accordingly if the German Government were willing to release Jews in position of extreme distress or danger, His Majesty's Government and United States Government would be willing to examine the possibilities of moving to and accommodating in Spain and Portugal such persons as could be handled without prejudice to vital military operations.[2]

2. His Majesty's Government are informing Dr. Weizmann[3] in strictest confidence of this proposal, but are making no comment beyond saying that they are in touch with the United States Government. It is presumed that the latter will similarly inform Dr. Goldmann.[4] His Majesty's Government are anxious to learn at the earliest opportunity the views of the United States Government on what action, if any, should be taken. In particular they would be glad to know whether the United States Government would agree to instruct their Am-

[2]The Assistant Secretary of War (McCloy) stated in a letter of June 10 to the Under Secretary of State: "I think that you can take it that the War Department's views would coincide with subparagraph *e* of the *aide-mémoire* (5 June) sent you by the British Embassy." (840.48 Refugees/6–1044)

[3]Chaim Weizmann, President of the World Zionist Organization; President of Zionist Federation of Great Britain and Ireland.

[4]Nahum Goldmann of the Jewish Agency for Palestine.

bassador at Ankara, if he is approached by the Jewish Agency, to associate himself in a reply on the lines set forth above. His Majesty's Government would suggest that Dr. Shertok[5] should be told that we cannot sanction him or any other Allied citizen having any dealings with the Gestapo, but that we would agree to his conveying the substance of our observations to his Zionist friend from Hungary. This would show that, although we cannot enter into the monstrous bargain now proposed by the Gestapo, we are yet far from indifferent to the sufferings of the Jews and have not shut the door to any serious suggestions which may be made and which are compatible with the successful prosecution of the war.

3. His Majesty's Ambassador at Ankara has been instructed to communicate the foregoing information in strictest confidence to his United States colleague, informing him that it has been transmitted to Washington in order that the reaction of His Majesty's Government may be coordinated with that of the United States Government. His Majesty's Ambassador has been instructed to return no definite reply to Dr. Shertok until the essential common line of action has been established between the two Governments.

4. The Department of State may be interested to know that, on being informed of the Gestapo's proposal, Dr. Weizmann merely observed that it looked like one more German attempt to embarrass the United States and United Kingdom Governments. He said, however, that he would like to reflect on the affair and receive news of any developments.

WASHINGTON, 5 JUNE, 1944.

43. The Camps

German concentration camps and their satellites numbered in the hundreds. Six were used in the systematic

---

[5]Moshe Shertok of the Jewish Agency for Palestine at Cairo.

killing of Jews. They were set up, in the wake of the decision to annihilate European Jewry, on occupied Polish soil. More than half of all the deaths occurred in these enclosures. The summary table in this section lists the camps with basic facts about each; the numbers of the dead are approximate.

The camp commanders in the table are listed in chronological succession. In the case of Auschwitz, a reorganization in November 1943 resulted in the establishment of a "Senior Garrison Officer" and three subordinate camp commanders:

Commander, Auschwitz I
(base camp)
Commander, Auschwitz II
(Birkenau—gas chambers)
Commander, Auschwitz III
(outlying sites—industrial)

SS-Lieutenant Colonel Rudolf Höss was the first Auschwitz commander, SS-Lieutenant Colonel Arthur Liebehenschel the first Senior Garrison Officer and commander of Auschwitz I. In May 1944, Liebehenschel moved to Lublin and was replaced in his capacity as Senior Garrison Officer by Höss, while Auschwitz I was taken over by SS-Captain Richard Bär. Höss was thus involved with Auschwitz as its founder and again during the high tide of the gassings in mid-1944. Eichmann, who had met him several times, said of him in 1961: "This was an unhappy man, an unfortunate man. . . . I pitied him and I commiserated with him." (His testimony at the Eichmann trial, English transcript, session 95, Q1, U1.)

The Treblinka-Belzec-Sobibor complex in the General Government was coordinated from August 1, 1942, by [SS-Major] Christian Wirth. He was in his upper fifties (born 1885), with experience as a former criminal police councillor in Stuttgart, but his SS promotion to major had not been confirmed when he was killed by partisans in Trieste in 1944. Several of the commanders of the individual General Government camps were also low-ranking, over-age officers. Dr. Irmfried Eberl, first Treblinka commander, was an Innsbruck physician; he is reported to be deceased. SS-First Lieutenant Franz Stangl, another Austrian (second Sobibor and third Treblinka commander), had served temporarily with the Order Police and appears to have had difficulty establishing his rank and status in the SS Personnel Main Office. After the war he spent sixteen stable years in Brazil where he was employed in the Volkswagen plant at Sao Paulo before he was extradited to West Germany in 1967. SS-Captain Gottlieb Hering (born 1887, second Belzec commander) was a disciplinary case, tried and exonerated before an SS court in 1944. He too is believed dead. The personnel records, some of them incomplete, one of them semi-charred, are kept at the Berlin Document Center under U.S. control.

The camps were built over a period of many months, and the installation of cables, lines, chambers, and barracks was an almost continuous process, extending, especially in the case of Auschwitz, into the gassing phase. The two documents below are accounts of construction in Treblinka and Auschwitz. The first was written by Eberl to the German commissioner in charge of the Warsaw ghetto (Heinz Auerswald). The fact that the request was sent to the ghetto commissioner suggests that it was to be filled as a matter of Jewish self-financing from the resources of the community soon to be gassed in the camp. The second item is part of a correspondence within Auschwitz itself, between the SS construction office there and a company owned and operated by the SS, the German Equipment Works (Deutsche Ausrüstungswerke—DAW). The corpse cellar referred to in the letter is a gas chamber, and the term crematory is a designation of the combination unit which housed the chamber and cremation facilities.

Death Camp Commanders and Operations

	Supervising Authority	Commanders		Principal Time Spans of Systematic Killings	Number of Killed
Auschwitz	SS Economic-Administrative Main Office	Höss Liebehenschel Höss	Auschwitz I Auschwitz II Auschwitz III	Summer 1942–November 1944	over 1,000,000
			Liebehenschel Bär Hartjenstein Schwartz		
Lublin	SS Economic-Administrative Main Office	Opitz Koch Koegel Florstedt Weiss Liebehenschel		Late 1942: gassings in single chamber. November 1943: mass shootings	tens of thousands
Treblinka	Higher SS and Police Leader, General Government	Eberl Schemmerl Stangl Franz		July 1942–October 1943	over 700,000

Belzec	Higher SS and Police Leader, General Government	Wirth Hering	March–May 1942 July–November 1942	about 600,000
Sobibor	Higher SS and Police Leader, General Government	Thomalla Stangl Reichleitner	April 1942– October 1943	about 250,000
Kulmhof	Higher SS and Police Leader, Wartheland	Bothmann	December 1941– September 1942; late 1944	over 100,000

[Facsimile in: Jüdisches Historisches Institut Warschau, *Faschimus-Getto-Massenmord* (Berlin: Rütten & Loening, 2nd ed., 1961), p. 304.]

Warsaw, June 26, 1942
[Office of] SS and Police Leader/Palais Brühl
SS-2d Lieutenant Dr. Eberl
Warsaw
to
Commissar for the Jewish District [Warsaw ghetto]

Subject: Labor camp Treblinka

For the completion of the labor camp Treblinka the following items are still needed urgently:
120 rolls of wall paper (samples should be shown beforehand)
1000 nails for rails on field railway track
200 screws for field railway (⅜ inch thick, 40 millimeters long)
4 pair (metal) bands with support hooks (doorhinges) 40 centimeters long
1 starter button
1 ignition switch
5 meters ignition cable
5 meters starter cable
1 battery 12 volts/100–120 amperes
1 file (three-edged) to sharpen saws
5 2-meter measuring sticks
1 saw set
5 Zimmermann pencils
I would be grateful for rapid delivery, since the above-mentioned items are needed urgently.

Heil Hitler!
[signature]

[Nuremberg document NO-4465.]

Central Construction Office, Auschwitz, to German Equipment Works, Auschwitz, March 31, 1943

Your letter of March 24, 1943
[Excerpt]
In reply to the above letter, the three airtight towers are to
be built in accordance with the order of January 18, 1943, for
Bw 30b and 3c, in the same dimensions and in the same man-
ner as the towers already delivered.

We take this occasion to refer to another order of March 6,
1943, for the delivery of a gas door 100/192 for corpse cellar
I of crematory III, Bw 30a, which is to be built in the manner
and according to the same measure as the cellar door of the
opposite crematory II, with peep hole of double 8 millimeter
glass encased in rubber. This order is to be viewed as especially urgent. . . .

44. Behind the Fence

Belzec is seldom mentioned in literature, although it
was, after Auschwitz and Treblinka, the most deadly
site in Europe. Only one of the inmates is known to
have survived; hundreds of thousands did not live to
describe the camp. On the other hand, Belzec's location
astride a traveled railway line afforded quite a few
glimpses from passenger train windows and produced
a good deal of local talk. A meticulous German observer
recorded some of these impressions in his diary.

[Institut für Zeitgeschichte, Munich, document ED 81.]

OBSERVATIONS ABOUT THE "RESETTLEMENT OF JEWS IN THE
GENERAL GOVERNMENT"

1. Notes by a German noncommissioned officer [Wilhelm
Cornides] *of August 31, 1942*

Rawa Ruska (Galicia) German House
August 31, 1942 2:30 P.M.

At 10 minutes past noon I saw a transport train run into the station. On the roof and running boards sat guards with rifles. One could see from a distance that the cars were jammed full of people. I turned and walked along the whole train: it consisted of 38 cattle cars and one passenger car. In each of the cars there were at least 60 Jews (in the case of enlisted men's or prisoner transports these wagons would hold 40 men; however, the benches had been removed and one could see that those who were locked in here had to stand pressed together). Some of the doors were opened a crack, the windows crisscrossed with barbed wire. Among the locked-in people there were a few men and most of those were old; everything else was women, girls, and children. Many children crowded at the windows and the narrow door openings. The youngest were surely not more than two years old. As soon as the train halted, the Jews attempted to pass out bottles in order to get water. The train, however, was surrounded by SS guards, so that no one could come near. At that moment a train arrived from the direction of Jaroslav; the travelers streamed toward the exit without bothering about the transport. A few Jews who were busy loading a car for the Armed Forces waved their caps to the locked-in people. I talked to a policeman on duty at the railway station. Upon my question as to where the Jews actually came from, he answered: "Those are probably the last ones from Lvov. That has been going on now for 5 weeks uninterruptedly. In Jaroslav they let remain only 8, no one knows why." I asked: "How far are they going?" Then he said: "To Belzec." "And then?" "Poison." I asked: "Gas?" He shrugged his shoulders. Then he said only: "At the beginning they always shot them, I believe."

Here in the German House I just talked with two soldiers from front-line prisoner-of-war camp 325. They said that these transports had lately passed through every day, mostly at night. Yesterday a 70-car one is supposed to have gone through.

In the train from Rawa Ruska to Cholm, 5:30 P.M.

When we boarded at 4:40 P.M. an empty transport had just arrived. I walked along the train twice and counted 56 cars. On the doors had been written in chalk: 60, 70, once 90, occasionally 40—obviously the number of Jews that were carried inside. In my compartment I spoke with a railway policeman's wife who is currently visiting her husband here. She says these transports are now passing through daily, sometimes also with German Jews. Yesterday 6 children's bodies were found along the track. The woman thinks that the Jews themselves had killed these children—but they must have succumbed during the trip. The railway policeman who comes along as train escort joined us in our compartment. He confirmed the woman's statements about the children's bodies which were found along the track yesterday. I asked: "Do the Jews know then what is happening with them?" The woman answered: "Those who come from far won't know anything, but here in the vicinity they know already. They attempt to run away then, if they notice that someone is coming for them. So, for example, most recently in Cholm where 3 were shot on the way through the city." "In the railway documents these trains run under the name of resettlement transports," remarked the railway policeman. Then he said that after Heydrich ["Protector" of Bohemia-Moravia] was murdered, several transports with Czechs passed through. Camp Belzec is supposed to be located right on the railway line and the woman promised to show it to me when we pass it.

5:40 P.M.

Short stop. Opposite us another transport. I talk to the policemen who ride on the passenger car in front. I ask: "Going back home to the Reich?" Grinning one of them says: "You know where we come from, don't you? Well, for us the work does not cease." Then the transport train continued—the cars were empty and swept clean; there were 35. In all probability that was the train I saw at 1 P.M. on the station in Rawa Ruska.

6:20 P.M.

We passed camp Belzec. Before then, we traveled for some time through a tall pine forest. When the woman called, "Now it comes," one could see a high hedge of fir trees. A strong sweetish odor could be made out distinctly. "But they are stinking already," says the woman. "Oh nonsense, that is only the gas," the railway policeman said laughing. Meanwhile— we had gone on about 200 yards—the sweetish odor was transformed into a strong smell of something burning. "That is from the crematory," says the policeman. A short distance farther the fence stopped. In front of it, one could see a guard house with an SS post. A double track led into the camp. One track branched off from the main line, the other ran over a turntable from the camp to a row of sheds about 250 yards away. A freight car happened to stand on the table. Several Jews were busy turning the disk. SS guards, rifle under the arm, stood by. One of the sheds was open; one could distinctly see that it was filled with bundles of clothes to the ceiling. As we went on, I looked back one more time. The fence was too high to see anything at all. The woman says that sometimes, while going by, one can see smoke rising from the camp, but I could notice nothing of the sort. My estimate is that the camp measures about 800 by 400 yards.

2. *Additional Eyewitness Reports*

a) A railway policeman at the switch yards in Rzeszow told me the following on August 30, 1942. "In Rzeszow a marble plaque with golden letters will be erected on September 1, because then the city will be free of Jews. The transports with the Jews pass almost daily through the switch yards, are dispatched immediately on their way, and return swept clean, most often in the same evening. In [from] Jaroslav 6000 Jews were recently killed in one day."

b) An engineer told the following in the evening of August 30, 1942 in the German House in Rawa Ruska: "Jews, who for the most part have now been transported away, were employed next to Poles and prisoners-of-war in the work on the drill field which is being built here. The productivity of these construction crews (among them also women) was on the average 30% of what would have been achieved by German workers. To be sure, these people received from us only bread—the rest they had to provide themselves. In Lvov recently I have accidentally seen a loading of such a transport. The cars stood at the front of a slope. How these people were driven down by the SS, sometimes with sticks and horsewhips, and how they were pushed into the cars, that was a sight I won't forget for the rest of my life."

As he told this story the man had tears in his eyes. He was about 26 and wore the party emblem. A Sudeten German peasant official, who sat at the same table, remarked on that: "Recently a drunken SS man sat in our canteen and he was bawling like a child. He said that he was on duty in Belzec and if that was going to go on for another 14 days he will kill himself because he can't stand it anymore."

c) A policeman told the following in the beer hall in Cholm on September 1, 1942: "The policemen who escort the Jewish trains are not allowed in the camp. The only ones who get in are the SS and the Ukrainian Special Service (a police formation of Ukrainian volunteers). But these people are doing a good business over there. Recently a Ukrainian visited us, and he had a whole stack of money in notes, and watches and gold and all kinds of things. They find all of that when they put together the clothing and load it." Upon the question as to how these Jews were actually being killed, the policeman answered: "They are told that they must get rid of their lice, and then they must take off their clothes, and then they come into a room, where first off they get a hot blast of air which is already mixed with a small dose of gas. That is enough to make them unconscious. The rest comes after. And then they are burnt immediately."

In answer to the question why this whole action is being undertaken in the first place, the policeman said: "Up to now the Jews have been employed as auxiliaries everywhere by the SS, the Armed Forces, and so on. Naturally they snapped up quite a bit of information and they pass on everything to the

Russians. That's why they must go. And then they are also
responsible here for the entire black market and driving up
prices. When the Jews are gone, one will be able to put into
effect reasonable prices again."

Note: Rawa Ruska is located about 50 miles northwest of
Lvov. Belzec is located on the Lvov-Cholm railway line, about
25 miles northwest of Rawa Ruska.

45. Selection

On the railway platform of Auschwitz, some of the new
deportees who looked as if they might be capable of
work were separated from the victims who were to be
gassed immediately. This procedure was known as selection. Several survivors have described those first
hours in the camp—the growing awareness of what
Auschwitz meant, the gradual realization of what selection signified. The following is such a description by a
physician. He was born in Vienna in 1905, was as-
sociated with the Neuropsychiatric Clinic of the University of Vienna from 1930 to 1938, and headed the
Neurological Department of the Viennese Rothschild
Hospital from 1940 to 1942. He does not say when or
from where he was deported to Auschwitz, but he deals
broadly with three phases of an inmate's life: shock on
arrival, apathy during incarceration, a sense of unreal-
ity following liberation. The account was originally
written in German shortly after the war. This excerpt,
on the initial phase of the author's stay in Auschwitz,
is from the printed English translation.

[Viktor Emil Frankl, *From Death Camp to Existentialism* (Boston: Beacon Press, 1949), pp. 6–12.]

When one examines the vast amount of material which has been amassed as the result of many prisoners' observations and experiences, three phases of the inmate's mental reactions to camp life become apparent: the period following his admission; the period when he is well entrenched in camp routine; and the period following his release and liberation.

The symptom that characterizes the first phase is shock. Under certain conditions shock may even precede the prisoner's formal admission to the camp. I shall give as an example the circumstances of my own admission.

Fifteen hundred persons had been traveling by train for several days and nights: there were eighty people in each coach. All had to lie on top of their luggage, the few remnants of their personal possessions. The carriages were so full that only the top parts of the windows were free to let in the grey of dawn. Everyone expected the train to head for some munitions factory, in which we would be employed as forced labor. We did not know whether we were still in Silesia or already in Poland. The engine's whistle had an uncanny sound, like a cry for help sent out in commiseration for the unhappy load which it was destined to lead into perdition. Then the train shunted, obviously nearing a main station. Suddenly a cry broke from the ranks of the anxious passengers, "There is a sign, Auschwitz!" Everyone's heart missed a beat at that moment. Auschwitz—the very name stood for all that was horrible: gas chambers, crematoriums, massacres. Slowly, almost hesitatingly, the train moved on as if it wanted to spare its passengers the dreadful realization as long as possible: Auschwitz!

With the progressive dawn, the outlines of an immense camp became visible: long stretches of several rows of barbed wire fences; watch towers; search lights; and long columns of ragged human figures, grey in the greyness of dawn, trekking along the straight desolate roads, to what destination we did not know. There were isolated shouts and whistles of command. We did not know their meaning. My imagination led me to see gallows with people dangling on them. I was horrified, but this was just as well, because step by step we had to become accustomed to a terrible and immense horror.

Eventually we moved into the station. The initial silence was interrupted by shouted commands. We were to hear those rough, shrill tones from then on, over and over again in all the camps. Their sound was almost like the last cry of a victim, and yet there was a difference. It had a rasping hoarseness, as if it came from the throat of a man who had to keep shouting like that, a man who was being murdered again and again. The carriage doors were flung open and a small detachment of prisoners stormed inside. They wore striped uniforms, their heads were shaved, but they looked well fed. They spoke in every possible European tongue, and all with a certain amount of humor, which sounded grotesque under the circumstances. Like a drowning man clutching a straw, my inborn optimism (which has often controlled my feelings even in the most desperate situations) clung to this thought: These prisoners look quite well, they seem to be in good spirits and even laugh. Who knows? I might manage to share their favorable position.

In psychiatry there is a certain condition knows as "delusion of reprieve." The condemned man, immediately before his execution, gets the illusion that he might be reprieved at the very last minute. We, too, clung to shreds of hope and believed to the last moment that it would not be so bad. Just the sight of the red cheeks and round faces of those prisoners was a great encouragement. Little did we know then that they formed a specially chosen elite, who for years had been the receiving squad for new transports as they rolled into the station day after day. They took charge of the new arrivals and their luggage, including scarce items and smuggled jewelry. Auschwitz must have been a strange spot in this Europe of the last years of the war. There must have been unique treasures of gold and silver, platinum and diamonds, not only in the huge storehouses but also in the hands of the SS.

Fifteen hundred captives were cooped up in a shed built to accommodate probably two hundred at the most. We were cold and hungry and there was not enough room for everyone to squat on the bare ground, let alone to lie down. One five-ounce piece of bread was our only food in four days. Yet I heard the senior prisoners in charge of the shed bargain with one member of the receiving party about a tie-pin made of platinum and diamonds. Most of the profits would eventually be traded for liquor—schnapps. I do not remember any more just how many thousands of marks were needed to purchase the quantity of schnapps required for a "gay evening," but I do know that those long-term prisoners needed schnapps. Under such conditions, who could blame them for trying to dope themselves? There was another group of prisoners who got liquor supplied in almost unlimited quantities by the SS: these were the men who were employed in the gas chambers and crematoriums, and who knew very well that one day they would be relieved by a new shift of men, and that they would have to leave their enforced role of executioner and become victims themselves.

Nearly everyone in our transport lived under the illusion that he would be reprieved, that everything would yet be well. We did not realize the meaning behind the scene that was to follow presently. We were told to leave our luggage in the train and to fall into two lines—women on one side, men on the other—in order to file past a senior SS officer. Surprisingly enough, I had the courage to hide my haversack under my coat. My line filed past the officer, man by man. I realized that it would be dangerous if the officer spotted my bag. He would at least knock me down; I knew that from previous experience. Instinctively, I straightened on approaching the officer, so that he would not notice my heavy load. Then I was face to face with him. He was a tall man who looked slim and fit in his spotless uniform. What a contrast to us, who were untidy and grimy after our long journey! He had assumed an attitude of careless ease, supporting his right elbow with his left hand. His right hand was lifted, and with the forefinger of that hand he pointed very leisurely to the right or to the left. None of us had the slightest idea of the sinister meaning behind that little movement of a man's finger, pointing now to the right and now to the left, but far more frequently to the left.

It was my turn. Somebody whispered to me that to be sent to the right side would mean work, the way to the left being for the sick and those incapable of work, who would be sent to a special camp. I just waited for things to take their course, the first of many such times to come. My haversack weighed me down a bit to the left, but I made an effort to walk upright. The SS man looked me over, appeared to hesitate, then put both his hands on my shoulders. I tried very hard to look smart, and he turned my shoulders very slowly until I faced right, and I moved over to that side.

The significance of the finger game was explained to us in the evening. It was the first selection, the first verdict made on our existence or non-existence. For the great majority of our transport, about 90 per cent, it meant death. Their sentence was carried out within the next few hours. Those who were sent to the left were marched from the station straight to the crematorium. This building, as I was told by someone who worked there, had the word "bath" written over its doors in several European languages. On entering, each prisoner was handed a piece of soap, and then——but mercifully I do not need to describe the events which followed. Many accounts have been written about this horror.

We who were saved, the minority of our transport, found out the truth in the evening. I inquired from prisoners who had been there for some time where my colleague and friend P——had been sent.

"Was he sent to the left side?"

"Yes," I replied.

"Then you can see him there," I was told.

"Where?" A hand pointed to the chimney a few hundred yards off, which was sending a column of flame up into the grey sky of Poland. It dissolved into a sinister cloud of smoke.

"That's where your friend is, floating up to Heaven," was the answer. But I still did not understand until the truth was explained to me in plain words.

But I am telling things out of their turn. From a psychological point of view, we had a long, long way in front of us from the break of that dawn at the station until our first night's rest at the camp.

Escorted by SS guards with loaded guns, we were made to run from the station, past electrically charged barbed wire, through the camp, to the cleansing station; for those of us who had passed the first selection, this was a real bath. Again our illusion of reprieve found confirmation. The SS men seemed almost charming. Soon we found out their reason. They were nice to us as long as they saw watches on our wrists and could persuade us in well-meaning tones to hand them over. Would we not have to hand over all our possessions anyway, and why should not that relatively nice person have the watch? Maybe one day he would do one a good turn.

We waited in a shed which seemed to be the anteroom to the disinfecting chamber. SS men appeared and spread out blankets into which we had to throw all our possessions, all our watches and jewelry. There were still naïve prisoners among us who asked, to the amusement of the more seasoned ones who were there as helpers, if they could not keep a wedding ring, a medal, or a good-luck piece. No one could yet grasp the fact that everything would be taken away.

I tried to take one of the old prisoners into my confidence. Approaching him furtively, I pointed to the roll of paper in the inner pocket of my coat and said, "Look, this is the manuscript of a scientific book. I know what you will say, that I should be grateful to escape with my life, that that should be all I can expect of fate. But I cannot help myself. I must keep this manuscript at all costs; it contains my life's work. Do you understand that?"

Yes, he was beginning to understand. A grin spread slowly over his face, first piteous, then more amused, mocking, insulting, until he bellowed one word at me in answer to my question, a word that was ever present in the vocabulary of the camp inmates: "Shit!" At that moment I saw the plain truth and did what marked the culminating point of the first phase of my psychological reaction: I struck out my whole former life.

46. The Gas Supply

In Auschwitz the Jews were killed with hydrogen cyanide, an efficient lethal agent for use in large chambers. Its trade name was Zyklon B, and it was stored in canisters small enough to be held in one hand. Inside the canister, Zyklon consisted of bluish pellets which turned into gas when they were poured through an aperture into a chamber. The SS man who handled the canister and the inmates who subsequently dragged out the bodies wore gas masks with special filters.

The gas was manufactured by the Dessauer Works for Sugar and Chemical Industry and distributed by the German Corporation for Combating Vermin (Deutsche Gesellschaft für Schädlingsbekämpfung m.b.H.—DEGESCH), whose managing director was Dr. Gerhard Peters. The Zyklon was used for fumigating ships, army posts, and camps as well as for killings in Auschwitz, and the allocation of the gas to the various users, both military and SS, was the responsibility of the Armed Forces Main Sanitation Park. Specific quantities within the allocation were ordered for Auschwitz by the SS Economic-Administrative Main Office's Group D, located in Oranienburg and headed by SS-Brigadier General Richard Glücks. The chief of D I (Central Office), who signed two of the following letters, was at that time Liebehenschel. Payments for Zyklon purchased by the SS were made by SS-First Lieutenant Kurt Gerstein, whose DEGESCH accounts for 1943 and 1944 totaled about 17 million Reichsmark. The letter written by Gerstein on May 24, 1944, coincided with the arrival in Auschwitz of the first transports from Hungary. Gerstein was fictionalized under his own name in Rolf Hochhuth's play *The Deputy*.

[Nuremberg document NO-2361.]

[SS-Colonel] Glücks
to Concentration Camp Auschwitz
July 29, 1942

Permission is hereby given for dispatch of a truck from Auschwitz to Dessau to load gas needed for disinfection of the camp.

[Nuremberg document NO-2363.]

SS-Lieutenant Colonel Liebehenschel to Concentration Camp Auschwitz
August 26, 1942

Permission is hereby given for dispatch of a truck to Dessau to load material for special treatment. Permit is to be given to the driver.

[Nuremberg document NO-2362.]

SS-Lieutenant Colonel Liebehenschel to Concentration Camp Auschwitz
October 2, 1942

Permission is hereby given for 5-ton truck with trailer to go to Dessau and back, to load material for Jewish resettlement. This permit is to be given to the driver.

[Nuremberg document NI-9909.]

Surgeon General of the SS and Police/Chief of Sanitation Materiel
(signed Bremenburg)
to Dr. Peters, DEGESCH
April 5, 1944

Request is made for the immediate release from the Dessauer Works for Sugar and Chemical Industry, of 12,000 pounds of Zyklon B, already allocated by the Main Sanitation

Materiel Command of the Armed Forces, and urgently needed by the Armed SS. Please inform Office of Chief of Sanitation Materiel at Surgeon General, SS and Police, Berlin W 15, Knesebeck Street 51, of availability.

[Nuremberg document NI-9908.]

Surgeon General of the SS and Police/Chief Sanitation Officer
(signed 1st Lieutenant Kurt Gerstein)
to Dr. Peters, DEGESCH
May 24, 1944

Request is made for bills still outstanding, so that I may pay the amounts owed in full.

Furthermore I would like to know how you view the durability of the special deliveries made to Oranienburg and Auschwitz. In case there are doubts about the duration of storage, we would have to use up the earlier shipments for disinfection and keep only fresh deliveries. Up to now there has not been any need to use anything. On the other hand, major quantities—that is actually the whole of the stored quantity—may under certain circumstances be needed all at once. But safety and durability are naturally to be considered first.

47. Revolt

Between 1942 and 1944 transports were moving almost constantly into the barbed-wire enclosures of the death camps. To kill all these people smoothly, month after month and year after year, the SS had to rely on the psychological unpreparedness of the deportees. It was essential that the victims not know precisely what was going to happen to them, and that they not believe such information as they had. Camp commanders were consequently nervous over any leakages of information, and in the document below the administration of Auschwitz admonished the SS and Police in the west to make sure that guards on the transports did not reveal any secrets to the Jews.

The death centers also had inmates who had survived an initial selection and could not help observing the continuous gassings and burnings. Although the camps were surrounded and laced with fences and machine guns, revolts did break out in them. Treblinka had such an uprising on August 7, 1943, Sobibor on October 14, 1943. A report of the Sobibor revolt follows the item from Auschwitz.

[Israel Police document 1208.]

Reich Security Main Office IV B 4 (signed Guenther)
to Commanding Officer of Security Police in France—attention SS-Lieutenant Colonel Knochen
  Commanding Officer of Security Police in Netherlands—attention SS-Major Zoepf
  Commanding Officer of Security Police in Belgium—attention SS-Major Ehlers
  Copy to Commander of Security Police in Metz
April 29, 1943

Immediate concern has prompted camp Auschwitz to renew a request that Jews about to be evacuated receive no disturbing revelations of any kind about the place or manner of the utilization which is in store for them.

May I ask for your attention and cooperation in this matter.

In particular, I should ask you to take pains to instruct the accompanying guards before every journey not to instill thoughts of resistance in the Jews by voicing in their presence suppositions about types of quarters etc. Auschwitz is most desirous that in view of urgent construction programs the receipt of the transports and their further distribution may be carried out as smoothly as possible.

[From the Archives of the Polish Interior Ministry in: Jüdisches Historisches Institut Warschau, *Faschismus-Getto-Massenmord* (Berlin: Rütten & Loening, 2nd ed., 1961), p. 565.]

REPORT OF THE ORDER POLICE IN DISTRICT LUBLIN
OCTOBER 15, 1943 [CITY OF] LUBLIN

On October 14, 1943, at about 5 P.M., revolt of the Jews in SS-camp Sobibor, 25 miles north of Cholm. They overpowered the guards, seized the armory, and after firefight with camp garrison fled in unknown direction. Nine SS murdered, 1 SS man missing, 2 foreign guards shot to death.

Approximately 300 Jews escaped, the remainder were shot to death or are now in camp. Military police and armed forces were notified immediately and took over security of the camp at about 1 A.M. The area south and southwest of Sobibor is now being searched by police and armed forces.

48. Liberation

During the last year of the war, Jewish work parties that had been mobilized in Hungary, deportees left alive in Auschwitz, and remnants of the Jewish labor force in Poland and the Baltic region were pulled westward out of reach of the approaching Red Army. They were relocated in concentration camps close to or inside the old German boundaries. One such camp was Stutthof, a mile or so from the Baltic coast and east of the Vistula River. On the western side of the river, about twenty miles from the camp, lay the city of Danzig; to the east were East Prussia and Lithuania. Stutthof had compartments for men and for women, and at the end of 1944 most of its population was female.

The Russians began a major advance on June 22, 1944, and, overrunning Lithuania and eastern Poland, came to a stop on the Vistula River in front of Warsaw on August 29. In the months that followed, while the front was static, Jewish women of Stutthof were employed under harsh conditions in the AEG (General Electric) at Torun and on agricultural projects in the open fields around Elbing. The Soviets resumed their offensive on January 12, 1945, and by the end of the month had formed a wedge into Germany which passed a few miles south of Stutthof to a point on the Oder River within forty miles of Berlin. In Stutthof, the nearness of Soviet guns prompted a partial evacuation of the camp between January 25 and 31; some of the inmates were moved west and others farther east along the coast. Near Königsberg, in East Prussia, hundreds of Jewish women were shot on the shore or pushed into the icy sea.

In February the Soviets launched an assault on Pomerania between the Oder and Vistula rivers, and by the end of March they had captured the port cities of Gdynia and Danzig. The German defenders were now pinned to the sea in isolated pockets which included the Hela peninsula jutting into Danzig Bay and beachheads from Stutthof to Königsberg. On April 9, Königsberg fell to the Russians, and one week later the Red Army began its envelopment of Berlin from the Oder-Neisse line, leaving Hela, Stutthof, and the coastal hinterland to the east in German hands. Between April 24 and 28 the Germans evacuated most of the remaining Stutthof inmates by sea to Hela, and then by trawler-drawn barges to Lübeck Bay. At Neustadt in Holstein, the concentration camp survivors were debarked under Royal Air Force bombs while SS and German naval personnel shot at them. This was the end, on May 3, 1945, three days after Hitler's death.

A personal account of Stutthof was written in Israel by one of the persons who had made the trip to Neustadt, Mrs. Liuba Daniel. She was born near Leningrad in 1919 and spent her youth in Kovno, Lithuania, where she was married in 1940 and where she became a nurse in 1941, shortly after the start of the German occupation. She relates how she restrained her husband "forcibly" from voluntarily reporting for what the Germans described as labor service, and how most members of her family were killed during the first months of German rule. She and her husband lived in Kovno until 1944. "In May," she reports, "my husband died. The terrible experiences were too much for him." On August 13, 1944, Mrs. Daniel was loaded into a cattle car on the last train departing from Kovno. The transport halted at Tiegenhof; the men were sent to Dachau and the women to nearby Stutthof. After three weeks in the camp, she began agricultural labor, driving a pick into the freezing ground. She was then returned to Stutthof until its final dissolution.

[Yad Vashem Oral History Depot, Tel Aviv, document 2568/74.]

DEPOSITION BY MRS. LIUBA DANIEL, NOVEMBER, 1965
[EXCERPTS]

We were loaded standing up in small open railway freight cars, and rode to Stutthof. The trip has remained a sharp memory, because that was the first time I began to feel a helpless, suffocating hate. We passed through the peaceful landscape, towns, villages, fields, and woods, and somehow it seemed unnatural to me that the sun was shining and that men went about their normal business. . . .

The sight of Stutthof, surrounded by high double fences of barbed wire with watchtowers, hundreds of SS men and trained dogs, was shattering. The unloading was even more cruel than at Tiegenhof station. Inside the camp, one's first view was fixed on a mountain of children's shoes. To tell the truth I did not understand what that meant. Then we noticed hundreds of shadowy female figures. They were Hungarian women with shaved heads, barefoot, in gray prison uniforms. I should like to stress that these Hungarian Jews had left their homes only four months before.

We were driven into huge barracks where we were assigned with shouts to our beds of wooden planks. Next morning we went to the delousing station.

Today when so many ask why all of the Jews in the diverse concentration camps did not simply hurl themselves with bare hands at the Germans, I want to say only one thing: There is no better method of depriving people of their last measure of human dignity than to undress them completely. . . .

We stood trembling, but not because we were cold and not even because of shame, between SS men who strolled back and forth trying their whips on their polished boots. Various uniformed women and women in civilian clothes (who later turned out to be inmates) shoved us in various directions. Mouths, hair and other places were examined for valuables. (Our luggage had already been taken from us.) Then we came to the doctor and he too looked for jewels. Thereafter we were subjected to an ice cold dripping shower with soap as hard as stone (of questionable origin), and given striped rags. We were now full-fledged inmates of a German concentration camp.

We stayed for three weeks in the barracks where some members of my group were not even able to find wooden planks for sleep. Everything was so full that we slept on the floor in the so-called dining area of the barracks. We saw very few uniformed Germans in the camp. They of course sat in their watchtowers, and every approach to the electrified barbed wire—which did not even lead to freedom, but only to another part of the camp area—was greeted with wild laughter and a salvo of bullets. Corpses were hanging on the fences like drying laundry.

Our true bosses were ethnic German [women] who—we learned later—were all criminals and were doing time here for robbery, murder, or theft. They wore civilian clothes, the most wonderful suits from the huge storehouse which grew daily with some of the best belongings of Europe's Jewry. . . .

[Winter] The prison garb, which we were given for our civilian clothes, had been washed, but all the same it harbored eggs of lice. Everyone had diarrhea at best and often it was dysentery. No one dreamt of the end of the war anymore—

only of a piece of wet bread or another potato and a day
without beatings. For the capos beat us without mercy, when
we were lined up for food or during the count. . . .

The corpses in front of the blocks accumulated daily. We
passed them with indifference. Even the glimpse of a familiar
face that had belonged to a person with whom one had con-
versed only a few days before produced no reaction. It wasn't
even hunger the way normal people feel it, but an indescrib-
able emptiness.

It came to the point that a woman was discovered trying to
open the belly of a corpse with a rusted knife. When we heard
the sudden commotion and loud crying in front of our barracks, curiosity conquered our physical weakness and we
shuffled to the scene just as the inmate block elders were about
to drag away the woman whom they had almost beaten to
death. When she was brought to the Germans and asked why
she had opened a corpse, she replied that she had been *so*
hungry and that she wanted to eat only the liver. Apparently
that was too much for the German masters; the woman was
dismissed without a word and then came instructions that she
should be given a second portion of soup.

On April 24 [1945] an order was issued for the evacuation
of Stutthof. Apparently the front line was already close, for
the Germans were panicky. Everybody was rushed to his feet.
Those who could not get up any more were routed from their
wooden planks with giant dogs. Everyone received a loaf of
bread—which we had not seen in three months—and we
marched, stumbling and limping for a whole day, to the shore.
There we were loaded like cattle during the night into a completely closed-off hold of a freighter. This was the most terrible night of my life. We were so crowded that one could not
move an arm. Since no air came in, some began to lose consciousness, but they were unconscious standing up. Besides,
most of us had stomach ills. Even if there had been a toilet
somewhere, we were unable to take a single step. People
howled, cried, pleaded, beat about wildly—all in vain.

I do not know how many bodies were left behind on the
Hela peninsula next morning.

We were disembarked and shunted through Hela all day.

The place was clogged with military in all kinds of uniforms. We saw concrete bunkers, machine guns, anti-aircraft artillery, but we did not know that Germany was breathing its last breath. The sky blackened with Russian aircraft and bombs rained down. We did not even throw ourselves to the ground, for it was too difficult to get up again. The military was gripped with panic, ran to and fro, barked orders at the top of their voices, and looked anxiously at the sky. I learned later that Hela was an exceptionally important strategic base.

During the evening we were driven back to the harbor and loaded into the hold of two large open barges. We had air and could sit. Both barges were drawn by motor ships which contained the entire crew and guard. This is how we traveled for eight days along the Baltic coast, squatting on dirty straw between Polish and Russian prisoners, without bread or water. Our companions were mostly men—the Jewish component of the transport consisted almost wholly of women—and although they found themselves in the same position with us, they did not behave as comrades toward us. They were hungry though not as hungry as we, and they were stronger than we. If at night one had to climb the single ladder to relieve himself, they would beat our legs, and if we had saved a little of our bread, they would try to tear it from us, cursing and shouting all day long.

Parallel to us, the second barge carried Jewish women as well as Norwegian and Danish inmates. One day the Germans gave the Scandinavians even some cans of food and these men shared the cans with the women.

We all had the impression that the Germans did not know where they were going. Several attempts were made to land, but the local authorities refused permission.

Hunger and thirst increased daily and we began to drink sea water. The guards showed up more and more seldom for inspection; we had the feeling that they feared a mutiny, inasmuch as the Christian inmates, who were men, represented a certain amount of power. Their hunger and thirst were such that they might have hurled themselves at the Germans with bare hands. Tension increased hourly.

During the night of May 2–3, we lay still for several hours and changed directions. We were turning back. Rumors had it that we were near Lübeck and that the city had fallen to the British.

Suddenly everything was quiet—the motors had stopped. On deck there was a disturbance that we in the hold could not understand. We heard running and yelling; boards above us broke and people fell down on our heads. The only ladder had vanished and it took some time before I climbed on arms and shoulders to the top. Then it became clear that our guards had disappeared with the motor ship. We were alongside a huge vessel which towered over the low barges. It was a swimming concentration camp with about 7000 inmates from Neuengamme. They were all men and threw down bread to us. That had been the reason for the wild stamping and fighting. The men were wrestling on the decks and a few even fell overboard. We women did not dare get close.

We had no guards, but we were in the middle of the water. In our helplessness—for almost four years we had not taken an independent step—we asked the captain of the big ship to take us on. After a short deliberation the request was refused with the reason that there were no orders for such a transfer.

Among the inmates of both barges, there were apparently some former seamen. The large side planks were broken off and used as oars to move the barges toward the shore line. It was a cold, light spring night. At 3 A.M., a little over 60 yards from shore, we hit sand. Slowly we got off on the single ladder. Each boat had 1000 people and the ladder could hold only one at a time. At the bottom the rest of the way was a path through ice cold water which welled to the hips. Ground under our feet after eight days. No rifle pointed at us after four years. We formed small groups and looked for roads. Slowly we moved on as it became dawn.

All of a sudden the morning quiet was broken by the fierce barks of dogs and the loud bang of motorcycles. Each machine carried two uniformed Germans and the wolfhounds ran alongside. They moved toward us shouting and driving us back to shore. People were still getting off—the sickest and oldest had not yet left the barges. Now we were made to stand in groups of four and naturally the debarkation proceeded much faster. Whoever did not negotiate the ladder fast enough was pushed off or shot. Four times a young bastard shot at an old woman; when she still swayed on the ladder, he hit her over the head with a rifle butt. The Germans were going berserk. As we discovered later, they had fled into town from a camp in order not to be caught by the British as camp guards, but the English had not yet come and their superiors, threatening disciplinary proceedings, ordered them back to their posts. There was still order in Germany.

We stood on the shore and did not dare to breathe. We looked at the reddening water . . . now it was our turn. Gradually we realized that we were standing at a canal and that on the opposite side stood tall houses amidst which we could make out moving silhouettes of people.

And now the last chase of life and death. We were made to run on a small path parallel with the sea while to our right on a soft hill lay elegant villas in whose gardens German officers with movie cameras were filming the scene. Whoever could not move fast enough was simply kicked down the hill into the sea. Then we crossed a bridge and were in the city. The run continued through the streets until we reached a huge military camp.

The sky had filled with enemy [Allied] planes and bombs came down like hail. The sirens did not stop and guards disappeared every minute in air raid shelters, while fires raged on all sides. Somewhere someone was handing out food and the smell was reaching us, but the crowding was too great and we could not make the effort. Naked people appeared from somewhere—the survivors of the huge ship which was now at the bottom of the sea. The British had ordered all ships into the harbor by twelve o'clock and when the captain wanted to move the vessel, an SS-captain shot him and the large swimming concentration camp sank with all but a few hundred of its inmates.

Then at four in the afternoon we heard shouting—the first British tank with a torn swastika on its tub passed us by. Our reaction was nil. Mentally and physically we were too much exhausted to feel anything at all.

49. Who Is Who in Postwar Germany

When West Germany became an independent state in the 1950's, it faced an immediate problem in dealing with its past. Civilian officials, military officers, and corporate executives had been implicated by the thousands in destructive activities. Who was to be cast aside as part of the old regime, and who was to be "reutilized"? The decision in the main was to single out SS men who had participated in killings for investigation and trial, and to rehabilitate almost everyone else.

Among the following selections, the first set of documents is taken from the 1963 hearings of the Senate Foreign Relations Committee on "Activities of Nondiplomatic Representatives of Foreign Principals in the United States." One of the nondiplomatic representatives was the public relations firm of Julius Klein in Chicago, Illinois. Klein, a delegate to several Republican national conventions and a retired major general of the U.S. Army Reserve, had also been a national commander of the Jewish War Veterans. His clients included the West German government as well as German firms. The committee records contain some of the firm's interoffice correspondence about publicizing the arrest in Germany of Richard Bär, former SS-captain who had been a commander of Auschwitz I. Bär died later while awaiting trial. The paragraphs reprinted below are parallel excerpts from the public relations draft and a speech in Congress.

In the second set of items, material in the right-hand column was taken from the German *Who Is Who*. The additional notes to the left were gathered from German documents and should provide a fuller understanding of the brief biographies.

[U.S. Senate, Committee on Foreign Relations, Hearing on "Activities of Nondiplomatic Representatives of Foreign Principals in the United States," 88th Congress, 1st session, Pt. 13, May 13, 1963, pp. 1840, 1841.]

JULIUS KLEIN PUBLIC RELATIONS

INTEROFFICE CORRESPONDENCE

To: Washington, Gen. Klein, Chicago.

From: Harry Blake.

Date: Jan. 5, 1961.

Subject: Draft of speech for Congressman Celler.

Attached is a draft of a speech which is to be passed on to Congressman Celler.

[Hand written note: (Germany) Neo-Nazism—Libonati— Put in Cong. Record by Cong. Libonati on Jan. 16, 1961, page A187.]

Mr. Speaker, the recent success of police of the Federal Republic of Germany in tracking down and arresting Karl Richard Baer, the last chief executioner at the notorious Nazi death camp at Auschwitz, is a salutary example of the spirit of contemporary West Germany. It affords a glaring contrast to the doctrines that prevail in the eastern half of Germany which remains in the grip of Communist captivity. In the self-styled People's Republic of East Germany, former Nazis such as Baer have been given mass amnesty in return for joining the Communist Party. Today, about one-third of the so-called East German Parliament is a rogues' gallery of Hitler alumni.

I believe this contrast is important to keep in mind. Memories of the World War II regime in Germany are still vivid. Understandably, emotions are quickly stirred at any report of incidents that recall the dark and lamentable period of the Nazis' sway. But what seems to me to be important to keep in focus is that the Germany of today is not one but two countries, each with a distinct leadership and with sharply differing political, ethical, and moral philosophies.

Under that remarkable survivor of Hitlerism, Konrad Adenauer, West Germany set out to build from scratch a political structure guided by the rule of law and respect for the dignity of the individual. History will acclaim this great statesman for his leadership in the stupendous task of physical and moral national reclamation. The Federal Republic's domestic and international program of restitution for the victims of Nazi persecution was a historic undertaking and the conscientious effort that has been made to meet obligations of unprecedented complexity is striking evidence of the integrity of West German leadership. . . .

FADING INFLUENCE OF NEO-NAZI GROUPS IN GERMANY

Speech of Hon. Roland V. Libonati, of Illinois, in the House of Representatives, Monday, January 16, 1961

MR. LIBONATI. Mr. Speaker, it is to the credit of Western Germany under the powerful leadership of Chancellor Adenauer and his sagacious Foreign Minister, Heinrich von Brentano, that the influence of neo-Nazi propagandists has faded into weak, splintered groups, reliant upon the soapbox variety of oratory to justify their beliefs in Hitlerism.

The ultranational youth movements fostering antidemocratic dogma and hate doctrines have attracted a negligible number of West German youths.

And, although neonazism is to be found in several forms, the recent success of police of the Federal Republic of Germany in tracking down and arresting Karl Richard Baer, the last chief executioner at the notorious Nazi death camp at Auschwitz, is a salutary example of the spirit of contemporary West Germany. It affords a glaring contrast to the doctrines that prevail in the eastern half of Germany which remains in the grip of Communist captivity. In the self-styled People's Republic of East Germany, former Nazis such as Baer have been given mass amnesty in return for joining the Communist Party. Today, about one-third of the so-called East German Parliament is a rogues' gallery of Hitler alumni.

I believe this contrast is important to keep in mind. Memories of the World War II regime in Germany are still vivid. Understandably, emotions are quickly stirred at any report of incidents that recall the dark and lamentable period of the Nazis' sway. But what seems to me to be important to keep in focus is that the Germany of today is not one but two countries, each with a distinct leadership and with sharply differing political, ethical, and moral philosophies.

Under that remarkable survivor of Hitlerism, Konrad Adenauer, West Germany set out to build from scratch a political structure guided by the rule of law and respect for the dignity of the individual. History will acclaim this great statesman for his leadership in the stupendous task of physical and moral national reclamation. The Federal Republic's domestic and international program of restitution for the victims of Nazi persecution was a historic undertaking and the conscientious effort that has been made to meet obligations of unprecedented complexity is striking evidence of the integrity of West German leadership. . . .

[*Wer ist Wer?* XV, 1967–68, Pt. I West (Berlin: Arani Verlags GmbH, 1967), pp. 383, 558, 1529, 2023, 2062.]

Involvement in Destructive Activities

Wer ist Wer?

EISFELD, Kurt

I.G. Farben official, sent to Auschwitz 1943 as head of Division II (chemicals) of I.G. Farben plant in camp.

Ph.D. sc., member, exec. comm., bd. of dir., Dynamit Nobel, Inc., Troisdorf, dir., Chemische Werke Witten, Inc., Witten/Ruhr—521 Troisdorf, dist. Cologne, Am Prinzenwäldchen 10 (Tel. office 50 51)—b. Jan. 12, 1904 Gröningen near Magdeburg (Fath. Tankmar E., M.D.), m. 1938 Lore Hartnacke, 6 childr.—Univ. Jena (chem.)— since 1929 chem. ind.—hobby: hunting.

GLOBKE, Hans

Author of several anti-Jewish decrees, including requirement that Jews in Reich carry middle names "Israel" and "Sara."

Undersec., ret., 53 Bonn, Dietz St. 10 (Tel. 2 37 24). B. Sept. 10, 1898 Düsseldorf (Father: Josef G., cloth merchant, mother: b. Erberich), Cath., m. Augusta Vaillant 1934, 3 children (Hans, Marianne, Werner), Kaiser Karl Gymnasium Aachen; then participant in W.W. I (arty.), Univ. of Bonn and Cologne, asst. judge and govt. assessor, from 1925; dep. police pres. Aachen; 1929–45 sup. govt. councillor and ministerial councillor, Pruss. respectively Reich Interior Ministry, 1949– vice-pres. prov. ct. of accounts Nordrh.-Westf. 1953– office of Fed. Chancellery, ministerial director and undersec. 1963 ret. High decorations inclu. Grand Cross of Service Order of Fed. Rep. Germany. Hobbies: Numismatics (Armenia, Axum), Rotarian.

RAHN, Rudolf

In France, was involved in deportation talks with Laval. As Foreign Office representative in Tunisia, instrumental in establishing forced labor for Jews and levying fines on them. Ambassador to Fascist Italian Republic during deportations of Italian Jews.

Ph.D. Ambassador ret. 4 Düsseldorf, Pempelforter St. 10 (Tel. 35 39 46). B. Mar. 16, 1900 Ulm/D., Luth., m. Martha Gerhardy 1934, 2 children. Univ. Tübingen, Berlin, Heidelberg (grad. 1923). 1927 League of Nations Secretariat, Geneva; from

1928 For. Office (foreign posts: 1931–34 Ankara, 1937–39 Lisbon, 1940–43 Paris, 1943–45 Rome and Fasano), 1945–47 interned; since then active in writing and commerce. 1951 member presidium Rhine-Ruhr Club, Ger.-It. and Ger.-Tunis. Soc.; currently dir. Lions Internat. Auth.: *Restless Life* 1948 (also Ital. and Span.); *Talleyrand* 1949. Hobbies: Music, lit., golf, lang., Engl., Fr.

Topf & Sons, oven builders, installed crematoria in concentration camps, including Auschwitz.

TOPF, Werner
Manufacturer; manager, Oberndorfer Gardinen- u. Spitzen-Webereien Inc., Oberndorf, Spitzen-Manufaktur Inc., OGUS-Wohnbau Inc., Oberndorf, Textilfärberei u. Ausrüstung Inc., Super & Co., both in Durmersheim/Baden, chmn., bd. of dir., Bergische Gardinen-Ind. Inc., Marienheide.—7238 Oberndorf/N. Eichendorff St. 9—b. June 2, 1905 Erfurt/Thür. Currently chmn., Assoc. of Ger. Curtain Material Industries, Neuss/Rh.—descended from well-known Erfurt industr. family (Topf & Sons).

As official in Reich Comm. Ostland/Finance, signed di-

VIALON, Friedrich Karl
Dr. jur., prof., undersec., ret., 53 Bonn, Am Buchenhang 15,

rective August 27, 1942, on financial aspects of ghetto formation in Lithuania, Latvia, White Russia.

b. July 10, 1905 Frankfurt/M., from 1927 badisch. judiciary (pros. atty.), 1932–35 badisch. Prov. Jus. Ministry (govt. councillor), then Sup. Prov. Ct. (judge), from 1937 Reich Finance Ministry; wartime service: military and civil at home and in occup. terr., 1950–58 Fed. Finance Ministry (last posit. ministerial councillor/budget), 1958–62 Office of Fed. Chancellery (economy, finance, social policy), 1962–66 Fed. Ministry for Econ. Cooperation (undersec.), from 1959 teaching commission & honor. prof. (1961). Various books (inclu. *Commentary on Budget Law, Public Finance Adm.*)

50. Amends

Since the end of the war, Jews have received restitution, reparations, and indemnification. The German term for all three of these measures is "amends." In their essence, however, they are designed to provide benefits only for the surviving victims—they are not compensation to Jewry for five million dead.

Restitution was the earliest regulation. It consisted of the return of identifiable property, such as a business or real estate, to the original owner or—if the owner did not wish repossession—payment to him for its retention. Reparations were West German contributions to the absorption of survivors in Israel and elsewhere. Indemnification payments, in turn, have been made to victims or their heirs for a personal or property loss inflicted on them by the Nazi regime. Each of these programs has its own history, and together they rival in complexity and exceed in duration the original German destruction process which gave rise to them.

Restitution laws were instituted by military governments in the western occupation zones of Germany from 1947 to 1949. The laws enabled Jewish owners to recover assets which had been "Aryanized" or, alternatively, to realize their full value in German currency from the "Aryanizers." The property of deceased victims without heirs was made available in the western zones and also in several western states to Jewish successor organizations for survivor rehabilitation. Overall, restitutions have amounted to the equivalent of several hundred million dollars.

Reparations, the second major program, were fixed in a treaty signed by West Germany and Israel on September 10, 1952, in Luxembourg. They were paid between 1953 and 1966 in the form of commodity shipments to Israel, and their dollar value, at 1952 rates of exchange, was $822,000,000. Israel's share of the reparations was $715,000,000 for absorbing a large number of the surviving victims in its territory, while $107,000,000 was payable by Israel to a Jewish Material Claims Conference for assisting survivors in other countries. The principal categories of deliveries, expressed in percentages of the total value of the reparations, were as follows:

	Percentage of Total
Oil (purchased in the United Kingdom)	29.1
Ships	17.0
Iron and steel for construction	11.3
Machinery (cranes, pumps, etc.)	9.2
Electrical products (generators, etc.)	6.5
Chemicals	4.7
Railway equipment, pipes, etc.	3.8
Other items, including textiles, leather, timber, specialized vehicles, optical instruments, coin presses, and agricultural products	11.0
Services, including obligation assumed by West Germany for indemnification of German owners of property sequestered in Israel and transferred to Israel	7.4
	100.0

The largest of the three programs is indemnification under the Federal Indemnification Law of 1953, the Federal Restitution Law of 1957, and a number of other enactments, including agreements between West Germany and various countries whereby Germany provided lump sums to those countries to satisfy claims presented by their citizens. The laws and treaties constitute a network of stipulations for coverage and eligibility which do not allow for any overlapping but do leave some gaps.

The most important measure is the Indemnification Law, which authorizes compensation for loss of support because of the death of a father, husband, or other provider, incarceration in ghettos or camps, the infliction of the yellow star, damage to health, or impairment of economic or professional advancement. Limited compensation is also allowed for property destroyed, damaged, or abandoned in territory defined by the Reich boundaries of 1937 and Danzig, and for special taxes, loss of good will, emigration costs, and so on. In addition, the Federal Restitution Law recognizes major claims for destruction or confiscation of identifiable property which was located in an area bounded by the postwar frontiers of West Germany, West Berlin, and East Berlin, or which, having been lost elsewhere, was brought into this territory by the German confiscators during the war.

Losses are indemnifiable only if they are the direct or indirect consequence of official German action. Thus, a death in the Bucharest pogrom of January 22, 1941, is *not* covered, because Roumania is considered to have been outside the German sphere of influence at that time; but the situation in which a Jew who, having escaped from German-occupied Athens to the partisans, succumbed to hardships in the course of his stay with them, is recognized because of the origin of the flight. Duodenal ulcers and gall bladder trouble usually are considered problems of personal constitution, but the failure of parents impoverished by persecution to provide special training for a retarded child is indemnifiable as an impairment of economic advancement. Again, most manic-depressive disturbances are not included since they are ruled to be "endogenous," but the suicide of a Jew who had felt himself severely threatened immediately after listening to a Hitler speech is ground for an admissible claim.

Compensation is payable only to persons who satisfy geographic requirements. The full benefits of the Indemnification Law are restricted to persecutees who resided on German soil at some time. If the victim was not an inhabitant of West Germany at the end of 1952 (or if he did not arrive there from behind the Iron Curtain afterward), he must have been a displaced person in the western zones of occupation or West Berlin on January 1, 1947, or he must have lived in the territory delimited by the German borders of 1937 or in Danzig during the Nazi regime. Indemnification for personal losses (death, health, freedom) is accorded to victims from eastern Europe who never set foot in Germany, provided they emigrated to a western country before 1966. They are eligible only for death benefits or compensation for loss of freedom if they took up residence in Israel.

Under the Federal Restitution Law, the territorial principle is established by the location of the property rather than the residence of the rightful owner. The geographic history of the claimant is consequently immaterial, except for the requirement that the claim be presented during a specified period from a country outside the area which became communist after the Second World War.

The federal laws do not provide for the Jews of Austria. The Austrian Jews, who are often considered the "stepchildren" of indemnification, obtain small payments for various losses from the Austrian state, and these allowances are partially financed by a German-Austrian compensation treaty.

The German payments have been made in lump sums or monthly checks. A single reimbursement is awarded for property losses and the loss of freedom, while allotments for indefinite periods of time are authorized for widows and orphans, disabled persons, those who suffered impairment of advancement, and claimants for insurance and pensions. In 1969 the cumulative amount received by Jewish victims passed the $5 billion mark. At the same time, 160–170,000 Jews were being indemnified month by month. The number of the recipients is declining gradually because of deaths, but the amounts of monthly compensation are being adjusted from time to time in accordance with a key geared to German civil service schedules. The West German government calculates that its obligations will continue beyond the year 2000, though numerically the beneficiaries, including victims and their heirs, will have declined to some tens of thousands.

For a documentary compendium of postwar German-Israeli relations, see Rolf Vogel, *The German Path to Israel* (Chester Springs, Pa.: Dufour Editions, 1969).

A NOTE ON THE EDITOR

Raul Hilberg received his doctorate in Public Law and Government at Columbia University. He was a member of the War Documentation Project in the Federal Records Center at Alexandria, Virginia, and subsequently taught at Hunter College and the University of Puerto Rico. Professor Hilberg is the author of *The Destruction of the European Jews,* a monumental, definitive history of the destruction process. Since 1956 he has been in the Department of Political Science at the University of Vermont.